DATE DUE

DEMCO 38-296

Gender and the Formation of Taste in Eighteenth-Century Britain

The Analysis of Beauty

Beauty is one of the most important and intriguing ideas in eighteenth-century culture. In *Gender and the Formation of Taste in Eighteenth-Century Britain* Robert Jones provides a new understanding of how emergent critical discourses negotiated with earlier accounts of taste and beauty in order to redefine culture in line with the polite virtues of the urban middle classes. Crucially, the ability to form opinions on questions of beauty, and the capacity to enter into debates on its nature, was thought to characterise those able to participate in cultural discourse. Furthermore, the term 'beauty' was frequently invoked, in various and contradictory ways, to determine acceptable behaviour for women. In his wide-ranging book, Jones discusses a variety of materials including philosophical works by William Hogarth, Edmund Burke and Joshua Reynolds, novels by Charlotte Lennox and Sarah Scott, and the many representations of the celebrated beauty Elizabeth Gunning.

ROBERT W. JONES is a lecturer in English at the University of Wales, Aberystwyth. He has published articles and reviews on several aspects of eighteenth-century culture, and is the editorial adviser in English literature for *The British Journal of Eighteenth-Century Studies*.

GENDER AND THE FORMATION OF TASTE IN EIGHTEENTH-CENTURY BRITAIN

The Analysis of Beauty

ROBERT W. JONES

CAMBRIDGE
UNIVERSITY PRESS

OF THE UNIVERSITY OF CAMBRIDGE
n Street, Cambridge CB2 1RP,
ingdom

VERSITY PRESS
The Edinburgh Building, Cambridge CB2 2RU, United Kingdom
40 West 20th Street, New York, NY 10011-4211, USA
10 Stamford Road, Oakleigh, Melbourne 3166, Australia

© Robert W. Jones 1998

First published 1998

Printed in the United Kingdom at the University Press, Cambridge

Typeset in 11/12.5pt Baskerville [CE]

A catalogue record for this book is available from the British Library

Library of Congress cataloguing in publication data
Jones, Robert W., Dr.
Gender and the formation of taste in eighteenth-century Britain:
the analysis of beauty / Robert W. Jones.
p. cm.
Includes bibliographical references and index.
ISBN 0 521 59326 3 (hardback)
1. English literature – 18th century – History and criticism.
2. Art and literature – Great Britain – History – 18th century.
3. Social classes – Great Britain – History – 18th century.
4. Sex role – Great Britain – History – 18th century.
5. Feminine beauty (Aesthetics) in literature.
6. Aesthetics, British – 18th century.
7. Ethics, Modern – 18th century.   I. Title.
PR448.A77J66   1998   97–44331   CIP

ISBN 0 521 59326 3 hardback

Contents

Illustrations

Preface

This book examines the concept of beauty as it was understood in eighteenth-century Britain. Concentrating mainly on the latter half of the century, the account which follows examines what shaped and defined what was thought to be beautiful, worthwhile or merely pleasing in the eyes of a diverse group of eighteenth-century writers and philosophers. Most importantly, this a study of what the discussion of beauty meant in a period during which a reference to the concept of beauty constituted a claim to cultural fluency and intellectual capacity. The changing pattern of wealth distribution which shaped eighteenth-century society, ensured that a greater number of people, particularly amongst the merchant and professional classes, were anxious to express their refinement as a means to cultural distinction. The newly charged atmosphere in which cultural debate took place led to an increased interest in the nature of taste, with more commentators wishing to lay claim to the final definition of what was good or beautiful. Indeed, one way to characterise eighteenth-century discussions of beauty is as a means through which those eager to enter the cultural sphere signalled their involvement. With this context in mind, it will be my contention throughout this book that an attentive reading of British critical opinion reveals that definitions of taste and beauty were implicated in wider cultural changes, as participants in theoretical debate sought to establish positions inflected by the nuances of class position and the uncertainties of gender roles.

Given these preoccupations, the analysis of beauty, as William Hogarth termed it, was an area of literary and cultural life that necessarily produced a number of competing theories, each seeking to valorise a particular set of judgements or modes of taste. For although eighteenth-century accounts of the beautiful were delimited by a general commitment to the 'standard of taste' and to 'correctness' in question of moral judgement, there was often little to unite the competing opinions offered on the subject. As Edmund Burke candidly revealed there was 'not the same obvious concurrence in any uniform or settled principals which relate to taste'.[1] In part this book explores why that was so and seeks to examine the wide variety of uses for, and opinions about, the beautiful found within eighteenth-century Britain. Indeed any book which focuses on eighteenth-century ideas of beauty is faced with a particular challenge: that of following the term through the multitude of its diverse functions and often opposing applications. For while it is undoubtedly true, that the beautiful represents one of the most enduring, and certainly one of the more important concepts in eighteenth-century British thought, it is also one of the most mobile terms the period has to offer. The briefest survey reveals it moving between a number of different locations, both discursive and social. The mobility of the notion of beauty frustrates any attempt to offer a simple account of the meaning of the term, or narrative of its function. The term has a mundane currency, a near ubiquity, that seems almost to make any specialised usage or significance impossible; but despite the equivocal meaning of the term, the question of beauty and its definition remained one of the most abiding concerns of eighteenth-century culture. Debates about taste, culture, refinement and desire were all conducted with reference to the idea of the beautiful during the eighteenth century; as Burke conceded it was the very diversity and plausibility of the term which made the debates about it so compelling and yet so uncertain.

While there has, in recent years, been a considerable amount of work published on the nature of aesthetics – alongside studies of manners and painting – this work has been deficient in its failure to examine the social and discursive relationships which structure eighteenth-century culture. Too frequently single instances from the highly charged realm of 'Taste' have been selected for isolated, if exhaustive, study; work undertaken on the nature of sublimity is perhaps the most obvious example of this trend. Within eighteenth-century studies the sublime has often been read as if it represented a purely phenomenological experience devoid of explicit social reference. By contrast my investment lies in the exploration of diverse and divergent areas of cultural practice and social discourse. I take my lead from the mobility of the term itself and pursue it in a number of its particular locations, within, for example, the mores of

polite society (Joseph Spence and James Usher), but also the practice
of a commercial portrait-painter (Joshua Reynolds); in the complexities inherent in the philosophical disputes of the mid-century
(Hogarth and Burke), and in the moral politics of two women
novelists (Charlotte Lennox and Sarah Scott). The power and
authority of each of these aspects of eighteenth-century culture can
be most fruitfully examined when their interconnections are explored. The idea of the beautiful forms a strong link between these
areas, which might otherwise seem to be divergent, or merely
coincidental in their chronology, and permits a greater understanding of eighteenth-century culture and society and the connections
upon which it is structured.

Careful analysis of texts by Hogarth, Burke, Reynolds and others
can provide an understanding of the ways in which definitions of the
beautiful were manipulated during the eighteenth century so as to
establish not only the refinement of the speaker but also their sense
of their social and cultural distinction. It was, however, the gendering of this debate which remains its most remarkable feature.
Throughout the period poor taste could be dismissed as effeminate,
the product of an unmanly desire for fripperies and extravagance or
the unwonted product of women's involvement in properly masculine deliberations. Particularly in the 1750s and 1760s the effeminising force of luxuriant appetites preoccupied those writing about
taste. It is necessary to read the work of Burke, Lord Kames and, to
an extent, Reynolds in the light of this concern. More directly, the
perceived beauties of women received minute attention as the signs,
alternately, of virtue or depravity. Therefore while the beautiful was
the object of judgement in cultural debate, it also functioned as a
guarantor of moral discourse, this was particularly true of those texts
which addressed the conduct of women. In this context the uneasy
division between the politeness of female society and the corruption
of effeminate fashion made for a compelling, if uncertain, debate. It
is this intersection of class and theory, gender and culture which
makes the beautiful so interesting, and yet so elusive. And it is
perhaps for this reason that critics have recently begun to request a
history of the eighteenth century written in relation, not to the
individuating claims of the sublime, but to the complex bonds and
sympathies represented by the beautiful. Given these conjunctions,
the beautiful demands serious appraisal as a category of thought; in
this vein Ronald Paulson has recently claimed that a 'narrative of the

Beautiful . . . seems to me, a corrective long-due'.[2] By agreeing with
Paulson, I wish to suggest that the 'analysis of beauty' is an activity
which will illuminate and enrich our understanding of the social and
textual processes at the heart of eighteenth-century British culture.

Acknowledgements

Many people have contributed generously to the final version of this book. I wish to thank all those who have read or responded to chapters and papers in the course of the last five years, including Malcolm Baker, Stephen Copley, Robert Devens, Lucy Hartley, Robert M. Jones, Tony Lake, Jo Littler, Jon Mitchell, Mary Peace, Dominic Rainsford, Shaun Regan, Philip Thomas, and members of the eighteenth-century research group at the University of York. John Barrell's work first inspired me to study eighteenth-century culture and I remain grateful to him for his wit as well as his wisdom. Marcia Pointon was a sympathetic as well as shrewd external examiner and I am thankful to her for her subsequent encouragement and support. I am also grateful to Helen Deutsch and Felicity Nussbaum whose invitation to talk on Sarah Scott at the Clark library in Los Angeles helped to clarify my ideas on ugliness and deformity. My biggest debt, however, is to my DPhil supervisor, Harriet Guest whose patience and perspicuity were invaluable. Her criticism and advice has prevented numerous errors and absurdities. I should also thank Josie Dixon of Cambridge University Press for her editorial guidance. My parents, Chris and Derek Jones, also deserve an acknowledgement for all the support they have given me since I began my research.

I would also like to give thanks to the Pro-Vice Chancellor's Learned Societies Fund and the Staff Research Fund of the Department of English at the University of Wales, Aberystwyth for providing me with the money to attend conferences and visit libraries. An earlier version of chapter three appeared as 'Such Strange Unwonted Softness to Excuse: Judgement and Indulgence in Joshua Reynolds's Portrait of Elizabeth Gunning', *The Oxford Art Journal*, vol. 18, no. 1 (Spring, 1995): 29–43. I am grateful to the editors for allowing me to reprint the essay here. I would also like to thank the Metropolitan Museum of Art, New York, the Royal Collection, Windsor Castle, the Witt Library at the Courtauld Institute and the Walker Art Gallery, Liverpool, for allowing me to reproduce images from their collections in this volume.

Introduction
The Empire of Beauty and the cultural politics
of taste

Commonplace, yet endlessly suggestive, discussions of beauty can be found within a surprisingly large range of eighteenth-century discourses. Not only can the question of beauty be discovered occupying a prominent position in debates about the nature of taste, but it can also be found within texts covering art criticism, moral philosophy and social commentary. The term, though, was perhaps most strikingly deployed in relation to the role of women in cultural and social debate. Writers as apparently diverse as Edmund Burke, William Hogarth and Joseph Spence all sought to employ the concept of beauty within inquiries which, while they were concerned with the rigours of philosophical discrimination, did not preclude a discussion of women's social place or her moral capacity. Spence, for example, successfully united an investigation into the question of taste with an account of how women should behave, claiming that a woman's beauty could make manifest her inner virtue.[1] Notions of beauty, therefore, had a wide applicability across a number of otherwise discrete areas, and as such the term gained a fashionable as well as critical currency. According to Charlotte Lennox's quixotic heroine, Arabella, few subjects afforded a 'Matter for a more Pleasing Variety of Conversation than [that] of Beauty'. Although Arabella's subsequent use of the term beauty to signal a woman's authority is used by Lennox to evidence the extent of her delusion, Arabella's sense of the term's significance and the generality of its application was not without its less obviously deluded adherents.[2] A reference to the concept of beauty was often used to describe the role and significance of women in eighteenth-century society; moreover it was a reference which could both damn and endorse the presence of women, suggesting either that they refined society or that, as in the case of Arabella, they disgraced it with their absurdity and presumption.

I

With these connections in mind, I want to ascribe two distinct, but closely connected, meanings to the phrase 'Empire of Beauty'. In the first place the expression describes, much in the manner of Pierre Bourdieu's notion of a field of cultural production or the discursive practices analysed by Michel Foucault, an area of investigation organised around a consideration of eighteenth-century taste and of the beautiful in particular.[3] However, such deliberations were never far removed from a conception how members of a polite society should conduct and express themselves. It is, I should imagine, obvious that one of the more commonplace uses of the word 'beauty' in the eighteenth century was to signify visual appearance. The word denotes, within the variously hierarchical schemes within which it exists, a sense of whether, and how, a particular object or person gratifies the viewer. However, the term is also connotative of appearance in a more specific and social sense. Beauty could be used to assess the morality or conduct of a woman, her likely authority or the extent of her charms. My second defintion of the phrase 'Empire of Beauty' is intended to capture this social and judgemental use of the idea of physical beauty. This definition of the 'Empire of Beauty' will be used to explore how debates about taste were transformed into a means of accounting for the place and representation of women. The fact that beauty was seen as the most appropriate term for defining women will be explored throughout this book; the story of Arabella, the female quixote, is, I will argue, governed by these assumptions.

This book is not therefore intended as a history of aesthetics; I am not setting out to produce a strictly philosophical reading of British debates between the publication of Francis Hutcheson's *Inquiry into the Original of our Ideas of Beauty and Virtue* in 1725 and Archibald Alison's *Essay on the Nature and Principals of Taste* at the century's end. There is to be no account here of the debate on what causes the beautiful to be felt by the perceiving subject, nor will I focus on, though I will have cause to mention, qualities of utility, fitness or variety. These considerations, whilst proper to the study of a particular evolution in British philosophy, are not mine.[4] My investigation is concerned with a different interpretation of the 'Empire of Beauty'; with the political uses and social affiliations which it was possible to describe, and to participate in, because one was able to discuss what was considered tasteful, or thought beautiful. In the rapidly changing environment of the mid-eighteenth century, which, as J.G.A. Pocock points out, was not an era of Augustan serenity, but an 'age of bitter and confused debate over the relations between reason, virtue, and passion', an ability to talk knowledgeably and with authority on the beautiful served as a sign of philosophic disinterestedness and political suitability.[5] It was the capacity which traditionally established the character of the subject of political discourse; the citizen himself.

It is here that the ambiguities of the Empire of Beauty begin to unfold, and its divisions and tribulations become apparent. Most people living in the eighteenth century believed that they were living through a period of great and perhaps unpleasant change. Commerce was most frequently held to be the cause of this, however, it was not the 'emergence' of commerce *per se* that was at issue. The processes of commercial exchange could, of course, be dated back to the Middle Ages. What troubled the majority of eighteenth-century commentators was the fact that the status of commerce, as much in discourse as in reality, was changing beyond recognition. Paul Langford has observed that commerce 'not only expressed the peculiar modernity of the Hanoverian age, it also indicated the problems which preoccupied contemporaries and the uncertainties which clouded their confidence'.[6] As Langford's study makes clear, what occurred in the eighteenth century is not the coming of mercantilism, but the fact that from the end of the seventeenth century onwards there was a move to reformulate the social and cultural importance of commercialism. As Lawrence Klein points out, 'it was at the beginning of the eighteenth century that the English began to absorb the experience of commerce into their political self understanding'.[7] This change can be seen in terms of a shift from discourse on commerce, one which described its particular practices and laws, to a discursive dynamic which sought to speak of and for commerce. Accounts of commerce no longer spoke merely of trade, but sought to represent the commercial classes as a vital and thriving community, a section of society which both sought and deserved a greater say in the running of the kingdom.[8]

Within a changed social order apparently propelled by a rapidly expanding commercial sector, the number of subjects desiring to be or claiming that they were already capable of participation in cultural debate was set to increase.[9] The transformation of the cultural sphere into an arena of class aspirations was naturally attended by a high level of anxiety and snobbish competitiveness. In this context the relations between 'reason, virtue, and passion' would indeed be fraught. To those who wished to uphold aristocratic privilege, commercial wealth threatened to unsettle the established orders of taste and criticism as they were handed down by Lord Shaftesbury in the second decade of the century. Mercantile wealth and the successes of financial speculation provided both new consumers, ready and willing to acquire, and new goods for them to buy; there were new forms of wares, from the East and West Indies, China and Africa as well as from the Americas and Europe. In this new environment there were not only more and different things to buy, but the objects bought had a new and, for some, unpleasant significance: the commodity had arrived.[10] Broadly speaking, the dominant modes of taste before the Restoration had been based on objects acquired without apparent commodification, inherited or held in trust; neither the owner nor the object were thought possessed by any notably 'grotesque ideas'.[11] Capital, acquired with the stateliest of exploitation and the most accomplished rack-renting, had been lavished on goods and estates purchased with a calm glance to endless futurity. At least this is the idea behind the policy of patrician taste and acquisition.[12] Not so by the start of the eighteenth century as, with an almost Falstaffian disregard for form and restraint, the merchant classes launched themselves on the spending spree of an epoch; demand began to appear insatiable: new plate, new chairs, new houses, new portraits (even of those long since dead), and wherever possible new relations, new friends and new occupations; in short, newer, richer lives.[13] With such spending came the consumer: monied, acquisitive and interested in the novelty of the commodity. Consumption on this scale caused something of a sea change in both the conceptualisation of ownership and the discussion of society. It had still been possible during the early seventeenth century for people to represent their purchases as if they were not commodities; but by the end of the century the expanding market had introduced too many new goods and too many new consumers for such patrician disclaimers to have any credibility. It is this crucial conflict between aristocratic and non-aristocratic forms of taste and consumption, which, as J.H. Plumb suggests, marked the emergence of a recognisably commercial, bourgeois modernity.[14]

The enormous expansion in the consumer economy was, when viewed from the position of the aristocracy, looked upon with a weary disgust. For the new acquisitions of the suddenly wealthy merchant classes were seen by traditionalists as an abnegation of all that was prudent management and good taste.[15] It was a vile, effeminate consumption, the stuff merely of the moment. Taste was corrupted; the word itself appeared to have lost something of the respect and assurance it was due; as one commentator put it, 'who has not heard it frequently pronounced by the loveliest mouths in the world, when it has evidently meant nothing'.[16] Within this discourse the taste of the city merchants was represented in such a way as to deny them concomitant cultural, as well as political, enfranchisement. What is striking in these polemics is the extent to which the repudiation reflected gendered concerns; middle-class tastes were not thought to be virtuous, they were the work of weak, unregulated passions, womanly cravings after fripperies, fancies and all manner of Chinese trash.

That the tastes of the middle classes should be figured within an explicitly gendered discourse, which represented anything less than stoic resolve as degenerate and unmanly, is crucial to any account of the culture of taste in eighteenth-century Britain. However, it also indicates the second, equally important, signification that I wish to attach to the phrase 'Empire of Beauty'. In this second sense, I have a more extensive sanction in terms of eighteenth-century usage, when the phrase was employed, not to define an area of research or philosophical speculation, but to name the particular area of women's government; the 'domain' of the fair. This meaning is something of a commonplace throughout the eighteenth century. The phrase is an integral part of the vocabulary of an established masculine sensibility, at once patronising and yet wary of women's potential authority, while also denominating a particular set of feminine tactics for gaining authority in a situation of dis-advantage.[17] Lady Mary Wortley Montagu writing in the guise of a 'Humble Admirer of the Fair Sex', dissects the unevenness of the situation with characteristic perspicuity:

I do not only look upon them as Objects of pleasure, but I compassionate the many Hardships both Nature and Custom has subjected them to. I never expose the Foibles to which Education has enclin'd them; and (contrary to all other Authors) I see with a favourable Eye the little vanitys with which they amuse themselves, and am glad they find in the imaginary Empire of Beauty, a consolation for being excluded every part of Government in the State.[18]

Having delineated the position of women as being in possession of only an 'imaginary Empire' the 'admirer of the Fair Sex' does an abrupt about face, claiming to be 'shock'd when I see their Influence in opposition to Reason, Justice, and the common Welfare of the Nation'. Women at first do not, and then later do, have considerable influence over the actions of men; they can be merely the 'Ornamental halfe of Mankind' and yet a threat to the fabric of the state.[19]

The dual position of women as both agents of corruption and idle ornament is one of the most often repeated ideas about women – at least society women – in eighteenth-century culture. It is something to which Richard Steele, writing twenty or so years earlier, also alludes, though in slightly different terms. Early in the run of the *Tatler* its fictional editor, Isaac Bickerstaff, is called away leaving his half-sister, Jenny Distaff, in charge. Jenny is portrayed by Steele as relishing the opportunity which has left her with a measure of command, a position she uses to question writings she has found in her brother's closet:

The first I lay my Hands on, is, a Treatise concerning *The Empire of Beauty*, and the Effects it has had in all Nations of the World upon the publick and private Actions of Men; with an Appendix, which he calls, *The Bachelor's Scheme for Governing his Wife*.[20]

Jenny outlines what Bickerstaff's proposals for such government entail. In the main they consist of an attack on what Bickerstaff sees as the follies and excesses of femininity. In the eyes of Jenny's big brother, women are the cause of quarrels, an effeminising presence which is to be guarded against, as their charms give them an authority over men wholly disproportionate to what is sensible, prudent and virtuous. It is this mixture of command and flippancy which disturbs Bickerstaff. The virtuous wife should, according to the Bickerstaff plan, forsake public assemblies, dote on her husband and remain utterly and steadfastly faithful. For Jenny this means that 'she shall be no Woman', as it means forsaking the very social pleasure which for Jenny constitutes the business of being a woman.

Steele, however, wants to have it both ways, and, in effect, to eat his syllabub and still have it. Through the character of Jenny, Steele is able to reintroduce the authority of feminine beauty as a positive, even improving, force while equally maintaining his masculine disapproval of women's potential command via her brother's writing. In line with this cautious two edged approach, Jenny announces her approval of the opinion – actually one of her brother's – that 'no Man begins to make any tolerable Figure, 'till he sets out with the Hopes of pleasing some of us'.[21] This is a sentiment with which Jenny agrees, adding that 'Every Temper, except the downright insipid, is to be animated and softened by the Influence of Beauty.'[22] It is testimony to the polite audience that Steele addresses, that animation and softening can be taken to occupy the same space. For many of Steele's contemporaries to be animate was the opposite of softness, and a choice between them was required. Indeed 'to be animated' was to embody masculine qualities of exertion and resolution, yet, in this instance, animation entails an activity which is merely sociable; visits are the example offered by Jenny. Beauty, then, is accorded a significance and a demonstrable influence upon the actions of men, so that it reforms, as well as corrupts.

Although Jenny does not give any details as to the exact contents of *The Empire of Beauty*, it is possible through a careful reading of the *Tatler*, *Spectator* and, from later in the century, the *Rambler* and the *Adventurer* to glean the substance of Bickerstaff's fears, and moreover to begin to examine the ambiguities which attended a discussion of feminine or female beauty. In essence, beauty became in the eighteenth century a contested term used to signify a woman's public presence; for some it marked the spectacle women ought to make in society, whilst for others, feminine beauty remained the symbol of corrupting pleasures, appetites which were best avoided and if possible extinguished. As a form of moral evaluation, the ascription of beauty was most often made with reference to society ladies, who found their arrival in public described with reference to their beauty regardless of whether the writer sought to give praise, or to offer condemnation. That a description of the beautiful woman often entailed a discussion of her moral worth is a theme to which I will return throughout the course of this book. However, before I can begin to expand on the nature and extent of my concerns, it is necessary to locate them within a more specific consideration of their relation to eighteenth-century society. While the argument will necessarily become more complicated as it is extended, I do not want to lose sight of this central conjunction between eighteenth-century accounts of taste and the account of woman's social presence.

TERMS OF VAGUE AND EXTENSIVE MEANING: BEAUTY, TASTE AND CULTURAL CHANGE

If Steele had discovered that beauty was the best term through which to signify the power he believed women might be able to exercise over men, then for writers, such as Lord Kames and Joshua Reynolds, the word beauty was used to exhort artists and their patrons to greater effort, for the beautiful continued to represent all that was pure and free from luxuriancy. Intriguingly, key thinkers, notably Burke, Hogarth and Joseph Spence, combined both these uses of the term, together with a sense of how the idea could be used to confer social and personal merit. The range of ideas which could be made manifest by an appeal to the notion of beauty is vital, for it distinguishes the discourses of early commercial modernity from our own late-capitalist postmodernity. In particular it indicates that the process of ideology, which in the nineteenth and twentieth centuries separated the aesthetic from the social was not yet fully in place.[23] For though, as we shall see, the precise nature of taste the grounds upon which it could be debated were hotly contested, discourses which sought to describe beauty remained available to, and formative of, arguments across a much more capacious field. It is therefore necessary, to be clear about what constituted eighteenth-century conceptions of beauty and how the various theorisations of the beautiful participated – in a way unparalleled in the twentieth century – in the social and cultural fabric of the period.[24]

Eighteenth-century discussions of beauty belonged not to the closed and specific branch of philosophy, known since the nineteenth century as aesthetics, but within a much more capacious field: that of taste, an inquiry which sought to account for art, morality and the natural world. Importantly, the term 'aesthetic' does not appear in eighteenth-century discussions of the beautiful, neither does its sense of an appropriately separable form of inquiry.[25] For, although the category of the aesthetic can refer to an account of particular pleasures and sensations, it addresses that issue in terms of why particular forms and objects are appreciated, whereas an account of taste, especially in its eighteenth-century usage, seeks to provide an account of 'correct taste' and to discriminate against that which is false.[26] It is not a question of defining what is 'correct' in the literal sense of veracity or accuracy in the delineation of the causes of sensation, but of finding and defining what is the right thing to say, to look for, to feel, and, perhaps most tellingly, to own. At the most basic level, to discern a thing of beauty remained, throughout the century, a process of registration and approval. To be tasteful entailed noting and defining the worth of any one of a number of objects. However, the beauty of the perceived object could take the form of a series of apparently diverse entities, including, for example, the harmony of a well-proportioned figure; an estate laid out in the latest style; the usefulness of a tool; or the calculable pleasure of a worthy action, ably performed. These images provide snapshots, perhaps merely the marginal details, of the project I hope to define and explore. They are expressions alongside which may be placed the harsher analytic terms of fitness, utility and uniformity, as appellations or as signs of what, within the broad compass of eighteenth-century philosophical criticism, was termed beautiful. These phrases fail, however, to register the ambiguities and frustrations which defining and monitoring the beautiful involved throughout the period. A more persuasive list would have to address, not only the relation of beauty to virtue, but the supposed sensibility of the observer and the known pleasures of appreciation and ownership.

These latter revisions will serve to reintegrate the profoundly ethical nature of most eighteenth-century accounts of the beautiful. The point can be evidenced via a reading of John Gilbert Cooper's rejection – his distaste – for the environs of London in the mid-1750s:

I am sick . . . of the splendid Impertinence, the unmeaning Glitter, the tasteless Profusion and monstrous Enormities, which I have lately seen in a Summer's Ramble to some of the Villas in the Neighbourhood of our Metropolis.[27]

Cooper has in mind (and we can assume his readers did as well) particular houses and developments, probably those at Twickenham and Richmond, to which wealthy merchants were retreating in droves by the mid-century. It is not only the probable novelty of these habitations which causes Cooper so much disquiet, but the fact that the 'tasteless Profusion' they embody can be taken as representative of impending moral collapse and artistic atrophy. Cooper viewed this trend in grandly historical terms, writing that 'history informs us, that in all Empires a similar depravity of Taste for Arts and Sciences and natural Beauty, has ever attended a national Corruption of Morals'.[28] On these terms the new wealth of the merchant classes, unfettered by either classical schooling or stoic restraint, causes a visible weakening of the national fabric. Clearly a moral and political issue, the discussion of taste necessarily becomes responsive to, if not actually structured upon, the dynamics of class culture and the politics of gender, especially when presented in the quasi-patrician discourse offered by Cooper.

Once a conception of beauty had been recruited into the social and moral discourse from which Cooper speaks, it was possible to employ the term to realise a variety of cultural ambitions. The various social groupings of eighteenth-century polite society – from the well-heeled country sets comprising the nobility, gentry and squirearchy through to the city crowd of merchants, bankers and shop-keepers – each sought a mode of address which would give sanction and credence to the propriety of its property. It is arguably for this reason that there was such a hectic debate upon the meaning of these terms. The result was an ambiguous oscillation of terms and meanings, and a high degree of diversity of application. Therefore, while it is possible, within the analysis of a particular species of beauty, say that of equipage, to isolate particular qualities which form the basis of approbation, this is not what I wish to discuss. Such a level of debate concerned with axles, wheels and their bearings, while perhaps offering a pleasing side-exhibit in the history of carriage making and its excellences, reveals little about the notion of beauty employed by political and social thinkers, or why it might be so vigorously contested within the periodical presses. This is because, above all else, the beautiful raises the question, not of particular taste for this phaeton or that, but of general taste. Taste, once it is figured as a claim to a discernment which rises beyond immediate use or gratification, could grant its user, if successful, a prestige and licence in other areas of social life; most notably political and cultural debate. The question of taste becomes, therefore, a means of distinction.

With so many different constituencies attempting to define what the words 'Taste' and 'Beauty' encapsulated and how they were to be defined, it is not surprising that the situation grew as confused as it did by the middle decades of the century. One writer was to claim 'of all our favourite Words lately, none has been more in Vogue, nor so long held its Esteem, as that of TASTE'.[29] The comment captures something of the uncertainty of the debate, as it refers to both the changing nature of fashion and the more certain qualities which have held the debate 'so long' in public view. Most thinkers in the period engaged to write something on the nature of taste or beauty, often aiming to 'fix' or to 'ascertain' the 'true' standard of taste in the process. The most persuasive thinkers were those who looked on the issue as a social one, and looked for cultural causes of appreciation and difference of opinion. David Hume, for example, in his essay 'Of the Standard of Taste', aimed to explore the diversity of opinion in this matter – its 'great inconsistence and contrariety' – and to provide at least some measure of regulation.[30] His opening remarks are significant for the way in which they highlight the predicament of beauty as a discursive counter:

The sentiments of men often differ with regard to beauty and deformity of all kinds, even while their general discourse is the same. There are certain terms in every language, which impart blame, and others praise; and all men, who use the same tongue, must agree in the application of them. Every voice is raised in applauding elegance, propriety, simplicity, spirit in writing; and in blaming fustian, affectation and false brilliancy: But when critics come to particulars, this seeming unanimity vanishes, and it is found, that they have affixed a very different meaning to their expression.[31]

Samuel Johnson was of much the same mind, observing that, 'the idea of beauty is vague and undefined, different in different minds, and diversified by time or place'.[32] Cooper remained less charitable, writing of the 'poor prostituted word TASTE', and representing the word as a term used without discrimination to sanctify every passing fancy, or current whim.[33] For Cooper, true taste must ever be in conflict with what is merely the 'motley production of modern refinement'. However, his drive to clarify what constituted taste ultimately led to precisely the forms of instability which he sought to remove.[34]

Burke wrote more specifically, comparing the misuse of the word 'sublime' to the ways in which 'beauty' is employed, claiming that: 'the abuse of the word *Beauty*, has been still more general, and attended with still worse consequences'.[35] Accordingly, Burke writes with the aim of fixing and setting what is truly beautiful. It was, however, a near impossible task. Unlike the sublime, the beautiful is not confined to a given nomenclature or range of experiences. It was possible, in the eighteenth century, to agree that the sublime was manifested in a certain greatness or obscurity. This is not so in the case of beauty, as the properties to which it can refer were apparently innumerable and certainly highly mutable. Writing half a century

after Burke, Richard Payne Knight was able to give a clear picture
of the problem:

The word Beauty is a general term of approbation, of the most vague and
extensive meaning, applied indiscriminately to almost everything that is
pleasing, either to the sense, the imagination, or the understanding;
whatever the nature of it be, whether a material substance, a moral
excellence, or an intellectual theorem. We do not, indeed, so often speak of
beautiful smells, or flavours, as beautiful forms, colours, and sounds; but,
nevertheless, we apply the epithet to a problem, a syllogism, or a period, as
familiarly, and (as far as we can judge from authority) as correctly as to a
rose, a landscape, or a woman. We speak also, and, I believe, with equal
propriety, not only of the beauties of symmetry and arrangement, but of
those of virtue, charity, holiness &c. The illustrious author, indeed, of the
Inquiry into the Sublime and the Beautiful, chooses to consider such expressions
as improper, and to confine beauty to sensible qualities of things.[36]

Burke wanted, as Payne Knight suggests, to exclude several forms of
beauty and to tie the term to a much narrower range of signification.
In this endeavour, Burke largely failed. Knight thought that this was
inevitable; it is impossible, he argues, to change the meaning of
words, to make them more precise and yet still be understood. The
problem is not merely one of language, however. Frances Ferguson
comments that, 'the beautiful continually needs watching, because it
can never be purified enough – for the very reason that it is allied
with society'.[37] Ferguson is writing here about Kant, but the remark
also makes sense in relation to Burke. Burke's desire to define
conclusively that which pleases was therefore frustrated by the
project itself. Too much was engaging, a fact which, as Neil Hertz
suggests, left beauty as a kind of wish-fulfilment, a hoped for end to
signification.[38]

What Knight's appraisal of Burke's predicament suggests, is that,
by the middle of the century, the word 'Beauty' had itself become an
over-abundant commodity. As a result its meaning in any given
context was ambiguous. I can borrow a description of a similarly
uncertain moment – Raymond Williams's description of the 'languages' of post-war Cambridge – to make clear my point and my
sense of its importance:

What is . . . happening through these cultural encounters, which may be
very conscious or may be felt only as a certain strangeness or unease, is a
process quite central to the development of a language when, in certain
words, tones and rhythms, meanings are offered, felt for, tested, confirmed,

asserted, qualified, changed. In some situations this is a very slow process indeed; it needs the passage of centuries to show itself actively, by results, at anything like its full weight. In other situations the process can be rapid, especially in certain key areas.[39]

It will be my contention throughout this study, that the eighteenth-century preoccupation with the beautiful is one such rapidly moving 'key area'. As so much of Williams's work demonstrated, the 'development of a language' constitutes one of the foremost processes of cultural evolution. For Williams, language and culture exist in a productive relation to one another, he writes that: 'a definition of language is always, implicitly or explicitly, a definition of human beings in the world'.[40] It is important to Williams's account of these fraught linguistic encounters, that 'no single group is "wrong" by any linguistic criterion, though a temporally dominant group may try to enforce its own uses as "correct"'.[41] This is an important distinction. The intention of this study is not to decide which judgements about beauty were correct or which misplaced, but to explore the claims made for that discernment. In particular, close attention will be given to the instabilities and ambiguities of competing modes of social address, viewed in terms of their class and gender politics.

Strikingly, the indeterminacy of the debate was a fact of which participants were only too well aware, in Burke's fine and accurate assessment:

We find people in their disputes continually appealing to certain texts and standards which are allowed on all sides, and are supposed to be established in our common nature. But there is not the same obvious concurrence in any uniform or settled principals which relate to taste.[42]

Burke's comment seems to me characteristic of much of the writing on taste produced in the mid-century. Uncertain in its address, and perhaps of the terms of the argument, Burke's *Enquiry* attempts to clarify the nature of taste. But as Burke concedes, 'the term Taste, like all other figurative terms, is not extremely accurate . . . and it is therefore liable to uncertainty and confusion'.[43] It is a mood captured by the *Connoisseur* in a vitriolic article, first published in May 1756, a little under a year before Burke's *Enquiry* was first offered to the public:

Taste is at present the darling idol of the polite world and the world of letters; and, indeed, seems to be considered as the quintessence of almost all the arts and sciences. The fine ladies and gentlemen dress with Taste; the architects, whether *Gothic* or *Chinese*, build with Taste; the painters paint with Taste; critics read with Taste; and in short, fiddlers, players, singers, dancers and mechanics themselves are all the sons and daughters of Taste. Yet in this amazing superabundancy of Taste, few can say what it really signifies.[44]

The term taste attains on this reading an unpleasant, near useless ubiquity, so that it either fails to define or to discriminate. For the *Connoisseur*, taste is being appropriated by those who have no legitimate claim upon it; the fashionable, the foreign and the mechanic. Its superabundancy signifies not its triumph, but its exhaustion. There is much here in common with Cooper's condemnation of the villas by the Thames, as both texts desire a delimitation both of modern wealth and new consumption in ways which mirror Burke's concern with words.[45]

As my quotations from Hume, Cooper and Burke have indicated, changes within cultural discourse can happen frequently – and noticeably – in this 'key area' of eighteenth-century debate. The discussion of the beautiful was taken up within several discourses and within divergent genres. As a result there is not one account of beauty, but several – a fact which produces the superabundance and promiscuity of which Cooper and the *Connoisseur* complain. A given author might refer his or her readers to a variety of objects – this could include the beauty of landscape, that of classical poetry, women or virtue. Equally, the argument of a particular text could present those judgements in distinctive ways, which are reliant on different criteria and particular notions of approval. It is possible therefore to think of beauty as a concept which was articulated within a series of distinct, yet overlapping discourses, each subject to the requirements of a particular genre or the persuasions of an individual writer.[46] It is important, therefore, to employ a theoretical model which can successfully discover the level of conflict, hesitation and interrelation such a complex, discursive situation necessarily produces. Peter de Bolla describes such a situation, when he writes that 'at any specific historical juncture a discursive network articulates the real, it allows and controls the possibilities for representation':

This network is made up of a number of discrete discourses which interact sometimes without hostility, at other times with considerable violence. The distances and line of force between specific discourses vary to a great extent, so that a particular discourse present to a specific discursive network may have almost insignificant connections to all the other discourses within the network.[47]

According to de Bolla, different discourses are present at any one cultural moment, furthermore how they relate to each other is variable – the discourses which describe beauty in the fine arts may or may not have cause to refer to an appraisal, say, of women, or poetry – consequently, there is a considerable 'difficulty in describing the precise distances or connections discrete discourses have to one another'.[48] What is persuasive in this model of the network is its capacity to accommodate not only a diversity of discourses, but a difference of reading and function. With the interconnections of discourses conceived as an open-ended 'network', de Bolla's analysis allows for different points of access and assessment within the same framework of discourses and texts.[49] This enables an effective consideration of diverse reading positions: philosopher and dilet-tante, aristocrat and merchant, male and female. This is precisely the commitment demanded by diverse and often conflicting eighteenth-century constructions of the beautiful.

In the light of de Bolla's model, it is possible to see how a focus on eighteenth-century discussions of the beautiful can highlight the term's participation, as a keyword, within a wide variety of appar-ently divergent or merely coincidental areas. Although it would be foolish to suggest that a reference to beauty pervades every sphere of activity, it does not seem unreasonable to suggest that a reading of the debates about taste and beauty offer potentially valuable insights into the culture as a whole. With this in mind, I want to use the remainder of this chapter to explore how it is possible within the eighteenth-century discussions of the beautiful to move from an account of the appeal of a given object to a less bounded, more socially and morally active form of address. This address can take the form, as it did for the third Earl of Shaftesbury, of a simultaneous selection and appeal to those capable of apprehending beauty (alongside order and proportion) and a call to the performance of civic virtue. However, for writers less concerned than Shaftesbury with the political significance of beauty, a reference to debates about taste constituted a more modest claim to culture and refinement. Such claims were based not on Shaftesbury's austere public of male citizens anxious about their virtue, but were directed instead towards a polite and sociable environment in which both sexes are present. As a result, beauty can have a different signification, a difference which is dependent on not only the object to which the reference is made, but, perhaps more importantly, to the status of the speaker making the assessment in relation to his and, less frequently, to her audience.

FROM CIVITAS TO CIVILITY: THE RE-EDUCATION OF HERCULES

To a large degree, the uncertainties attending any description of the beautiful arose because of the way in which discussions of beauty were located within texts which argued for profoundly ethical positions. One such discourse was the republicanism articulated by Shaftesbury, and later, on slightly different terms, by Joshua Reynolds. Both Shaftesbury and Reynolds employ a theory of the beautiful, not merely as a way of making claims about art, though this is important, but as a way of forming arguments about morality and politics as well as the conduct of public and social life. For Shaftesbury, the proper order of society and indeed the universe, could be visualised by reference to the beautiful. Furthermore, an appreciation of that beauty would encourage the subject both to seek and to preserve that order, thereby maintaining the political and social status quo. It is to this ideal, that Shaftesbury refers when he writes that:

the admiration and love of order, harmony and proportion, in whatever kind, is naturally improving to the temper, advantageous to social affections, and highly assistant to virtue, which is itself no other than the love of order and beauty . . . if the order of the world appears just and beautiful, the admiration and esteem of order must run higher, and the elegant passion or love of beauty, which is so advantageous to virtue must be improved by its exercise in so noble and magnificent a subject.[50]

Shaftesbury's sense of what is entailed by 'beauty' and 'virtue' was distinctive, and was to have repercussions throughout the eighteenth century. As John Barrell has argued it was possible from the publication of Shaftesbury's *Characteristics of Men, Manners, Opinions, Times* in 1711 through almost to the 1830s to use the beautiful to signal a particular kind of affiliation, defined as membership of the republic of taste.[51] This was an affiliation which sought to establish a distance from the individual concerns of private life and, perhaps more importantly from the sordid preoccupations of commercial practice.

Shaftesbury's firm ideological commitment to the function of beauty as the sign of virtue rested upon the ability of the citizen to distinguish between the universal good embodied by the state and their own particular interests. This is a claim that Shaftesbury underlines when he writes that:

to deserve the name of good and virtuous, a creature must have all his inclinations and affections, his disposition of mind and temper, suitable, and agreeing with the good of his kind, or of that system in which he is included, and of which he constitutes a part. To stand thus well affected, to have one's affections right and entire, not only in respect of oneself but of society and the public, this is rectitude, integrity or virtue. And to be wanting in any of these, or to have their contraries, is depravity, corruption and vice.[52]

In these terms virtue is defined by the ability to rise above particular concerns or personal interests. All personal gratification is deferred, even denied. Public identity, the allegiance to the universal good, becomes, as a result, an existence beyond the self. Shaftesbury makes public virtue paramount, but restricts the capacity to act publicly to men of his own social position.[53] Within such a culture, Shaftesbury believed that it was possible to instil the kind of lesson which would ensure that liberty was preserved and corruption thwarted. It was a lesson he had learned from reading ancient histories; early Greek and Roman citizens were, he wrote, disciplined from an early age for 'the command of others; to maintain their country's honour in war, rule wisely in the State, and fight against luxury and corruption in times of peace and prosperity'.[54] According to Shaftesbury, it was as a result of this stern self-regulation, and guided by the pursuit of beauty and virtue, that the ancient republics maintained their freedom and their dignity. There was no area of life which Shaftesbury regarded exempt from the need for such discrimination:

Even in the Arts, which are mere imitations of . . . outward grace and beauty, we not only confess a taste but make it part of refined breeding to discover amidst the many false manners and ill style the true and natural one, which represents the real beauty.[55]

Spoken of in these terms, appreciation of the beautiful provided an analogy with entrance into the more ideal world of the public sphere and the realisation of true citizenship. Without this discrimination, the ability to grasp the universal, it is impossible to 'represent merit and virtue, or mark deformity and blemish', whether in the political realm of the citizen or in the appreciation of the connoisseur.

We have come to describe this form of republicanism as 'civic-humanist', and it is in reference to this conception of politics that recent discussions of the formation of taste in eighteenth-century Britain have been conducted. The term owes its origin to the discipline of intellectual history, most prominently to the work of J.G.A. Pocock.[56] In this context it is used to describe the resurgence of the idea that political life was to be organised around the classical ideal of the citizen's allegiance to, and participation in, a free and secular state. In British thought, this revival is most marked in the seventeenth and eighteenth centuries, and is most illuminated by a consideration of the careers and opinions of John Harrington, and Viscount Bolingbroke, before the discourse's sentimental revision by Burke.[57] A convenient summary of this version of republican ideology has been provided by Pocock himself:

Since the revival of the ideal of active citizenship by Florentine civic-humanists, there had been a gathering reemphasis on the ancient belief that the fulfilment of man's life was to be found in political association, coupled with an increasing awareness of the historical fragility of the political forms in which this fulfilment must be sought. *Virtue* could only be found in a *republic* of equal, active, and independent citizens, and it was a term applied both to the relations between these citizens and to the healthful condition of the personality of each one of them; but the republic was peculiarly exposed to *corruption* – a state of affairs often identified with the dependence of citizens upon the powerful, instead of upon the public authority – and the corruption of the republic must entail the corruption of the individual personality, which could only flourish when the republic was healthy.[58]

Translated into a British context of aristocrats and parliaments, the ability to be a citizen was thought to rely on the practices and principles of patrician landownership. In what is arguably one of the most blatant fulfilments of Marx's dictum that 'the ruling ideas are nothing more than the ideal expression of the dominant material relationships', the ownership of land was not thought of as owner-ship at all.[59] Or if it was, it was not the possession of anything as vulgar as a commodity, but rather the possession of a permanent fixed interest in the state, held in trust for succeeding generations. So conceived, aritistocratic landowners were thought to be above the particular and divisive economic interests which debarred the East India merchant from the exercise of citizenship fully as much as the cobbler and the tallow-chandler.

The most comprehensive account of this political position, in terms of a theorisation of taste and the Arts, was provided by Shaftesbury himself and was directed towards those 'conceived of by the discourse of civic humanism as a ruling class'.[60] In strict adherence to the civic-humanist doctrine of free citizenry capable and willing to exercise its virtue as much as its discrimination, the triumph of the arts described by Shaftesbury is a vision of a free polity:

Everything co-operates, in such a State, towards the improvement of art and science. And for the designing arts in particular, such as architecture, painting and statuary, they are in a manner linked together. The Taste of one kind brings necessarily that of the others along with it. When the free spirit of a nation turns itself this way, judgements are formed; critics arise; the public eye and ear improve; a right taste prevails, and in a manner forces its way.[61]

In such an environment, all art becomes good and a 'right taste', unmarked by fashion or caprice, reigns supreme. In civic-humanist terms, true beauty can only exist in such a state, as it is only in such an environment, that taste can be free from luxury and despotism. That Shaftesbury is locating his account of the arts within a conception of the state indicates something of the nature of his civic-humanist politics.[62] Civic humanism, as Pocock makes plain, laid great stress on the integrity of political office as the guarantor of liberty.[63] As such the condemnation of corruption was offered alongside a call for disinterested virtue and public spiritedness as the basis of the civic description of the social. To read Shaftesbury's remarks on painting and on the arts in general is to discover that language transposed into an account of taste, such that the 'public eye and ear' comes to expect and to judge only that which is free from the taint of particular customs and affectations. Painting, argued Shaftesbury, can only exist in a free polity; the point being that Britain should be made one, and if it could not then it was necessary to imagine that it could.[64]

This ideal was to remain the prevailing fantasy of English theorists and proponents of art for the next century and a half. Reynolds certainly endorses it, while Mark Akenside, one of Shaftesbury's

earliest adherents, describes the process of rejuvenation of the arts
thus:

> Arm'd with a lyre, already have we dared
> To pierce divine Philosophy's retreats
> And teach the Muse her lore; already strove
> Their long-divided honours to unite,
> While tempering this deep argument we sang
> Of Truth and Beauty. Now the same fair task
> Impends; now urging our ambitious toil,
> We hasten to recount the various springs
> Of adventitious pleasure, which adjoin
> Their grateful influence to the prime effect
> Of objects grand or beauteous, and indulge
> The complicated joy.[65]

The 'complicated joy' is that of taste as it returns to an England
finally gaining the trappings of true greatness. The image refers at
once to the refinement of all judgement and to the reunification of
truth and beauty in the form of the reconnection of 'Philosophy' and
'Imagination'. However, Akenside takes the debate beyond the
ground upon which Shaftesbury was prepared to travel. Continuing
his celebration of the return of true taste Akenside writes of art's
rejuvenation in terms of the pleasure given to the faculty of the
'Fancy', making it much more sensuous than does his predecessor:

> . . . The Sweets of sense,
> Do they not oft with kind accession flow,
> To raise harmonious Fancy's native charm?[66]

That Akenside is moving the debate along, elaborating and changing
what he takes from Shaftesbury, will be important in later chapters.
Here, though, I want to stress that Akenside, like Shaftesbury, is
engaged in a project in which the beautiful is closely related to the
political as a representation of the political order and public
obligation.[67] Indeed his confidence that the arts will improve is
based on the precisely civic hope of a return to 'public Liberty'.[68]

However, despite the confident predictions made in the texts such
as *The Pleasures of the Imagination*, Shaftesbury and his immediate
followers stumbled when it came to the detailed application or
elaboration of their ideas. While Shaftesbury could argue that 'the
order of the world appears just and beautiful', he was far less able to
describe what this order might be, or what form it might take. It is
suspended, with a circumlocution typical of Shaftesbury, as a kind of

general category – 'order, harmony and proportion' – and a general-ised mode of reception, 'the elegant passion or love of Beauty'. What 'Beauty' might entail, and who and what may possess it, is left unstated, for to state it would be to render it visible, and hence to vulgarise it. This is the problem which besets civic accounts of the beautiful throughout the eighteenth century, for in order to be represented it must take a particular form, once embodied it necessarily loses much of the generality which originally gave it moral and rhetorical force. For civic-humanists like Shaftesbury, the problem lay in the very founding exclusions of civic humanism itself: in the forms of particularity it could not and would not tolerate. Particular tastes were to be the major source of problems for civic theorists. There were two principal forms of 'bad' particularity which could corrupt the civic virtuosi: the quest for commodities, or the consumption of particular goods and services; and the desire for (and ultimately the desires of) women. The exclusion of commercial wealth – in particular the luxuries Shaftesbury chose to call 'Lady fancies' – became an increasingly intractable issue for civic theory from the 1720s onwards. The claims, which could be made against or on behalf of commerce, were critical by the mid-century, largely because of the questions trade provoked about the practice of virtue and formation of political (or public) personality. From the civic perspective, the growth of commerce made for a new depravity; Akenside described 'Taste' as shrouded in a 'Gothic Night' of ignorance and interest.[69] While commerce polished and improved, it also assaulted and softened the basis of republican personality. As Pocock writes, from a civic perspective 'the growth of refinement was the corruption of personality':

In a commercial society, men became more refined, more enlightened, and more specialised – women aiding them in this to the limits of the capacity that social theory assigned them – but they moved away from the single-minded devotion to the city which characterised the warrior, the citizen, the patriot.[70]

Some of Shaftesbury's writings, most notably, the *Inquiry into Virtue and Merit*, indicate that he was prepared to go someway towards accommodating the requirements and aspirations of a flourishing commercial society.[71] However, Shaftesbury remained deeply suspi-cious of any attempt to privilege individual interest over the public good. His texts may attempt to accommodate desire, but they do so only after Shaftesbury had rendered that impulse subservient to a general end.

Accordingly, while Shaftesbury's conception of the beautiful possessed enough of the sensual for it to function, as Terry Eagleton argues, as a 'political unconscious', it remained little concerned with the appreciation of the body, or even of particular forms.[72] Current taste, in particular, was derided and represented as effeminate consumption, represented throughout the *Characteristics* as the product of women's unwanted intrusion upon men's reasoned and reasonable society. Women presented an especial problem for Shaftesbury, who frequently counselled his readers against association with the 'fair sex' as an activity likely to prove injurious to their civic virtue and to their public reputations. To Shaftesbury's mind, the presence of women led to adoration that was far from manly. Furthermore, he thought their beauty too particular and too sensual to lead to the contemplation of a higher order of being. As a result, the ability to define real beauties and not just passing fancies or mere pleasures (of the kind women might offer) was crucial to the exercise of the civic mind. The concept of beauty was, therefore, endowed with great power as well as ambivalence by Shaftesbury. Within his discourse, beauty acts as both a conception of the order of the universe and, as a kind of test against which the citizen can be measured. Shaftesbury writes on the latter issue counselling an avoidance of the corrupting charms of individual beauties and their luxuriance.[73]

The most explicit example of this formulation occurs in Shaftesbury's 'A Notion of the Historical Draught or Tablature of Hercules'. The text is an account of how to represent the 'Choice or Judgement of Hercules' in the historical style.[74] According to Shaftesbury, Hercules should be shown standing between the emblematic figures of Virtue and Pleasure. Following the story taken from Xenophon, the ancient hero is to be depicted choosing between the two and, in so doing, determining the course of his life. The decision is of immense importance, as 'it is on the issue of the controversy between the two, that the character of Hercules depends'.[75] If Hercules chooses Pleasure, he will sink into inactive luxuriance; if his choice, however, is for Virtue, then he will pursue a life of honour and courage. It was the 'agony' of this choice which made in Shaftesbury's mind for the principal action. For, wrote Shaftesbury, 'the interest of Hercules himself is at stake. It is his own cause which is trying. He is in this respect not so much the judge, as he is in reality the party judged.'[76] Hercules' judgement, if he chooses correctly, is an act of self-preservation. To attain virtue, Hercules must renounce sensual gratification. In performing this action he will have proved himself able – like the true citizen – to proceed beyond his own concerns and to have become a man capable of virtue, in its highest civic sense. The choice would appear to be easily apprehended. It is to decide between a preference made on the basis of instinct and that promoted by reason. Shaftesbury's position in the 'Notion' is one of stern disavowal: Hercules as the patriot hero, must reject all the temptations of the recumbent Pleasure and ascend instead the rugged path of virtue. The choice facing Hercules is, therefore clear cut; moreover, were he to choose wrongly, the false trail would be difficult to leave. In this late piece Shaftesbury is clear that to do other than one's civic, public duty is to fall into an insipid, amoral effeminacy, for the particular, sexualised pleasures of luxury drain the vigour required for proper conduct.

Notwithstanding Shaftesbury's tremendous influence of the development of taste as an object of intellectual inquiry, many of the writers who succeeded him were reluctant or unable to pursue the issue of beauty's relation to civic virtue with quite the consistency which Shaftesbury would have desired. By the mid-eighteenth century, for reasons I shall later describe, it no longer appeared necessary or even possible to exclude the particular pleasures Shaftesbury found so debilitating. By contrast, later writers reformulated taste in a way which brought bodily pleasure within the orbit of virtue. Joseph Spence was one such writer, significantly his monumental work *Polymetis, or an Enquiry Concerning the Agreement Between the Works of the Roman Poets and the Remains of the Ancient Artists* exhibited a more sensual appreciation of beauty than Shaftesbury could have accepted. In broad outline, Spence's history of the Roman poets employs a historical narrative which follows poetry's progression from early rude force through various glories before the arts sink, into what Spence describes, as 'a certain prettiness, and glitter, and luxuriance of ornaments'. It is an account which in proposing a 'kind of sympathy between all the polite arts', sees them 'languish and flourish' together, according to the prevailing morality of the times.[77] Thus far Spence is in agreement with Shaftesbury, who in the *Characteristics*, similarly charted the decline of the ancient arts into luxuriant corruption exemplified by the pursuit of false beauties.[78] Spence believed, in common with Shaftesbury, that it was only by a robust resistance to the unmanly pleasures of luxury and effeminacy that a society and its arts could proceed.[79]

Despite the importance of these connections, Spence abandons his distaste for the pretty and the luxuriant and begins to appreciate, even to enjoy, that which is mere softness and sensual delight; principally, the *Venus di Medici*. The statue, a copy of which is in Polymetis' garden temple, is the object of his devotions, she has in fact, 'one of the prettiest faces that can be conceived'. Hers is a figure which he can describe only in less than disinterested terms. In a passage which terminates with Spence's delight at the softness and delicacy of the breasts, the statue is said to be a 'bewitching' and 'wanton' piece; moreover, she is 'the standard of all female beauty and softness'.[80] As the excited prose makes clear, there is less sense in Spence's account of the need for restraint, or for seeing the *Venus di Medici* in terms other than those expressing one's sexual preferences. Throughout the passage pleasure is at issue, and it would appear pleasure alone. Accordingly, Spence delights in describing how Mars was entrapped by her charms, claiming that it is a 'pretty' act of imagination to recount the story.[81] Mars's fate can be repeated, so that it is possible that the goddess has 'made a conquest of you'. Spence was aware of what is at stake here, confessing that:

to confess the truth to you, I am so much in love with the Venus di Medici, that I rather choose to court this impropriety, than to prefer any other figure to hers. The thing is not perhaps quite so reasonable, as it should be; but when did lovers ever act with reason?[82]

There is then some retention of the civic sense of the danger of 'galante' adoration, of the idea that it represents a loss of the self. However, Spence increasingly displays an interest in the idea of Venus' character, speculating that, while she is often thought of as 'treacherous', she is, in reality, 'all graceful, and bewitching, and charming'.[83] By degrees Spence has cautiously changed the terms of the debate. While for Shaftesbury, the 'character' of Hercules was secured by abstaining from pleasure, for Spence, it is the pursuit of what pleases, which is the ground of character. The relationship between the virility of the male subject and the chastity of the feminine object is made the issue. As a result, the character who is judged is more likely to be Venus, than Hercules. Having freed himself from suspicion, Spence can insinuate, for example, that though Venus 'is not really modest, [she] counterfeits modesty extremely well', because he is not being judged as Hercules was by Shaftesbury.[84]

What Spence's text suggests, I think, is that although the account of taste favoured by patricians like Shaftesbury had been formed in a visibly homosocial environment wedded to the ideal of aristocratic male independence, women, as participants of refined society, had become the most readily available example of beauty, and sign of the instant gratification which attended its comprehension.[85] These new attitudes towards beauty, those which were encouraged by this changed definition of social roles, were necessarily different from that envisaged for the princely schoolroom outlined by Shaftesbury. This shift in emphasis and address is something to which Spence, even as he compiles an essentially civic rendering of the arts, cannot but draw attention. Returning to the excellences of the *Venus di Medici* he remarks that:

From her breasts, her shape begins to diminish gradually down to her waist; which I remember to have heard an English Lady at Florence, criticising at first sight, as not fine and taper enough. This probably proceeded from our beauties in England carrying this nicety generally too far; as some of the Grecian beauties did formerly too, at Athens. And I am more persuaded that this was the case, because the same lady (who one would think should be a good judge of beauty, because it is what she must see, at least, every time she looks in her glass,) after having seen the Venus di Medici several times, had the grace to own herself in the wrong; and even to exclaim against the excess of this mode among us. The Venus di Medici, with all her fineness of shape, has what the Romans call corpus solidium, and the French embonpoint; (I do not know that we have any right word for it in English). And her waist in particular, is not represented as stunted by art; but as exactly proportioned by nature, to all the other parts of her body.[86]

According to Spence's account the English seem to lack an appropriately specialist vocabulary for this kind of appraisal. If English connoisseurs were to acquire a special word for the beauties embodied by the *Venus di Medici*, it would, on this reading, have to accommodate a vision of aestheticised plumpness or a pleasingly curvaceous form. The inability of the English language to provide Spence with an appropriate set of terms, reveals the uncertain discourse in which his remarks are written. On the whole, Spence, as I have already observed, is concerned with the public lessons it was possible to draw from the consideration of ancient statuary and classical poetry. Here, however, he wanders from that theme. His account of the statue may begin coherently enough, but he soon slides into an account of the depredations of contemporary dress. The woman's poor judgement is represented as entirely owing to the commodifying nature of current fashion. According to Spence, when she finally judges aright, it is a move propelled by a narcissism which collapses the difference between subject and object. However, her acceptance of a better taste is a concession accomplished with a refined and pleasing 'good grace'.

More important, perhaps, than these specific points, is the sense that the commentary on the judgement of Venus, the high point of a civic act of repudiating manliness, becomes a judgement more particularly concerned with women and their conduct, for which the touring 'English Lady' stands as a metonym. Significantly, her function is twofold: to stand as representative of women as a whole and to represent all those whose taste is defective. Her appearance at this point, both in terms of her entrance into the text and the form of her personal charms and fashionable foibles, is then important, if ambivalently so. What might have begun in terms of an obligation (perhaps playfully made) for men to restrict their sexual appetites, becomes a required renunciation for women to give over fashion, judgement and the capacity to be anything more than the recipient of male pedagogy. The 'English Lady at Florence' becomes the object of culture – the fetishised object of beauty and taste – and only occasionally the subject of that discourse.[87] However, while Spence has disparaged and exploited the figure of the 'English Lady', she remains included, and her presence is recorded. This represents an important change in English thinking about judgement and society. *Polymetis* begins with a gathering of male worthies tired after 'the business of a long session'.[88] It was therefore a social gathering, characterised by the apparently private leisure interests of public men. In this passage, Spence has moved away from that arena, and describes a moment of polite sociability: discourse with, as much as about, women. He is anxious about the change, representing Polymetis as wary, though playful, about the role and effect of women and their beauty. In what follows it will become evident that this form of appraisal, based upon a consideration of femininity and feminine beauty, began first to intrude upon and then to dominate eighteenth-century accounts of taste.

DISPLAYS OF RENUNCIATION: DIVIDING PUBLIC AND PRIVATE
PLEASURE

It will be clear from my argument so far, that I have only begun to
describe why it was that the beautiful attained the prominence and
the currency it did in the eighteenth century. I have said little, as yet,
about how it could become the source of conflict and contestation
comparable to that described so vividly by Williams. In many
respects, what I wish to concentrate on is the very moment of
historical fragility (to use Pocock's phrase) that was occasioned by
the redistribution of wealth, and, to a much lesser extent, power, that
occurred during the middle years of the eighteenth century. Pocock,
together with other historians, has argued that the expansion of
commerce in the eighteenth century forced contemporary thinkers
to redefine personality; no longer could the participatory virtues of
civic humanism, with its strident requirements for public and
military life, operate in a society divided along conflicting lines of
private interest. As many cultural historians have suggested, the
discourse of civility offered at least a partial resolution of this
tension. Developed as a language and a code of social practice,
civility or politeness did not demand the martial and manly skills of
the seventeenth century, but sought instead a polite public culture; a
society, at once tasteful and polite, yet adapted to the business of
making money. It is in the space of such refinement, and within the
campaigns for the reformation of manners, that the majority of texts
on taste and beauty can be most profitably situated. In such an
environment masculinity and femininity were to change their
meaning and modalities. As both sexes sought the company and
conversation of the other, in the increasingly heterosocial world of
the market and the assembly room, it became necessary to redefine
the roles of each sex. In order to bring the sexes together, men
rejected or were at least expected to shed, their more violent and
boorish tastes, indeed men were expected to be easy in the company
of women. Simultaneously, women were increasingly required to
display an engaging fineness of feeling. It is without question, that
the realignment of social identities, required by the persuasive
rhetoric of civility had an enormous impact on the way in which
gender roles were prescribed during the eighteenth century.[89] It has
been with a sense of the importance of these changes that much
attention has recently been given to the complexities of the relation-

ship between the public or private spheres, together with a consideration of how these formations might establish class-inflected and gendered positions.[90]

A reading of debates about the nature and apprehension of beauty in the light of this history, reveals how middle-class intellectuals secured a formulation of taste by routeing it through the language of civility and politeness. This was a strategy, which could give primacy to private, sometimes individual, desire and gratification, without necessarily compromising virtue. Such a reconciliation of desire and virtue had not been possible at the beginning of the century, when the relationship between virtue and what was termed 'the interests' or 'the passions' caused Shaftesbury considerable difficulty (though the issue was treated rather more brazenly by Bernard Mandeville). Indeed expression of appetite, longing or even individual inclination had always threatened to disrupt the discussion of taste.[91] However, by mid-century, the separation between public good and individual interest required by civic humanism was less rigorously upheld. With the increased cultural significance of the middle class becoming more and more evident, a new rationalisation of conduct was required, one that gave at least some credence to desire. John Barrell defines eighteenth-century criticism as first opposing and then accepting what it appears to deny:

The prestige of a male ruling class, it is claimed by the civic discourse on the fine arts, has to be earned by that act of renunciation; but the prestige of the middle class critic and connoisseur comes to be earned in a more comprehensive fashion. It is won by a public *display* of renunciation, which by granting a legitimacy to an interest in the aesthetic gives a licence to what it appears to have renounced.[92]

Importantly, Barrell's account implies only an apparent renunciation, he leaves '*display*' hanging between honest practice and deliberate disingenuousness. I would like to expand upon the hesitation, which seems to me a shrewd one. It was, I will argue, a mere '*display* of renunciation' that characterised much eighteenth-century writing on taste.

Barrell's description of the process, by which a sexualised aesthetic pleasure is made acceptable by an act of stoic self-denial, turns upon the question of defining what constitutes the public sphere in which this act of disavowal is to take place. Barrell suggests that 'the public sphere is involved not in one but in two binary relationships with the private'; in the first 'the public is constructed as the *opposite* of a private sphere which is openly theorised by the discourse of civic humanism, and which defines what the citizen *should* do in his private capacity. In the second binary, there is another version of the private, constructed as the *contrary* of the public . . . and defines what the citizen *may* do in private, so long as he is not thereby disabled from maintaining his public character and performing his public function.'[93] Thinkers, such as Shaftesbury, who employed a civic-humanist vocabulary, had, therefore, a sophisticated notion of what the public entails; it was the space of political office and of magisterial, parliamentary and military responsibilities. Defined by public participation, its predominant mode of address is that of rhetoric, both moral and political. The opposition of this space to that which is considered 'private' is therefore conventional and easily apprehended. For the private, in its virtuous form, must be the practicalities of landownership, particular acts of personal generosity or mercy, and the formalities of the court and social round, as well as those areas of life which are considered intimate or merely domestic. The other form of the private, that which is illicit, would have included vices ranging from gambling and drinking to visiting prostitutes. What unites these divergent areas is that they are assumed to have no public significance, unless through their excessive or vicious pursuit they impinge on the practice of a public life.

This distinction is not compatible with the middle-class experience of public culture. Without the obligations of office to give it coherence, the idea of the public which defines middle-class virtue was less easily apprehended and less obviously separable from private life. For this largely unenfranchised class (at least in political terms) any definition of 'publicity' or 'public virtue' had to be distinct from the aristocratic vision of the state, if it was to be anything other than an unattainable ideal. What is so marked, therefore, in the first half of the eighteenth century, is an attempt by middle-class (and largely professional) intellectuals to reformulate the civic discourse on virtue or to promote a new account sanctioning the actions that the middle classes could accomplish – notably industry, compassion, prudence – actions which were to be given the status of genuinely moral or social virtues. Any description of this process requires a complication of the public–private model suggested by a narrow reading of civic humanism. For in the minds of middle-class intellectuals, unwilling to accept their exclusion from debate, the public could not be imagined as merely that which was defined by the political. Indeed, it had to include much of what had previously been defined as private.

In contrast to the political realm described by civic humanism, the notion of the public sphere described by the middle-classes, and in which they accomplish acts of self-regulation, was comprised of 'public spaces' conceived of as locations of polite assembly, commerce and leisure.[94] It was not fundamentally an arena in which gratification was expected to be denied, though it was to be controlled and channelled. Given the importance of this second, middle-class notion of what it is to 'be public', it is necessary to consider eighteenth-century Britain as a culture in which there are at least two accounts of the private and two forms of the public – the civic and the sociable – in circulation at any one time. Contemporary writers frequently focused on the ambiguous relationship between the two spheres, often exploring how one space secured its virtue by recruiting the other.[95] Addison and Steele, along with Defoe, are the foremost exemplars in this initiative. Addison, in particular, sought to refashion the public sphere into a space appropriate for what were previously thought of as private acts, thus making it a sphere open to middle-class influence. Lawrence Klein argues the programmes of reformers such as Addison are best understood in terms of the cultural change he had defined as the 'rise of politeness'.

The kernel of the phenomenon was given in a simple phrase: "the art of pleasing in company". As such politeness encompassed technique, norm, and social environment: it was a set of attitudes, strategies, skills, and devices that an individual could command to gratify others and thus render himself truly sociable.[96]

Klein argues, that politeness was the discursive technique through which the strategies of a commercially based social life were reconciled with the traditional claims of virtue.[97] As Nicholas Phillipson remarks, Addison 'set out to show anxious men and women how to reorganise their conduct by bringing their morals and manners into alignment and becoming acceptable, virtuous agents in the process'.[98] Phillipson further suggests, that 'Addisonian politeness [was] presented as a mechanism for integrating the modern citizen's moral and social self and of overcoming a form of alienation which commerce brought with it'.[99] To accomplish this process was, according to Phillipson, an 'historic achievement'.[100]

The moral programmes propounded by Addison and Steele are familiar to most scholars working in the field of eighteenth-century studies. Found in the pages of the *Tatler* and *Spectator*, they provide a convenient and relatively coherent picture of the realignment of virtue in the first two decades of the eighteenth century. To give a slightly different picture, I want to take my example from the writings of the mid-century portrait-painter, Joseph Highmore. Highmore is an appropriate, as well as a slightly novel, instance of bourgeois sociability. A professional painter of the generation before Reynolds, he represents a particularly good example of the kind of subject I have in mind: civil, restrained, prudent and above all polite. His work as an artist is remarkable for the exactness and nicety with which it replicates ideas of manners suited to a commercial culture.[101] Therefore, it is of no surprise that his essay, 'Of Politeness and Complaisance, as Contradistinguished' is noteworthy for the precisely bourgeois caste it places upon the nature of politeness. For Highmore, politeness is a means of interacting with the world, which at once allows him to appear courteous and refined, yet does not require either the possession of landed wealth or deferral of gratification for its accomplishment. It is a quality and a performance which Highmore can define with well-practised ease:

politeness may be considered as a habit of saying and doing obliging things, or an apparent endeavour to give pleasure, and to avoid giving pain; with a particular attention to the taste and inclination of all, in which the manner is as significant as the matter, and will be as visible in little circumstances as in greater.[102]

It was common, at least in aristocratic or traditional statements on politeness, to worry about, or to defend, the forms of social interaction it proposed against the charge that it was a mere show.[103] Highmore appears unconcerned with this critique, cheerfully allowing politeness to be an 'apparent endeavour . . . in which the manner is as significant as the matter'. What does concern him, however, is that politeness can overbalance into an 'indiscriminate subjection to the caprices of all'; such is the mere complaisance from which Highmore wishes true politeness to be 'Contradistinguished'. Politeness is, as he defines it, a moral good, a suitable companion virtue to personal benevolence. And yet he is cautious:

though benevolence is a most amiable natural quality, and politeness an
excellent and artificial accomplishment, of which the one is essential to a
good mind, and the other to a well-bred man; and both absolutely
necessary, to extend a man's influence in the world; yet he may possess and
exercise both these, in all the instances wherein they can be useful, without
subjecting himself to the tyranny of unlimited complaisance, which is so far
from being necessarily included in these, that it often interferes with them,
and sometimes unseasonably wears out an opportunity, not to be
recovered.[104]

On this account, complaisance is politeness and benevolence carried
to an excess; it is a 'yielding up of ourselves' to all and sundry. The
result is a waste of valuable time and money. Politeness, on the
contrary, allows you to 'dismiss' people when your duty – and
perhaps your pleasure – relies upon the avoidance of such supine
attentions. Highmore argues for the importance of opposing dissipation firmly – recommending that engagements are broken if they
are contrary to self-interest. For while 'politeness in the sense here
exhibited is to be industriously cultivated', it is not intended as a
blank cheque against which others can draw time, money or even
compassion. Instead, its purpose is to account for the day to day
exercises of a busy life in a courteous and morally respectable
manner. His 'opportunities' represent specific, local departures from
the pursuit of his business interests; Highmore is indeed making a
'*display* of renunciation'.

Highmore's sense of the necessity of moderation and prudence in
social and charitable expenses was one with which Addison was
broadly in accord. Though Addison praised charitable giving, he
noted that 'we should manage our Charity with such Prudence and
Caution, that we may not hurt our own Friends or Relations, whilst
we are doing good to those who are Strangers to us'.[105] What both
Addison and Highmore accomplished was the presentation of an
account in which benevolent action, polite conduct and the practices
of prudent social living are reconciled with a measure of personal
interest and appropriate self-regard. There is no requirement in
either account to be the selfless citizen who sets aside his needs and
aspirations in order to support the greater interest of the state. As
Addison's cautious remarks make plain, the discourse describing
virtuous sociability was distinctive in terms of its address to the
middle classes defined as prudent yet beneficent. This polemic was

consistent with Addison's most famous statement of intention in an early edition of the *Spectator*:

I shall be ambitious to have it said of me, that I have brought philosophy out of Closets and Libraries, Schools and Colleges, to dwell in Clubs and Assemblies, at Tea-Tables in Coffee houses.

I would therefore in a very particular manner recommend these my speculations to all well-regulated Families, that set apart an Hour in every Morning for Tea and Bread and Butter; and would earnestly advise them for their Good to order this Paper to be punctually served up, and to be looked upon as a Part of the Tea Equipage.[106]

Addison's description of a cultural consensus based upon both polite readers and 'well-regulated families' can be compared to Jurgen Habermas's description of the formation of the 'public sphere' in eighteenth-century Europe. Habermas defines the public as the coming together of private, atomised individuals through shared cultural interests and political assumptions. He writes:

The bourgeois public sphere may be conceived above all as the sphere of private people come together as a public; they soon claimed the public sphere regulated from above against the public authorities themselves, to engage them in a debate over the general rules governing relations in a basically privatised but publicly relevant sphere of commodity exchange and social labour.[107]

Habermas's account of the formation of the public, as this extract makes clear, is primarily concerned with how bourgeois subjects resisted political regulation enabling themselves to become free-thinking citizens. Throughout his study Habermas views this aspiration as one of the foremost achievements of European Enlightenment; as such, although Habermas indicates that the new public sphere was reliant on the private commercial activities of its participants, he does not explore the ambiguities such a dependence would have entailed in the eighteenth century.[108] Indeed Habermas has little interest in the conflicts and anxieties which accompanied the emergence of polite publicity in eighteenth-century Britain. Neither does he discuss how the idea of being public might have appeared dubious to contemporary moralists. As a result critiques of public culture, such as those propounded by civic humanists like John Brown or Samuel Fawconer, are largely ignored. Habermas omits their complaints because he considers opposition to the Public Sphere solely in the guise of the political resistance offered by an embattled executive. However, as J.G.A. Pocock has argued, nu-

merous eighteenth-century writers regarded the relationship
between the new public sphere and commerce as the source of
corruption and effeminacy, and not, as Habermas suggests, rationality and renewal.[109] Indeed for many in eighteenth-century Britain
commercial enterprise, far from providing an avowed and unquali-
fied imperative, was at once the source of a new culture and the
cause of imminent collapse. Part of the argument of this book will be
concerned with how this argument was conducted in British
accounts of both public judgement and private taste, and, most
importantly, how these debates were themselves reliant upon a
profoundly gendered language.

Without an appreciation of the significance of the gendered terms
in which debates about the nature of public culture were conducted
in the eighteenth-century it is impossible to understand the force and
range of the criticism of commercial culture which runs through the
writing not only of Addison and Steele, but also of Burke and
Reynolds. For example, the role of women in the sociable environment, described by Addison was central to its constitution as a
distinct social space, as to its claims to politeness and refinement.
According to Lawrence Klein, Addison's 'tea-table' philosophising is:

indicative of wider changes both in the maps of discourse and in the actual
landscapes which such maps attempted to interpret. Obviously, these
changes had implications for the gendering of discursive practices and for
women's relation to discourse in society.[110]

As Klein makes clear, the presence of women, an anathema to older
notions of the public (such as the civic humanism of Shaftesbury),
was one of the key features of polite society. Again Habermas's
account of modernity underestimates the significance and the
ambiguity of this aspect of public life and debate in the eighteenth
century.[111] Indeed Habermas's rather stilted treatment of the gendered nature of the public highlights the degree to which he is
unwilling to see the formation of the 'Bourgeois Public Sphere' as
the construction of only one version of the 'public', one which
existed alongside many others. The much used epithet of the 'public'
woman, provided cruel testimony of the degree to which definitions
of the public were subject to differing as well as uneven development. Indeed the very notion of the 'public' in the eighteenth-
century discourse is hugely contested, this is especially true when the
problematic issue of women's participation is addressed.

For male writers such as Steele, Shaftesbury and Spence, the issue of 'publicity' was related to a consideration of virtue, itself understood as a profoundly secular and innately masculine concern. The maleness and worldliness of the debate – observing women, watching against their effect on men – combines with the definition of the beautiful in the area of critical judgement to suggest an intersection of discourses which is profoundly social as well as thoroughly politicised. Shaftesbury deserves much credit for this alignment, as Robert Markley observes:

As an aristocrat, idealist, and Whig, Shaftesbury is an historically important figure because he shifts discussions of morality and virtue a way from the traditional rhetoric of religious orthodoxy to secular discourses of ideological power and prestige.[112]

While it is possible to dispute as to whether Shaftesbury was solely responsible for this shift – as a case could equally be made for Pope – he exerted considerable influence on subsequent discussions of beauty, and in particular on its relation to virtue. The movement of ideas from the patrician Shaftesbury to the polite philosophers of the mid-century is however a complex one. In what I take to be a suggestive but undeveloped remark, Markley writes of the 'new kinds of misreadings' to which Shaftesbury's work became available in the decades after its publication.[113] That a misreading, intentional or otherwise, provides a means of appropriating Shaftesburian ideas into the conduct and opinions of the middle classes is not perhaps the whole story. The processes of cultural transmission, which in the eighteenth century moved the debate on virtue further fom the terrain of religion and into the polite, worldly existence of the middle classes, was as tortuous as it was profound. For although Shaftesbury employed the beautiful as a sign of order within an idealised state, the writers who followed him were to deploy a notion of the beautiful as a way of representing a harmonious and polite sociability.[114] This key shift in the discursive location of the beautiful, can best be defined as a movement from a political discourse that endorsed the ideal form of beauty as a means of representing the nation-state, to a mode of cultural politics which used references to the beautiful as a way of signalling the Hanoverian age's capacity for sensibility and humanity as well as good taste.

It will be important for me to be able to refine and reformulate my argument as it progresses; however, much will be gained for the cause of clarity if I broadly outline the premises of my argument now, and then go on to complicate it later. I want to argue that the accounts of taste, and of beauty in particular, which were reworked in the mid-eighteenth century are remarkable for the ways in which they seek to provide – often within the form and repertoire of existing critical models, of which civic humanism is the most pressing instance – an explanation of taste which was an appropriate discourse for describing the more consciously private and domesticated lives of the middle classes. This is a move from philosophical representations of the order of the state to a means of representing the feelings and interactions of a middle-class and commercial culture. Once realigned in this manner, the discourses which define beauty become specifically committed to the emerging middle-class taste of the mid-century.[115] There was, however, no new dawn breaking in the 1740s, no wholesale or irrecoverable transformation. Rather, there was throughout the eighteenth century an attempt to redefine what constituted good or false taste, in a discourse, which borrows from and yet at other times contradicts, older and more authoritative texts.

Importantly, this will also be a narrative which reveals the changed identity of those participating in the discussion of taste and as such will reflect the turbulent nature of a culture in transition. At times the debate returns to a previous agenda, the Aristotelian or the Neoplatonic, and at other times develops new lines of inquiry; those determined by empiricism, sensibility and so forth. It is impossible, therefore, to construct a single history to explain the phenomenon of the beautiful in eighteenth-century culture. There is, for example, no direct transmission of ideas from the Neoplatonism of the 1690s through the associationism and sensibility of the mid-century, to find some resurgence, or at least restatement in such figures as Richard Payne Knight and Archibald Alison at the close of the period. Indeed, to confine the history of beauty to one narrative would be to obscure its nature and to deny its multiple intersections with the cultural fabric of the period. There are a number of ideas of beauty in circulation within the context of eighteenth-century society: the excellences of material objects; the attraction of beautiful women; painterly beauty; moral beauty; and theological and social graces. It is the aim of this book, to describe a history and a method which can bring some of them together.

CHAPTER ONE

'A Wanton Kind of Chase': gender, luxury and the redefinition of taste

The discursive nature of the beautiful made the concept an attractive ideological weapon for a number of constituencies within eighteenth-century society. In a period in which competing modes of social address sought to reflect class positions mediated through a discourse on taste and judgement, a reference to beauty could be employed to establish a wide range of social and cultural positions. The concept was variously and simultaneously used to signify the power and ambition of the aristocracy, while, alternatively, it could be used to describe the social relations which the middle classes found attractive. The feelings and the sensations which the beautiful was said to generate could therefore, depending on who was speaking (and for whom), announce claims to patrician excellence or bourgeois social affinity. Certainly, the huge number of treatises produced on the nature of taste during the course of the century provide weighty testimony to the assertion that the subject of beauty was an issue of more than philosophical interest. Recent critical studies have explored the scrupulousness with which writers such as David Hume, Alexander Gerard and Edmund Burke sought to define and to appraise the 'Standard of Taste'. It is important, however, not to miss, within the twists and turns of philosophical argument, the cultural urgency which animated and gave purpose to what might otherwise appear to be merely dense or over-sophisti-cated treatments of rather obscure problems.[1]

Current historical thinking about eighteenth-century Britain has suggested a country, and more ambiguously a 'culture', anxious to come to terms with its dual identity as a society both 'polite and commercial', or in Richard Steele's more mordant expression, 'the most polite age and the most vicious'.[2] Steele was not alone in finding society wholly given over to the pursuit of either personal gain or vicious pleasure.[3] Sympathy for such dour appraisals of the

37

country's fortunes arose because its was impossible (at least at the beginning of the century) to reconcile the prosperity and refinement of the age with traditional accounts of virtue. It was matter of common pride that society was no longer rude and unformed, but it was less widely accepted that the new affluence prompted a corresponding moral improvement. Indeed the reverse was often claimed. J.G.A. Pocock has argued that within the dominant mind-set of early eighteenth-century thought, 'the movement of history toward credit, commerce, and the market was defined as a movement toward culture but away from virtue'. Pocock is careful, however, not to claim a simple transition or an easy triumph for commerce. What he proposes instead is a 'bitter, conscious, and ambivalent dialogue' running throughout the century.[4] The debate about taste in the eighteenth century is both a comment upon and a product of this ambivalence.

For the citizens of a mercantile society, a society where the distribution of wealth is increasingly broad, there is a perceived need to have a clear idea of what to desire – which pictures, which plate, and what costume or coiffure. But there is also an urgent need for that desire to be expressive of difference and distinction, and not indiscriminate choice. It is not enough to wish to have one's portrait painted; one must know who is best equipped for the task, or more importantly, who has the most fashionable clientele. A country retreat is no marker of taste if it is only a 'Cit's Country Box'. This last example makes plain a process which is distinctive to the eighteenth century.[5] The expansion of wealth production and distribution, particularly among the merchant classes, enabled a far greater number of people to participate in high culture, both as consumers and connoisseurs, than ever before. Certainly the number exceeded those able to play an active role in politics. The result of such a change was an intensified interest in the nature of taste, with more and more people wishing to know what was good or beautiful.

Despite this general requirement, arbiters of taste tended to write for recognisably different constituencies. For example, the elite tastes and high political aspirations of aristocrats such as the Earl of Shaftesbury did not countenance the poorly resourced judgements of the middle classes, who were seen as deficient in both delicacy and wealth. Embracing a form of politics most conveniently described as civic humanism, Shaftesbury's account of taste sought to explain how taste was connected to political and moral integrity. Although Shaftesbury had his successors (in art theory, Reynolds is the most famous example), his account of taste and the politics upon which it rested did not go unchallenged. By the second quarter of the century it is possible to identify writing on the nature of taste wholly divorced from the civic priorities of the noble Earl. This alternative discourse emerges with Addison and Steele and with Jonathan Richardson, one of England's first theorists of art. Denied access to the realms of politics and large scale landownership, these figures fashion a discourse on the beautiful which articulates the aspirations of the minor gentry and the middling classes. This discourse is not concerned with patrician, political claims, but with justifying a mode of cultural consumption based on the ownership and appreciation of goods which had previously been derided as luxuries.

In this context Richardson, an accomplished portrait-painter and keen propagandist for British art, makes for an interesting example of a more general trend. In his major critical works, *The Two Discourses* of 1719 and *An Essay on the Theory of Painting* published some years later, Richardson attempted to define good taste by advocating a new 'Science of the *Connoisseur*', indeed it was his intention to promote British painting by finding the critical tools which could best express its value.[6] Throughout, the critical language was defined by emphasis on personal pleasure and individual discernment. Richardson expressed an eagerness to 'open to Gentlemen a New Scene of Pleasure, a New innocent Amusement'; it was to be furthermore a space in which 'one Man may be as Good a Judge as another'.[7] Most radically, Richardson was committed to the notion that connoisseurship was a rational pursuit, a profoundly learnable activity improving to its practitioners. This is a crucial claim and Richardson makes much of defending his belief that connoisseurship should be considered as rational as any other form of knowledge.[8] To be a connoisseur was consequently to be divested of prejudice and to resist the impositions of arbitrary authority. According to Richardson, the good connoisseur thought for himself, and was as free from the persuasions of custom, as from the blandishments of aristocratic authority.[9] The rules employed in the judgement of painting had to be the connoisseur's own (or at least arrived at through their private study), and as such are a property of the connoisseur's personality. It is important not to under-estimate the importance of this dimension of Richardson's work. Making his point rather forcibly, Richardson argued that as connoisseurs his readers must '*establish to our Selves a System of Rules to be apply'd to what we intend to give Judgement of*; . . . And these Rules must be our Own'.[10] In these terms connoisseurs become a horizontally organised merit- ocracy, while connoisseurship itself is an independent, but acquired, knowledge. The necessity of free-thought and independence is enforced by Richardson's repeated reference to theological argu- ment as a supporting discourse.[11] The ideal of Protestant independ- ence and personal judgement was a vital influence; in the field of critical judgement, Richardson argued, 'we are all *Connoisseurs* as we are Protestants'.[12] There could be no priests in Richardson's account, no specialists who claim privileged access to appreciation of art. The correct judgement of a painting is consequently the product of 'General Consent'.[13]

In terms such as these the question of taste was opened to a far wider constituency than Shaftesbury would ever have envisaged. Accounts of taste no longer sought to restrict appreciation of the arts to aristocrats alone; William Hogarth, for example, argued that 'no one may be deterr'd, by want of such previous knowledge, from entring into this inquiry'.[14] Certainly the number who wished to gain access to what Burke termed 'the works of imagination and the elegant arts' increased enormously. Burke, like many other eighteenth-century writers, wanted to establish the 'principles' by which the 'Senses' formed 'Judgements' in this most enticing and yet vexatious area.[15] Burke's argument in the *Enquiry* was to suggest that the subject's response to beauty or refinement was an irrational though providentially necessary sensation.[16] It was a perception which, within certain rather broad limits, was 'common to all'.[17] In the context of a culture characterised by rapidly changing values and priorities, a more wary thinker than Burke could see easily the dangers (and the absurdities) inherent in such an account. For Hume, if taste was merely perception, then the possibility of defining taste rapidly receded.[18] To Hume's mind it was incumbent on the philosopher and the critic to exclude those perceptions which were erroneous, prejudicial or just misinformed. Hume, ever the politest of philosophers, entrenched on the grounds of refinement and education, asserting that only those of enlarged and delicate views could be trusted in their discernment as to what was genuinely tasteful.[19] In many respects, determining who was capable of possessing a refined judgement was the question which dominated criticism throughout the eighteenth century. Only rarely, such as in the case of the labourer-poet Stephen Duck, did the entitlement to creativity become a topic of debate. The critical issue was to define taste and to decide who was capable of exercising it.[20]

Hume's patient discernment was not always shared by his contemporaries. Periodicals such as the *Connoisseur* and the *World* provided a forum in which their contributors (most notably Bonnell Thornton, George Coleman and Soame Jenyns) lambasted the modern world for its sordid traffic in commodified goods and for its brazen pursuit of wealth and power. Accordingly, the pages of these essay-journals rifle to the sound of their furious condemnations. While most mid-century accounts of taste can best be understood as engaged in an uneasy negotiation with the emerging commercial culture, periodicals like the *World* remained bitterly opposed to any notion of expanding the community of taste.[21] Such polemics provide the most appropriate context in which to read writers such as Hogarth and John Gilbert Cooper, both of whom are discussed below. Hogarth, along with Addison and Richardson, produced an account in which the appreciation of the beautiful became a gratification acquired either from the senses, or most radically from property. Hogarth's apparent sympathy with commercial culture caught the *World*'s attention in April, 1753:

A great comic painter has proved, I am told, in a piece everyday expected, that the line of beauty is an S: I take this to be the unanimous opinion of all our professors of horticulture, who seem to have the most idolatrous veneration for that crooked letter at the tail of the alphabet. Their land, their water must be serpentine; and because the formality of the last age ran too much into right lines and parallels a spirit of opposition carries the present universally into curves and mazes.[22]

The satire is pointed, if a little wide of the mark. For all that, the essay illustrates a common strategy by representing the newly wealthy as capable of nothing save particular tastes and fragmented styles. The attack on modern commercial culture becomes more explicit when the paper describes squire Mushroom's villa, on the sight of which 'the eye is saluted by a yellow serpentine river . . . over which is a bridge, *partly in the Chinese style*'. Consequently the hapless Mushroom is portrayed as the 'chef d'œuvre' of 'modern impertinence'.[23] The fulminating condemnations of the *World* were perhaps not uncommon. With great consistency, periodicals, like the

World and the *Connoisseur*, portrayed the middle classes as able only
to spend, to consume without judgement, representing their tastes as
random, unprincipled and, above all, indecorous.[24]

To conservative commentators, eighteenth-century society appeared to be characterised by two incontrovertible changes. First:
the commodification of cultural production – the *Connoisseur's*
authors suggested that gardening, the book trade, theatre, criticism
and even marriage and military service had all succumbed to
commercial pressure.[25] Secondly: the explicit and unparalleled
'intrusion' of women into almost all spheres of social and cultural
life. By the middle of the century, therefore, it was clear that 'culture'
had to be thought about, made the subject of legislation and
consequently policed. Above all culture was self-evidently heterodox
and in need of rationalisation. John Brewer's description of the
diversity and vitality of eighteenth-century cultural production
makes the point clearly:

The marketing of culture became a trade separate from its production:
theatrical and opera impresarios, picture-, print- and booksellers, became
the new capitalists of cultural enterprise, peddling culture in almost every
medium and art. The publisher John Dunton was one of the first
booksellers to recognize the importance of women as cultural consumers.
J.J. Heidegger, the opera impresario who partnered Handel, orchestrated
the Hanoverian monarchy's public ceremonies, and introduced the
masquerade to English theater. John Rich, theatrical manager and
patentee, changed the format of the London stage, introducing pantomime,
comic dancing, complex machinery, and extravagant scenery. Jonathan
Tyers, the proprietor of Vauxhall Pleasure Gardens, patronized the painters
Hogarth and Hayman, and the musicians Handel and Thomas Arne.
Andrew Hay, having failed as a portraitist, became the first professional art
dealer . . . John Boydell, printseller, developed the English export trade and
established the Shakespeare Gallery as a shrine to British culture.[26]

To this frenetic activity it is possible to add the *Spectator* papers of
Addison, the moral essays of Pope, together with the conversation
pieces which were then beginning to adorn the homes of the affluent
and well-heeled. The question had become which of these activities
could be regarded as refined, thought of as 'culture' in the restrictive
sense of that term.[27] In attempting to differentiate between behaviour which could be considered as educated, polite and refined
and that which prompted avaricious or carnal appetites, eighteenth-
century writers began to establish new definitions of culture. Certainly not all the activities described by Brewer could easily be

considered as constituting the elegant works Burke had in mind when writing his *Enquiry*. Furthermore, as Terry Castle's work on the masquerades of eighteenth-century London has demonstrated, exuberance of cultural production did not guarantee its social acceptance.[28]

Eighteenth-century conceptions of culture, at least those produced by the end of the century, are the by-products of the debates about commerce and consumption, taste and pleasure which ran throughout the century.[29] When, as in the seventeenth century, the Court had defined what was acceptable, proper or worthy, there had been much less need to develop particular means of describing how those values were generated or to explain who might possess them. Decisively Court culture did not have this authority in eighteenth-century England. Indeed one of the most profound changes to take place in the period was the separation of the ability to be moral and cultured from the capacity to exercise political power.[30] This new distinction between the state and civil society, a move which had been gathering pace steadily since the Glorious Revolution, encouraged the great increase in social and cultural writing which characterised eighteenth-century debate. It was also a discrepancy which the newly propertied and yet unenfranchised could attempt to fill with their own polemics and intended reformations.[31] The newly active sphere of culture provided a context in which the discussion of taste and beauty began to be transformed. Foremost amongst these changes was the movement of the definitions of the beautiful from an abstract philosophical category to a sensuous thing upon which specific, and not universal, relations could be described. This chapter describes that transformation, and the forms of cultural politics it represented.

PROPER FEELINGS, PROPRIETORIAL TASTES: 'THE MAN OF POLITE IMAGINATION'

The most illuminating point at which to begin this inquiry is with Joseph Addison's 'Essay on the Pleasures of the Imagination', first published as a series of papers in the *Spectator* in 1712.[32] Addison's essay, which drew on the recent discoveries of Locke and Newton, can be considered as a new departure, indeed the discussion of taste was one which Addison thought, perhaps justifiably, to be 'entirely new'.[33] Addison wished to explore the causes and the sensations associated with tasteful perception, but it was beauty (rather than novelty or grandeur) which captured his interest. He writes that there is 'nothing that makes its way more directly to the soul than *Beauty* which immediately diffuses a secret Satisfaction and Complacency thro' the Imagination'.[34] Addison remained somewhat vague about what exactly caused the mind to apprehend beauty, merely asserting that 'by Experience' we know that there are 'several Modifications of Matter which the Mind . . . pronounces at first sight Beautiful or Deformed'. Addison is, despite this ambiguity, able to determine what makes certain objects pleasing to the eye. It is a property (a key word this) which consists: 'in the Gaiety or Variety of Colours, in the Symmetry and Proportion of Parts, in the Arrangement and Disposition of Bodies, or in the just Mixture and Concurrence of all together'.[35] The identification of pleasing qualities, however, is not an empirical assessment dependent on the perception of proper qualities; it is an act of imagination.

Addison's emphasis on imagination and its pleasures reveals an investment in the discussion of taste that goes far beyond the enjoyment of particular forms. In the course of the Essay, Addison develops what is a complex ideological understanding of the process of contemplation. In a crucial passage he explains what he regards as the capacities of the 'Man of Polite Imagination':

He can converse with a Picture, and find an agreeable companion in a Statue. He meets with a secret Refreshment in a Description, and often feels a greater Satisfaction in the Prospect of Fields and Meadows, than another does in the Possession. It gives him indeed a Kind of Property in everything he sees, and makes the most rude uncultivated Parts of Nature administer to his Pleasures: So that he looks upon the World, as it were in another Light, and discovers in it a Multitude of Charms, that conceal themselves from the generality of Mankind.[36]

The 'Man of Polite Imagination' is therefore in a position of some command. Empowered with an improving and active gaze, he appears at once to own everything, and yet nothing in particular. The concept of pleasure is left deliberately void of visible commitment. It is an apparently libertarian moment, an expansion of opportunities. The free movement of the eye enables the viewer to participate in the aristocratic survey of landed property. There is no inheritance of taste or property strictly speaking, for the person viewing the land is able to exchange his position with that of the owner to become, if only imaginatively, the lord of all he surveys.

At first glance, Addison's account seems to be in line with Shaftesbury's suggestion that the ownership of an object, even the mere ability to own it, would diminish its value, rendering it unbeautiful and the pleasure 'absurd'.[37] For Shaftesbury a notion of possession was unlikely to provide the key to pleasure, rather the reverse; his sense of the beautiful required the viewer to be disinterested, to rise above the concern for property. The notion that the 'Man of Polite Imagination' enjoys more in the 'Prospect of Fields and Meadows, than another does in the Possession' implies an accord with these sentiments. However, it is not clear how the 'Kind of Property' spoken of as the foundation of polite pleasure can be accommodated within such requirements. The meaning of this passage hinges upon whether 'Property' is thought to bestow the sensible gratification derived from actual property-owning or whether it offers an alternative pleasure, one which relies on an ability to rise above the pleasures of ownership. The situation may be made yet more complex by consideration of Addison's insistent attention to the privacy and particularity of the sensations he describes. Throughout the Essay the 'public' nature of beauty, endorsed by Shaftesbury, is noticeably absent. The pleasure of a beautiful landscape is a 'secret Refreshment' and the 'Gaiety or Variety of colours' correspondingly produces a 'secret Delight'.[38] These feelings appear as unique experiences belonging to a notion of the subject that is neither keen to deny personal gratification nor anxious to define universal truth. There is therefore a contradiction in Addison's account between the politeness of an imagination which is free from particular, property based desires, and the individuated pleasures which are associated with sensible gratification. In these terms Addison appears willing to endorse the language of acquisition as the basis of an account of sensation, though like Richardson he does so within the purview of gentlemanly distinction. The complexities of Addison's account indicate not only the peculiarly unstable nature of the eighteenth-century conceptions of imagination, but also the more immediate problem of trying to account for the elevated nature of taste without losing sight of the pleasures that made it both meaningful and desirable.

The difficulty of maintaining a connection between pleasure, taste and virtue, was also apparent in Francis Hutcheson's *An Inquiry into the Original of our Ideas of Beauty and Virtue*, which he published in 1725.[39] Following Shaftesburian principles, Hutcheson argued that the pursuit of virtue and beauty was independent from any consideration of need, interest or desire. To seek beauty was to quest for a pleasure which had no regard to future expectation, and still less to property:

> The Ideas of Beauty and Harmony, like other sensible Ideas, are *necessarily* pleasant to us, as well as immediately so; neither can any Resolution of our own, nor any *Prospect* of Advantage or Disadvantage, vary the Beauty or Deformity of an Object.[40]

It is clear from this passage that Hutcheson was, at least initially, committed to the notion that the love of beauty is disinterested, claiming that while an object could be valued from a consideration of advantage, true esteem was 'antecedent' to such calculation.[41] According to Hutcheson, appreciation happens too quickly for any calculus to take place; things either please, or they do not. It was in this connection that Hutcheson introduced his most pressing case; his conception of the 'Internal Senses' which, he argued, regulated pleasure. Put simply, Hutcheson suggested that the perceiving subject has an innate propensity for receiving pleasure, or displeasure (in the form of actual pain), from the impressions made upon them by 'complex ideas'. Throughout the *Inquiry,* beauty and taste were conceived as complicated ideas.[42] The disposition to respond is held by Hutcheson to be analogous to, if not actually identical with, that exhibited by the external senses of sight, hearing and touch when they apprehend the 'simple' ideas of colour, sound and texture.[43]

Having distinguished the internal sense from mere appetite, Hutcheson further divorced taste from the grosser forms of gratification by arguing that the beautiful ought to be considered as a matter of imagined apprehension, and not as the result of the existence of any characteristic inherent in any given object. Hutcheson makes this point when he writes in his treatise that 'the word *Beauty* is taken for *the idea rais'd in us,* and a *Sense* of Beauty our *Power of receiving this idea*'.[44] Although Hutcheson sets out to describe the 'qualities' which make an object beautiful, he suggests that it is a compound ratio of uniformity and variety, the process of perception and approval is so dependent upon internal sense that the role of such 'qualities' is undefined. True, he describes, as he puts it in a 'mathematical style', the manner in which the feathers of fowls are beautiful, precisely because of the qualitative relation of uniformity and variety, yet he keeps the location of the beautiful mental or sensory:

For Beauty, like other Names of sensible Ideas, properly denotes the *perception* of some Mind; so *Cold, Hot, Sweet, Bitter*, denote the sensation in our Minds, to which perhaps there is no resemblance in the Objects, which excite these Ideas in us, however we generally imagine otherwise.[45]

On this account beauty as the '*idea rais'd in us*' is not a property of the object itself but the perception raised in the mind as the result of viewing that object.[46] The operation of the internal senses is therefore represented by Hutcheson as being largely passive and without appetite. In common with Addison's 'Man of Polite Imagination' who has a 'propensity to receive' particular forms of gratification, Hutcheson's internal sense serves as a receptacle for refined pleasures. Although some confusion attends Hutcheson's contention that beauty is an idea of a kind which has what he terms a 'nearer resemblance' to objects, it is clear that Hutcheson is at least partially succesful in his attempt to distinguish taste from desire. Indeed, throughout the *Inquiry* Hutcheson espouses what is a relatively convincing account of how the idea of beauty functions independently of interest. However, he has far greater problems with the definition of judgement, and in accounting for why mankind should possess the capacity for such discriminations. Most disturbingly, Hutcheson does not appear able to differentiate between the perception of beauty and the inclination to be pleased, as a result his account of the 'Sense of Beauty' is unfulfilled and his account of judgement remains imperfect.[47]

Towards the end of the *Inquiry* Hutcheson attempts to rationalise and defend his argument. Revealingly enough, he suggests that the pleasures associated with the contemplation of objects of taste are the 'Chief ends for which we commonly pursue '*Wealth* and *Power*'. This suggestion is offered by Hutcheson to counter any possible charge that his speculations have been nothing more than the 'airy Dreams of an Inflamed Imagination'. Property is therefore a worthwhile object of pursuit for the 'sensible part of Mankind' as it allows them to enjoy pleasures impossible without that ownership.[48] In terms of the overall development of Hutcheson's case, the introduction of interest is belated, and perhaps somewhat contrived. Yet Hutcheson accords it great importance: 'beside this Consideration of *interest*, there does not appear to be any necessary Connection, antecedent to the Constitution of the AUTHOR of *Nature*' to associate beautiful objects with that 'sudden sensible *Pleasure* exalted in us upon observation of them'.[49] Given his earlier conviction that taste preceded a calculation of advantage, it would appear that the introduction of 'interest' at the end of the *Inquiry* is an attempt to prevent the collapse into mere pleasure which the discussion of beauty has generated. However, the connection also indicates the social group for whom he was writing. In the final pages of the *Inquiry*, Hutcheson makes repeated reference to the 'sensible' or 'busy part of Mankind'; in other words the propertied classes. Accordingly, the interests he describes are those of a restricted social group, those for whom luxurious rather than necessitous purchases are the order of the day. The desires which clarify and support his argument turn out, rather shrewdly, to be the 'interests' of the well-heeled, propertied classes.

In fact Hutcheson is prepared to give this 'interest' a distinctly proprietorial caste, alleging that the 'full Enjoyment' of music, dress, architecture and equipage is impossible 'without *Property*.'[50] That the 'interest' Hutcheson describes is conceived of as property, as objects owned so that they may be pleasurably consumed, indicates an important shift away from the idea that the consumption of individual goods has no social value.[51] Hutcheson, however, remains hesitant, and it is finally to the munificence of the Deity that he attributes the beauties of the created universe. His reticence on this point is indicative of the as yet poorly defined account of personal pleasure or feeling; it was not until later in the century that feeling and virtue were more clearly aligned. Embarrassed by the apparently mercantile cast of his conclusions, Hutcheson introduces a providential cause for the ownership of property. Hutcheson's problems emerge because, in Howard Caygill's terms, the 'establishment of the civility of a commercial society on the moral sense demanded the violent repression of the difference between sense and idea, private interest and public good'.[52] However, the 'repression' of such differences was not something Hutcheson could maintain consistently. Property forces its way back into his account, offering him both his most plausible explanation for why objects might please, but also an idea not entirely consistent within his stated aims. However, although Hutcheson was prepared to say that property and taste were connected, he was not prepared to suggest, as Bernard Mandeville had done, that the desire for such gratification was in itself conducive to public virtue.[53] Despite these reservations, Hutcheson's account remains significant for the way in which it connects the acts of possession with sensible gratification. The connection was new and important in the mid-century, but most significantly it would eventually allow a greater constituency of owners to justify their possessions within an authoritative moral framework. In order to account for later developments in this area it will be necessary to maintain an engagement with Hutcheson's emphasis on these sensible excitements derived from the contemplation of objects. The more so, because it was not always possible to define that reaction in terms which rendered it an adequately disinterested response.

THE THRILL OF THE NEW: HOGARTH'S ANALYSIS OF BEAUTY

Texts such as those written by Richardson, Addison and Hutcheson initiated a discourse through which the personal possessions and private tastes generated by commercial society could be endowed with greater significance. However, these early eighteeth-century theorists of taste continued to respond to the opportunities presented by commercial affluence by seeking to restrain it within the security of traditional connoisseurship. Hutcheson looked for 'uniformity amidst variety', and while he did not deny the diversity of objects thought beautiful he was anxious to incorporate that range within a permanent order or fixed 'Design'. William Hogarth, by contrast, was committed to the pursuit of novelty and variety as the foundation of visual pleasure. To an important degree Hogarth exploited the possibilities and opportunities represented by Addison's *Spectator* papers and extended them.[54] His position therefore, unlike Hutcheson's, embraced commercial modernity without embarrassment, and proposed a conception of taste in which variety, novelty and heterogeneity are given decisive roles.[55] This was indeed, in Addison's phrase, 'entirely new'.

The novelty of Hogarth's *Analysis of Beauty* can be detected on two levels. Firstly, there is the newness and variety described in the text, in Hogarth's discussion in 'Of INTRICACY', for example. Secondly, there is the novelty of the *Analysis* as an exposition of the beautiful. David Bindman has written of the 'essential loneliness' of Hogarth's position in the 1750s, suggesting that Hogarth's position was one

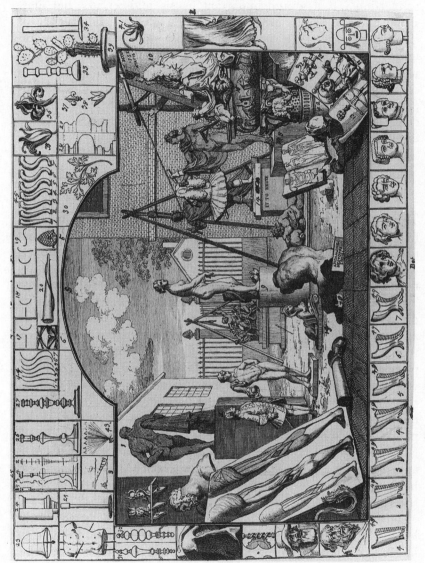

Figure 1 William Hogarth, *Analysis of Beauty: Plate 1 (Third State)*, 1753

upon which few would have ventured. Bindman argues that Hogarth's 'determined empiricism and attempt to reduce the Beau ideal to an observed method could hardly appeal to those influenced by the classical idealism of Rome'.[56] However, Hogarth's familiar yet highly detailed mode of observation allowed him to use everyday English speech as his analytical language and to extend his account of beauty to encompass the everyday sights of London. Most infamously, this new capaciousness included stays, candlesticks and smoke jacks.[57] It was this apparent lack of discrimination which, despite a number of favourable reviews, most notably in the *Gentleman's Magazine*, aroused the ire of his critics.[58] Hogarth, aware of opponents' likely response, attempted to face them directly:

I have but little hopes of having a favourable attention given to my design in general, by those who have already had a more fashionable introduction into the mysteries of the arts of painting and sculpture. Much less do I expect, or in truth desire, the countenance of that set of people, who have an interest in exploding any kind of doctrine, that may teach us to *see with our eyes.*[59]

The attack on the 'instructors and leaders' of fashionable society with which Hogarth begins the *Analysis* may be a disingenuous one (surely no one was quite as stupid as Hogarth implies?), but it was also motivated by his class consciousness. Hogarth's awareness of his class position as a professional artist dictated that his formulation of taste would reject, rather than emulate, patrician presumption.

With this position established Hogarth begins the *Analysis* by announcing that it is his aim to rectify the bad taste of the connoisseurs, and to enable a greater audience to appreciate the nature of beauty. To Hogarth's mind the connoisseurs were not, as Richardson described them, rational men guided by their own judgement, but were instead a group of fashionable, over-polished dilettanti. In short a set of people overly persuaded by the reputation of antiquity and by the effeminacy of foreign art.[60] In one of the most famous passages in the *Analysis*, he rounds upon them, asking 'who but a bigot, even to the antiques, will say that he has not seen faces and necks, hands and arms in living women, that even the Grecian Venus does not but coarsely imitate?'[61] Here, as throughout the text, the warm sensuousness of a living English woman is preferred to the dusty lure of the ancient statue.[62] The statement is curious in view of the subsequent remark that 'Ladies always speak skillfully of necks, hands and arms; and often will point out such particular beauties or defects in their make, as might easily escape the man of science'.[63] Hogarth is enlarging the community which is thought capable of judgement – butchers and smiths are also given some credit. However, the extent of women's judgement is restricted, most obviously by the exposure of the body: a restriction which keeps women's taste confined to that which can be seen with propriety. The restriction of women's judgement is social, as well as visual. It marks women's exclusion from the forms of pleasure which are associated with less chaste forms of beauty. Despite this reservation the face of the polite woman has considerable significance in Hogarth's account of visual pleasure. Hogarth writes:

The face indeed will bear a constant view, yet always entertain and keep our curiosity awake, without the assistance either of a mask or view; because the vast variety of changing circumstances keeps the eye and the mind in constant play, in following the numberless turns of expression it is capable of. How soon does a face that wants expression, grow insipid, though it be ever so Pretty?[64]

The face offered Hogarth a pattern of features and expressions from which he could read the 'index of the mind'.[65] Hogarth's account of the readable face suggests that a countenance composed of fine or intricate lines could offer both pleasure and definition, chastity and a more ambiguous pleasingness. Although Hogarth sought to avoid the imputation of being a 'physiognamist', what is suggested by his reflections is a reading of morals within a discourse on the physical appearance which Hogarth most readily applied to women.[66]

It will be important for my argument in subsequent chapters, that Hogarth's rejection of Shaftesburian Neoplatonism, accords closely with the forms of judgement found both in conduct books and in sentimental novels. Indeed, Hogarth's willingness to see physical appearance as an indicator of virtue connects him closely with developments in polite discourse almost entirely opposed to the public concerns of civic humanism. Despite his commitment to beauty as a mode of moral judgement, elsewhere in the *Analysis* Hogarth makes the spectacle of beauty a matter of excited exploration:

Intricacy in form, therefore, I shall define to be that peculiarity in the lines, which composes it, that *leads the eye a wanton kind of chase*, and which from the pleasure that gives the mind entitles it to the name of beautiful.[67]

Real excellence is therefore located in '*the beauty of a composed intricacy of form*'.[68] It is an image which is, once again, best exemplified by common examples. He remarks that the 'principal' of intricacy 'recommends modesty in dress, to keep up our expectations'. The folds of clothing and the lines of a face are successful because they encourage 'imaginary pursuits'.[69] These circuits of pleasure connect pleasure, feeling and polite sociability together. In Hogarth's polemic the '*beauty of a composed intricacy*' comes to be equated not only with the pleasures of variety, but with the sensations of delight which attend the sight of the women whose modesty and sexuality inhabit the same uncertain space. Beauty is therefore made into a mode of intricacy and pleasure which he terms a '*wanton kind of chase*', a moment of delight reliant on the excitement of the viewer's senses.[70]

In these terms, there is something genuinely innovative about the *Analysis*, though it may not, as has been suggested, be the 'first anti-academic treatise in the history of aesthetics'. Such an appraisal depends on the assumption that 'Hogarth places the onus of judgement on the sensitivity and training of the observer'.[71] More persuasive is Ronald Paulson's suggestion, that Hogarth's realignment of beauty with the sensory can be profitably located with the context of the new poetics of the 1740s and 1750s.[72] The poetry and criticism of the 1740s marks a transition from the moral deliberations of Pope, towards a poetic sensibility based upon the reaction of the subject to emotional rather than political or social events. Poets like Mark Akenside and James Thomson had begun this transition, but it was to find its greatest expression in the poetry of Edward Young, William Collins and Thomas Gray, and in the criticism provided by the Warton brothers.[73] The long digressive poems produced by Thomson and Akenside strove to find a language, not for the description of nature or ethics, but for the presentation of felt experience. Key passages in *The Seasons* and in *The Pleasures of the Imagination* suggest that it is through a sensational and emotive personality that beauty is to be found.[74] For example, it is only when Thomson has Lord Lyttelton joined by his 'lov'd LUCINDA' that 'Nature all/Wears to the Lover's eye a Look of Love'.[75] Akenside perhaps goes a little further. It has been observed of his poetics that he sought to 'use the beauties of nature as an occasion for discussing and describing the operations of the human mind'.[76] Certainly Akenside makes feeling – and particularly feelings of pleasure – central to his project, along with a liberated notion of the Fancy.[77]

According to Paulson, the shift to a more effusive account of the pleasures of the senses ensured an important change in the definition of beauty through which the indulgence of feeling replaced the stern nature of judgement. Paulson further argues that Shaftesburian assumptions embodied by the judgement of Hercules motif were increasingly rejected as part of this shift.[78] This suggestion is persuasive in relation to Hogarth's highly sexualised pursuit of beauty and pleasure as represented by the attractive living woman. For Hogarth, the interest and delight of beauty lies precisely, as it would for Burke, in the excitement of feeling. The beautiful is made sensuous, the product of a personal response. The pleasures of contemplating beautiful, intricate forms give rise to a:

kind of sensation . . . , which I have since felt at seeing a country-dance; tho' perhaps the latter might be somewhat more engaging; particularly when my eye eagerly pursued a favourite dancer, through all the windings of the figure, who then was bewitching to the sight, as the imaginary ray . . . , was dancing with her all the time.[79]

These terms perhaps indicate why the country dance as a moment of social complexity and aroused passion came to be such an important image for Hogarth.[80] For it was here that the sensual nature of both beauty and society could be most readily, and most exuberantly, realised.[81] In this respect the *Analysis* suggests that a consideration of sexual difference is central to the analysis of taste. For it is in this difference, one which can be apprehended by everyone, that taste can begin to be manifested with something approaching concreteness.[82]

The logic of Hogarth's *Analysis* places him, I think, as a defender of commercial culture. As in his conversation pieces, he conducts his account of taste so as best to accommodate the possessions and aspirations of an upwardly mobile audience.[83] This is a position, however, that it is possible to overstate or to treat reductively. In his most recent study, Paulson attacks David Solkin for making precisely this connection. To Paulson's mind, Hogarth is a dissident figure designedly outside the practices and the discourses in which Solkin sought to place him.[84] Although Paulson weakens his critique through an occasionally hasty identification of civic humanism with what he terms the 'Whig oligarchy', there is much in what he asserts. As Paulson points out, Hogarth was at times a vocal, not to say vociferous, opponent of fashion, luxury and commerce, and many of his prints make this point emphatically. However, despite his aversion to the importunities of fashion, Hogarth can be found advocating the advantages (or, at least, the potential advantages) of commercial prosperity; witness his *Allegory of George Prince of Wales as the Future Protector of the Realm* (1720), which reworks the iconography of Hercules' judgement as a sign of settled prosperity. From a discursive, rather than directly artistic perspective, this is equally true of the fragmented *'Apology for Painters'* in which Hogarth, like Richardson, advanced the argument that a prosperous commercial culture should advance the arts.

Analysis of Hogarth's attitude to commercial culture, therefore, necessitates careful consideration – it may have been Hogarth's point that for every prosperous Beer Street there was a debauched Gin Lane. In the present context, it seems more plausible to suggest that Hogarth was making a subtle differentiation between the kinds of commerce he valued as active, likely to produce opportunities for the worthy and the industrious, and that which merely promoted the modes of luxuriance which already characterised the aristocracy. If this is correct, and I would suggest that it is, then Hogarth's opinion of commercial culture is of a subtle and nuanced kind. He does not immediately regard commerce as degenerate yet withholds his judgement as to the advantages of affluence. The difference can be exemplified by the distinction between Johnson's view that a busy and active commercial life raised the mind from the 'insipidity' of those who live by the 'toil of others' and Goldsmith's satire on the presumption of the shopkeeper Jack Varnish found in *The Bee*.[85] Johnson's depiction of industry, in many respects similar to the exertions Hogarth's *Analysis* recommends, discovers value in the exertions of effort and enjoyment, whereas Goldsmith can only find ridiculous the affectation he detects in the newly prosperous. The disjunction between Johnson's and Hogarth's sense of the possibilities of commerce and Goldsmith's critique of luxury (as a position not always antithetical to Johnson or to Hogarth) is the fault line which runs throughout eighteenth-century culture. Moreover, the division of opinion is the product of a combination of discourses, prominent amongst which is the discourse on taste, which both half-accepts and

half-damns the successes of commercial prosperity. It is the purpose
of the rest of this chapter to explore how anxieties about Britain's
new wealth underwrote debate about taste in the 1750s and 1760s.

By far the most ambitious examination of taste in the eighteenth
century was that attempted by Burke in his *A Philosophical Enquiry into
the Origin of our Ideas of the Sublime and Beautiful*. Certainly, Burke's ideas
remain key indicators of how ideas about beauty were changing in
the mid-century.[86] According to Tom Furniss, Burke's *Enquiry*
deserves this prominent position in the history of British criticism
because it participated 'in a political, economic, and philosophic
project which contributes to what a recent historian has called the
"making of the English middle class"'.[87] Such a re-fashioning of the
discourse on taste required at least a partial rejection of civic
priorities, indeed Burke had little interest in the idea that there is a
connection between beauty and virtue.[88] On the contrary, Burke was
entranced by the pleasures which might be associated with beauty.
Uninhibited by the ideals of restraint which held back Joseph
Spence, Burke wrote enthusiastically of the pleasures which attended
the sight of beautiful objects. Like Hogarth's *Analysis*, Burke's *Enquiry*
focused on particular sensations and individual pleasures from which
he sought to draw more general conclusions. What an analysis of the
eager desires exhibited by Burke's prose will reveal is that during the
mid-century it was possible, within certain circumstances, to consider
forms of judgement and contemplation which indulged private
gratification. It was arguably this commitment that provided the
means through which the endeavours of the commercial classes can
find a favourable expression.

Throughout the *Enquiry*, Burke does little to disguise the fact that it
is women who provide the most exciting, as well as the most
privileged, form of beauty.[89] This is a problematic conjunction
which at once constitutes the beautiful, and yet threatens to disrupt
its appraisal through the unwarranted intrusion of desire. The
problem becomes clear in what is a justly infamous passage:

Observe that part of a beautiful woman where she is perhaps the most beautiful, about the neck and breasts; the smoothness; the softness; the easy and insensible swell; the variety of the surface, which is never for the smallest space the same; the deceitful maze, through which the unsteady eye slides giddily, without knowing where to fix, or whither it is carried. Is not this a demonstration of that change of surface continual and yet hardly perceptible at any point which forms one of the great constituents of beauty?[90]

Burke, here, as throughout the *Enquiry*, has rejected 'Fitness' and 'Harmony' in favour of minute observations of size, texture and form. The placidity and poise of civic proprieties have been replaced by an appeal to pleasure and variety. Tellingly, the headless woman is described as hurrying the male gaze, ever encouraging the pursuit of pleasure. The rejection of decorum flirted with by Spence in *Polymetis* is brought out into the open by a largely carefree Burke.[91] Although Burke notes that 'I can strengthen my theory in this point by the opinion of the very ingenious Mr. Hogarth; whose idea of the line of beauty I take to be extremely just', there is in reality little sense of anything very much having been demonstrated or theorised in any clear sense. Seeking to prove that 'perfectly beautiful bodies are not composed of angular parts', Burke has drifted lazily but excitedly from a consideration of a dove's 'downy' chest to a ravished appraisal of a headless woman.[92] In so doing Burke dispenses with utility (an idea never entirely rejected by Shaftesbury and emphatically endorsed by Hume), virtue and proportion as the efficient causes of the beautiful, replacing them with an aesthetic of heterosexual excitement.[93]

The recurrent reference to the beauties of women reveals the degree to which Burke sought to legitimate individual desire was via a discourse of sexual appreciation. However, in common with Hogarth, Burke sought to endow his giddy pleasures with a social and not merely sensory significance. In order to accomplish such a manoeuvre, the love of women had to be made into a social longing. Burke writes that:

Men are carried to the sex in general, as it is the sex, and by the common law of nature; but they are attached to particulars by personal *beauty*. I call beauty a social quality; for where women . . . inspire us with sentiments of tenderness and affections towards their persons; we like to have them near us, and we enter willingly into a kind of relation with them.[94]

By describing the improving 'social' qualities of tenderness and solicitude attendant on the love of women, Burke refuses to make the appreciation of women a solely private act. Accordingly, the pleasures associated with the contemplation of female beauty are made into the signs of both individual virility and social sympathy.[95] Furthermore, Burke suggests that these pleasures are of a social and socialising force that cannot be dismissed merely because they partake of the sensual. The sensual becomes for Burke, not the opposite of the public realm, but its sign.[96] What is most striking in this connection is the way in which the male observer's virility becomes central to Burke's account of taste. It is this identity which while it validates taste, is also that quality which is most easily debased or waylaid. As a result of this investment, Burke appears to suggest that the disposition to be pleased can be made acceptable with rather less regard to the general good than Hutcheson would have been prepared to countenance. So much so that, although Burke sought to elevate and refine taste, to reclaim it from depravity and misapplication, his account is in frequent negotiation with, and in part endorses, luxuriant pleasures.

However, the *Enquiry* falls a long way short of licensing pleasure as an end in itself. While Burke, like Hogarth, celebrates the pleasures of the 'deceitful maze', he is also careful to distance his analysis from that which is merely lewd appetite. It is possible to read the long 'Introduction on Taste' appended to the second edition of 1759, as a determined attempt to shore up the problems in his argument via an attempt to dispense with the tastes of the licentious.[97] Despite the distinctions envisaged by the introductory discourse, Burke continued to be concerned about the nature and extent of the desires he appeared to license. He did not want to accept corporeal desire as the principle for taste merely because it could be extended to any object the viewer found attractive. Love had to be distinguished from lust. By love Burke intended all that is elevated, socialising and agreeable:

I likewise distinguish love, by which I mean that satisfaction which arises to the mind upon contemplating any thing beautiful, of whatsoever nature it may be, from desire or lust; which is an energy of the mind, that hurries us on to the possession of certain objects, that do not effect us as they are beautiful, but by means altogether different.[98]

In this passage Burke is not concerned, nor did he wish to sully himself, with that which is mere appetite. Taste in its grosser application is not his concern. Burke was keen to remove his

conception of the beautiful away from that which might be possessed, and sought to represent beauty not as a corporeal object, but
as a gracious *je ne sais quoi*. Burke implied a similar distinction when
he directed his analysis of taste to the 'works of the imagination and
the elegant arts'; in both instances Burke is seeking to distinguish
between what he values as the embodiment of refined sensation and
that which offers only sensual gratification.[99] Despite the association
of the appreciation of beauty with a grasp of the rightful social and
political relations, Burke remained anxious about the effects of love
on the man of taste. In a key passage he elaborates the consequences
of an excess of affection:

When we have before us such objects as excite love and complacency, the
body is affected, so far as I could observe, much in the following manner.
The head inclines something on one side; the eyelids are more closed than
usual, and the eyes roll gently with an inclination to the object, the mouth
is a little opened, and the breath drawn slowly, with now and then a sigh:
the whole body is composed, and the hands fall idly to the sides. All this is
accompanied with an inward sense of melting and langour.[100]

Although Burke suggests that these effects are 'always proportionate'
to the beauty of the object and the 'sensibility of the observer', it is,
he claims, 'almost impossible not to conclude, that beauty acts by
relaxing the solids of the whole system'. The effect of love, therefore,
is a monstrous weakening of the entire constitution. While the effects
of such pleasures are damaging to the individual, the experience was
universal: 'Who is a stranger to that manner of expression so
common in all times and in all countries, of being softened, relaxed,
enervated, dissolved, melted away by pleasure?'[101]

Although Burke is much troubled by such an effeminate loss of
self-command and self-regard (he saw love as potentially disruptive
to the social order as well as to the individual), he remained willing
to extend the definition of taste to include particular desires.[102]
Burke's ambivalence indicates his participation in a range of discourses which sought to define not only taste, but also society.
Crucially, Burke's rhetoric about lost resolution and declining
powers parallels the critical language employed to describe the
experience of commercial Britain. Conservative writers, particularly
those in the periodical presses, similarly represent a loss of form and
restraint, but make it a national, rather than personal, characteristic.
Thomas Cole, for example, wrote fervently against luxury in his
Discourses on Luxury, Infidelity and Enthusiasm. Cole's text is suffused

with a sense of impending collapse of the national fabric on the verge of melting away:

We are already far advanced in the same destructive road of luxury, so far, that if some method be not, in due time, taken to refrain our progress, we must necessarily sink into contempt and wretchedness, as individuals, and not withstanding all our late successes, be lost, as an independent people.[103]

Cole is rehearsing here what was by the 1750s a well-established line of attack. He represents Britain's new prosperity, characterised most immediately by 'our late successes' in the Seven Years' War, as liable to produce, not national greatness, but degenerate luxuriance. Wealth is being produced, this Cole does not dispute, but he does question to what end (morally and historically) such affluence is tending. Noticeably, his text endorses the same tropes of loss, irresolution and sinking formlessness with which Burke endows the love-sick observer. The appeal for restraint, to 'refrain', is similarly common to both. If Burke is advising that individual appetites need to be confined within reasonable bounds, then Cole is suggesting that the culture as a whole has lost its sense of those proprieties.

The critique of luxury, as John Sekora has demonstrated, occupied a pivotal position in the texts and languages which articulated culture in the eighteenth century.[104] In many respects luxury (conceived of by Sekora as a Foucauldian discourse) provided a way of surveying and castigating the modern, one which permitted a surveillance of power, riches and commerce. In the changing circumstances of the mid-century, the attack on luxury was carried forward by a wide range of critics, however, John Brown's *Estimate of the Manners and Opinions of Our Times* provides a particularly acerbic instance of this form of critique. [105] Occupying a prominent place in Brown's polemic is the spread of luxuriant effeminacy, a contagion which Brown sees as injurious to the 'National capacity'. It is a malaise which weakens, invariably, though not irrecoverably, the ability of the nation to defend itself. Brown argues that the twin follies of fashion and commercial affluence combine to ensure the existence of only the most enervating and enervated of cultures. Brown argues that 'the character of the Manners of our Times: . . . on a fair examination will probably appear to be that of a *"vain, luxurious,* and *selfish* Effeminacy." '[106] Brown goes on to claim that modern luxury has robbed the nation of its moral fibre; martial and public values have in his opinion been forsaken for the giddy pleasures of the moment. Traditional English values have consequently been lost and along with them the masculine resolve which made the national defence, religious observance and sound reasoning possible. Brown can be specific in his isolation of a whole repertoire of contemporary evils, citing effeminacy of dress; the excessive use of carriages and chairs; the enervating impact of warm, carpeted homes; and idle, shallow talk; all of which culminate in a sickening 'vanity' and 'unmanly delicacy'.[107] This liturgy is consistent with a recognisably traditionalist polemic. Samuel Fawconer composes a comparable list of social ills.[108]

What is important about the *Estimate* is that Brown takes these depravities as evidence of a public body in decline.[109] Luxury, according to Brown, because it dissolves the ties which form the social fabric, abolishes the idea of a reputable, political public. In consequence, being public – a situation represented through the activities of prostitutes and the antics of 'pretty fellows' – becomes merely a show of lewdness, or at best a vain search for the 'Applause of Men'.[110] The apparent collapse of virtue, brought about, it was alleged, by the expansion of commerce and overseas-trade, prompted Fawconer to claim, somewhat furiously:

Generally speaking, the consequence of extensive commerce is exorbitant wealth: and exorbitant wealth naturally produces an attention to pleasurable enjoyments. For they, who have the means of luxury in their hands, seldom deny themselves any gratification, which their circumstances give them the opportunity of indulging . . . But here lies the danger: luxury is of that assimilating insinuating nature, that its infection, like a pestilence, runs thro' every order of the country . . . [and], whether tempted by inborn pride, or seduced by the power of all prevailing fashion, every impertinent inferior treads on the heels of his betters.[111]

For Fawconer, the transformation of the public into a realm of commerce, of interest, and, most of all, of pleasure ensures that political corruption follows.[112] For Fawconer it was logical that the creation of wealth and prosperity would, if unchecked and unregulated, lead to a decline in the more substantial values represented by the landed interest, the state and the church. This is a prospect which for Fawconer marks the end of England as a civilised, and civic, society.[113] Consequently, as both Brown and Fawconer make clear, luxury, the baleful fruit of commercial excess, marks a profound loss of both national identity and cultural certainty.

Figure 2 William Hogarth, *Analysis of Beauty: Plate 2 (First State)*, 1753

It is not unreasonable to suggest that Burke's *Enquiry* intercedes at precisely this point in the debate. Burke's distinction between the 'Society of Sexes' and 'Society in General' attempts to differentiate between a potentially lewd and lustful arena and an ordered and social mode of living.[114] In a very real sense Burke's disinction complements that implied by Hogarth between the effeminate and corrupt world of the connoisseurs (embodied by the dancing-master and the statuary yard depicted in *Plate One*) and the more innocent pleasures revealed in his depiction in *Plate Two* of the *Analysis* which features a vibrant, but largely innocent, country dance. Pursuing a slightly different line of argument, Lord Kames followed in Hutcheson's footsteps, and hoped to rescue Shaftesburian disinterestedness from Mandeville's attack.[115] In his *Elements of Criticism*, Kames describes, and similarly derides, the loosening of mind and limb occasioned by an excess of pleasure. The sentiment of love, according to Kames, 'doth not tend to advance the interests of society, but when in a due mean with respect to strength'.[116] Kames, like Burke, was anxious about the connection between individual feeling and more general good.[117] Certainly, he was worried by the excesses to which feelings could run, and the luxuriance which opulence could bring.[118] However, he was also committed to the notion that an affluent society could be a well-regulated one. To Kames's mind, a proper cultivation of the arts was the best way to ensure that mere wealth was transformed into something capable of virtue. In a fulsome dedication to George III, Kames makes the point emphatically:

The fine arts have ever been encouraged by wise princes, not singly for private amusement, but for their beneficial influence in society. By uniting different ranks in the same elegant pleasures, they promote benevolence: by cherishing love of order, they inforce submission to the government: and by inspiring delicacy of feeling, they make regular government a double blessing.[119]

Kames's advocacy turns on a commitment, not to the power of the King as such, but on his capacity to organise the hegemonic potential of the nation's cultural fabric of which the arts are a necessary part. The dedication is also instructive in that it discloses an attention to 'culture' (as that which is both refined and subject to 'cultivation') which runs throughout Kames's argument. Having made this commitment, Kames spends a considerable amount of time, not only in spelling out how a standard of taste may be defined, but also in seeking to prove the rationality and good sense which is associated with correct taste.[120]

Throughout, Kames is concerned that modern luxuriance will remove the distinctions upon which his notion of taste is based.[121] Despite these reservations, Kames did not feel the need to reach for the guidance offered by religious instruction as Cole had done. On the contrary, he is willing to advocate an acceptance of new-found wealth if it is properly channelled:

> We stand therefore engaged in honour, as well as in interest, to second the purposes of nature, by cultivating the pleasures of the eye and ear, those especially that require extraordinary culture, such as are inspired by poetry, painting, sculpture, music, gardening and architecture. This chiefly is the duty of the opulent, who have the leisure to improve their minds and their feelings.[122]

Kames, however, is unwilling to leave the arts as an end sufficient in themselves, for without something more substantial underpinning his scheme it will threaten always to topple back into mere ornament and voluptuousness.[123] Howard Caygill has suggested that Kames's sense of beauty was defined by a sense of obligation and rights which ensured that taste was necessarily differentiated from luxury. In these terms, Kames can be seen to continue the same anxious tradition as Hutcheson and Burke. His emphasis on the cohesion and responsibility required to maintain a well-regulated society recalls Hutcheson on labour and Burke on the sublime.[124] Kames, however, does not install the Burkean ⁄emphasis on effort and exertion, but demands instead that pleasures be enjoyed sociably. Kames argued that it was only when the 'capital pleasures' were 'enjoy'd in common' that they could really please. Without such intercourse, the result is either insipid or luxuriant. It is in such terms that the real spur to art is to be found. For it is in the shared pleasures which good taste encourages that the foundations of a truly great culture are located.

According to Kames, once uniformity of taste has been established within a society, then the large projects of a truly noble civilisation are underwritten by a shared set of cultural norms.[125] As such Kames's argument, if not altogether persuasive, achieved what Caygill describes as 'a settlement between the traditional fear of luxurious corruption and the aspiration to justify the virtues of commercial society'.[126] In these terms, Kames provided a way of accommodating the fruits of what Cole termed 'our late successes' which does not appear to damage the notion of virtue and decorum he sought to maintain. While there is clearly much in this assessment, a comparison with Adam Smith's advocacy of the pleasures which necessarily attend the acquisition of wealth and goods reveals just how guarded Kames was being. In his essay on the 'Imitative Arts' Smith was far less cautious, arguing that 'the idea of expense seems often to embellish, so that of cheapness seems as frequently to tarnish the lustre even of agreeable objects'.[127] Smith's breezy disregard for the proprieties of cultural acquisition was not one Kames felt able to endorse; like many mid-century theorists Kames was to continue to be sceptical about the connection between 'wealth' and what Hutcheson termed the 'full Enjoyment' of the senses.[128] Kames was not, however, rejecting pleasure or material possessions out of hand; rather, he is seeking a rapprochement between wealth and virtue, and offered the arts as the means to accomplish this project.

JOHN GILBERT COOPER AND THE LUXURY OF FEELING

A reading of Hogarth and Burke has proved their work to be highly sensitive to distinctions of gender. This investment took broadly two forms: firstly, the fear of effeminacy figured as a loss of restraint and a descent into luxury; secondly, and just as importantly, a concentration on woman as the sign of true beauty. Critically, as in Burke's case, the two ideas were dangerously entangled. I want to conclude this chapter by examining comparable developments in John Gilbert Cooper's *Letters Concerning Taste*, a text which offers an ambitious, if ultimately ambivalent, polemic on the nature of 'true' taste. Cooper is worth reading at length because his text reveals the way in which the gendering of the debate on taste participated in more general shifts in eighteenth-century culture. Previous critics, most notably David Solkin, have studied Cooper as an exemplar of 'patrician' culture.[129] For the most part, what interested Solkin was the extent to which Cooper could be read as a supporter of the aristocratic power and authority. Solkin goes so far as to suggest that 'Cooper's line of reasoning comes straight out of Lord Shaftesbury'. In so doing Solkin has concentrated on those passages in the *Letters* where Cooper images the rural retreat as the proper environment for tasteful and genteel contemplation. As a result, Solkin does not focus in the precise mechanisms through which value is attributed by Cooper. Had he done so, he would have discovered that for much of the *Letters*, Cooper consciously genders the problem of taste as feminine. To recover this gendered aspect of the text is to reveal a great deal more modernity in Cooper's polemic than Solkin is prepared to allow. However, as recent work has pointed out, including that by Solkin himself, the patrician, or in John Barrell's terms, the civic, represents one, and only one, language of value in a competing network of discourses.[130] A detailed analysis of Cooper will reveal, not his unequivocal affirmation of an unchanging aristocratic culture, but rather the position of his text as a point of intersection between conflicting modes of social and critical address.

A consideration of Cooper's use of the epistolary form, and the type of address which that form encourages, can provide a way into these complicated cross currents. In many respects the epistolatory form is ideally suited to Cooper's overall project, as it indicates all the associations of privacy, domesticity and leisured philosophical speculation which he wishes to convey. The letters represent an easy, almost complacent, certainly part-confessional medium, in which the author may ponder the intricacies and the ecstasies of a tasteful life in a relatively uninhibited way. The twenty letters which complete the text are arranged so as to appear as a collection written to a 'small circle of Friends, here concealed under fictious Names'.[131] The first of the letters which comprise *Letters Concerning Taste*, establishes Euphemius as a philosophical, as well as polite correspondent, one who contrary to the 'Example you afford us' is mistaken in his separation of truth and beauty:

Whence comes it, EUPHEMUS, that you, who are so *feelingly* alive to each fine Sensation that Beauty and Harmony gives the Soul, should so often assent, contrary to what you daily experience, *that* TASTE *is govern'd by caprice, and that* BEAUTY *is reducible to no Criterion?*[132]

Cooper replies to the dummy argument provided by his addressee by asserting the necessity and pleasure of good taste; a gratification resulting from, he claims, a 'chain of truths' leading back to God. The first nine letters, all addressed to Euphemius, constitute the most developed thesis of the text. Starting with a rehearsal of Shaftesbury, Hutcheson and Addison, Cooper moves through the categories of taste to define imagination and sense. Taken together, the letters to Euphemius attempt to fashion a coherent advocacy of the beautiful, and of proper taste for a correct conduct in all aspects of life.

The effect of these well-crafted appeals is to suggest a closed community which shares a common social, philosophic and class-based agenda. This is crucial; Cooper's text, unlike Shaftesbury's or Hutcheson's, has little to offer directly to the public sphere. Though not ignored – indeed the text is frequently ambiguous on the point – public life is placed at a distance so as to ensure the primacy of certain forms of privacy, and even seclusion. However, the isolation of a small community away from the rigours of life in civil society supports a distinct view of aristocratic life and sensibility, one which wishes to remain actively hegemonic despite its seclusion. Cooper is at pains to reassure his readers that he loves the 'Comforts of domestic Life and the Charms of Contemplation in Retirement'.[133] He does not wish, it appears, to be seen to offer himself to the corrupting influences of publicity or even publication. Cautious but noble seclusion is therefore made the order of the day.[134] Cooper seeks to produce subjects suitable for public life (and taste) even if they do not actually pursue a career in the senate. As a result, Cooper's argument relies on a rather curious, if not uncommon, double think which alleged that public values could only be upheld through virtuous non-participation in the very culture for which they were designed. A similar strategy is adopted in James Thomson's *The Seasons*, where Lyttleton is represented as a man capable of public virtue largely because he has the sense to remain aloof from the degradation of party and city.[135]

Throughout the *Letters Concerning Taste*, an ideal independence and domestic felicity form an integral part in his index of value, privileging those scenes which offer resistance to the corrupting influences of city and commerce.[136] Writing the text in the form of letters to friends establishes this agenda succinctly. Unlike a more formal treatise, *Letters Concerning Taste* is able to introduce instances of highly personal taste and experience into its argument. By appearing to be the product of private, relatively unguarded utterance the text claims the authenticity which came in the mid-century to be associated with a spontaneous declaration of feeling. Most importantly, experience can be represented as an instantaneous flow of feelings accurately re-presented through the letter form. It is something which is incontrovertible, coming as it does from the writer's '*Soul*'.[137] This direct reporting of these feelings or sensations enables the claims made elsewhere in the text to appear as the true declarations of a tasteful heart. It is in this mode that the author assures his readers that 'my Heart always flows from my Tongue and Pen'.[138] In this way *Letters Concerning Taste* establishes the author's privileged and domesticated seclusion; he is unhurried and unsullied by the outside world. Indeed the '*beautiful* Proportion', which for Cooper forms the 'science of living well', demands a healthy disregard for the corruption of public life.[139] Throughout, the attractions of public diversion are replaced by a cultivated sympathy for the 'PENSIVE PLEASURES' of a secluded life.[140]

In contrast to this well-ordered life, modern luxury leads to a deviation from natural and moral truths. Luxury is consistently presented as something which the man of taste must guard against. Luxuriance is a malign force which Cooper sees as degrading the arts by promoting styles and designs at variance with nature.[141] Luxury leads to depravity and corruption according to Cooper's account, leaving nothing but trashy exuberance. The architecture of modern buildings displays only a 'splendid impertinence'. It is brash and gross in its extravagance and ornamentation. The convenient unity and variety of the rural seat is lost in a gaudy show of excessive irregularity:

But in all these notable Distortions of Art, I perceived the poor prostituted Word TASTE, was constantly made use of to express the abortive Conceptions of distempered *Fancy*, you would be led to think, that the new Gentry of the City, and their Leaders the well-dressed Mob about *St. James's*, were seiz'd the moment they left the Town-Air with a *Chinese* Madness, and imagined a Deviation from *Truth* and *Nature* was an infallible Criterion of TASTE.[142]

The implications of 'well-dressed' are clear enough; the 'new Gentry' is merely wearing the trappings of refined society and does not possess the substance of true breeding or taste. The specific isolation of a depraved appetite for Chinese goods also indicates a traditionalist's fear of the newfound wealth of imperialism.[143] For it represents an importation which is taken to be an unpleasant introduction of the exotic, a force injurious to the nation, as well as a distasteful and unpleasant fashion. Moreover, Chinese tastes were generally perceived to lack coherence or uniformity; they were indeed a mere profusion of ornament. Cooper sees such taste as depraved and as corrupted as the men who offer them, weighted down as they are by false extravagance and wealth. Cooper's proposition is clear: social and ethical irregularity, if not overt vice, emerge concurrently with poor taste. Luxury, the wealth produced by commerce in producing an impoverished taste, represents a 'Deviation from *Truth* and *Nature*'.

Broadly speaking, then, Cooper's position is that true taste is, through divine ordination, the principle upon which beauty was founded, and that any deviation from beauty must therefore be an unsightly falsehood. Within this scheme, the approval of any given object rests upon an internal sense which, following the plan of the 'ALMIGHTY', ensures that 'all beauty without should make a responsive Harmony vibrate within'. At this level all terms are securely located within a coherent discourse, if only as a consequence of what Peter Kivy describes as the 'Deist dodge' of yielding to God responsibility for final causes.[144] Ostensibly Cooper is extending and justifying the doctrine advanced by Shaftesbury and Hutcheson, that whatever is beautiful, or true, will immediately strike the spectator with immediate and irrecoverable effect. He writes accordingly that taste is that 'instantaneous Glow of Pleasure which thrills thro' our whole Frame, and seizes upon the Applause of the Heart, before the intellectual Power, Reason, can descend from the Throne of the Mind to ratify its Approbation'.[145] Significantly, neither Shaftesbury nor Hutcheson dispense with the function of reason as quickly and as carelessly as Cooper has done here. Hutcheson, for example, maintained a sense of judgement through his distinction between the feelings prompted by the 'Sense' and those which were merely sensual. For Cooper, on the other hand, the role of reason is reduced to that of a rubber-stamp; on the throne it may be, but its office is restricted to the ratification of decisions taken by the more clamorous senses.

The problem is most apparent when Cooper describes the pleasures encountered by a social party on a recent tour of England. Their enthusiasm for the beauties of landscape, he concedes, was catching, and it was not long 'before it came in my turn to be not *touch'd* but *rapt*, and to *feel* the aetherial Glow of Admiration at the sight of a neighbouring Villa to SCARBOROUGH'.[146] Although Cooper's prose appears merely to relish a moment of pleasurable excitement, what is really significant is the total absence of judgement and the abandon of his rapture. Unlike Hutcheson, who retained, however ambiguously, a notion of both judgement and proper qualities (which he defined as '*Uniformity* amidst *Variety*') Cooper endorses an account of taste and beauty which is entirely reliant on the internal senses for its justification. Instead of Hutcheson's cautious and complicated 'mathematical style', Cooper offered a more immediate explanation based on responsive harmonies and felt excitement. Cooper's would appear to be an incontrovertible position, if only on its own terms; for, if the beautiful and the grand are instantly affecting, there should, theoretically, be no grounds for dispute. True taste ordained by God should appeal to all equally. In reality Cooper found such an idea unimaginable; for in no sense does Cooper believe in the open, inclusive potential of the internal sense model. The question becomes, therefore, one of deciding who can perceive or define what is tasteful, and from what position, social or analytical, they may presume to speak.

However, if Cooper is to establish his central point – that there are real criteria defining the beautiful – then he has to do more than merely state instances of depraved taste. He has to find some way of describing the divergence he describes in a way which maintains his stated aim that truth, value and beauty are coincident. At one level Cooper can, as Hutcheson had done, reflect that this disagreement is nothing more than the consequence of luxury and mis-education.[147] This might make the doctrine of the internal sense look almost worthless, and certainly makes the version of it which Cooper offers Euphemius look vulnerable. For, if it is to make any impact at all, the internal sense model must maintain the primacy of that singular and irrecoverable impulse which is at its philosophical centre. What Euphemius had suggested in his letter was that '*additional* Charms' may be granted to the 'human Form . . . from Education'. To an extent Cooper accepts the potential for association (rejected by Hutcheson) which his correspondent offers. As a result he accepts the prospect of legitimately '*acquir'd* Charms' as a way of thinking through the problem of disparate tastes.[148] These charms, he suggests, form a 'superaddition' which, while it maintains an address to truth as the sole point of origin for beauty, combines it with a 'look' and a 'disposition' so as to suggest that the existence of feelings of amiability and love sanction a diversity of tastes. The figure of wise and ancient 'Ethograph' is introduced at this point in the argument to describe the relation between harmony and love in a way which renders '*acquired* charms' consistent with divine truth:

our Souls are attun'd to one another, like the Strings of musical Instruments, and the Chord of one being struck, the *Unison* of another, tho' untouch'd will vibrate to it. The Passions therefore of the human Heart, express'd either in the living Countenance or the Mimetic Strokes of Art, will affect the Soul of the Beholder with a familiar and responsive Disposition. What wonder then that Beauty, borrowing thus the Look of Softening Love, whose Power can lull the most watchful of the Senses, should cause that Sweet *Nepenthe* upon our heart, and enchant our corresponding Thoughts to rest in the Embraces of Desires?[149]

Beauty by borrowing the 'Look of softening Love' has begun to be figured as a benign seduction. So that while some charms are not given through real criteria, and are merely associated (another example is the majesty given to a castle if a famous battle took place there), they strike the viewer as strongly as if they were real. Beauty becomes, on this reading, something which may 'steal more subtly on the Soul of the Beholder', tempting him to approval and acceptance. Cooper continues:

Sure then I am, that you will always allow Love to be the Source and End of our Being, and consequently consistent with Truth. It is the Super-addition of such Charms to Proportion, which is called the *Tasteful* in Music, Painting, Poetry, Sculpture, Gardening and Architecture. By which is generally meant that happy Assemblage which excites in our Minds, by Analogy, some pleasurable image.[150]

Love is internalised as an addition to or even the primary part of, taste. As a result, Cooper is combining, rather unwisely, what Addison, and later Burke, sought to distinguish: desire and appreciation.

Cooper's account of approval as the expression of desire gives rise to an image of the chords or strings of the heart.[151] The heart, the synecdoche for love and desire now appears as commensurate with the internal sense. For this analysis to succeed beauty must only be registered when there already exists a harmony within.[152] While this sensation may be supposed to rely on the receipt of such pleasure by a cultivated Man of Polite Imagination (fittingly, Addison himself is the example), this image of inner-chord changes leads to what Walter Jackson Bate terms a 'luxury of feeling':[153] an unrestricted outpouring which relies only on the movements and vibrations of the heart to control or direct it. Cooper's description of aesthetic sensibility goes beyond even Shaftesbury's rhapsodic invocations and might, as Kivy suggests, push the text tentatively towards a 'dynamic

relationship' of the reasoning faculties and senses which could then
'constitute . . . "a sense of beauty"'.[154] The text, though, is unclear
and a little hesitant about whether the account it offers is a move
away from Shaftesbury or merely a re-statement, in slightly different
terms, of his position.

Cooper has to be clear when writing to Euphemius about the
extent to which it is possible to create a 'happy assemblage' of
charms and graces around one beautiful image. This process, owing
to its origin in the contemplation of the (implicitly female) human
form has become necessarily an issue of gender and desire. Significantly, Cooper connects the pursuit of luxury with an effeminate
character. For example, when Cooper is censoring the Italian poets
he accuses them of writing an overly forced and vainly pretty form of
verse. Italian poets are, he claims, averse to the 'Dignity of the
Heroic' and the 'Simplicity of *Pastoral* poesy'.[155] However, with
feeling (a more properly feminine attribute) installed as the guarantor of taste there is a need for a candid confession of his own
potential for confusion: 'it may be easily conceiv'd how a luxuriant
Fancy may in the heat of poetic Rapture glow up into a Nonsense'.[156] A problem made worse by the author's decision to give
vent to his *'flow of soul'* when writing to Philimon.[157] It is difficult to
see how the propriety of being 'not *touch'd* but *rapt*' is significantly
different from the immoral seizure which afflicts the mob of St
James's. The cause of this instability may be conceived of as the
absence of any discourse which might limit the definition of the
beautiful outside of the pleasures and feelings of the perceiving
subject's mind. Addison and Hutcheson encountered this same
problem, and Addison, in particular, is ambiguous in his response.
However, Addison and Hutcheson ultimately deal with the potential
for conflicting opinion by attributing it to error, false association and
the like. Cooper on the other hand has sought to demonstrate how
this diversity may occur in terms of the seductiveness of the objects
themselves, alongside the procedure of the inquiring mind. The
situation described in these terms requires some 'Management' if
order is to be maintained:

You will observe from hence that a true relish for Life as well as for natural
Beauty depends upon a right Management of our Fancies; for if Fancy
presents Objects in false Appearances to these *Spirits of Sense*, the *Affections*
will embrace Vice and deformity with their caresses, which naturally
belong to Virtue and Beauty.[158]

Fancy is an idea close to luxury within the discursive position from which Cooper writes, which is, at times, that of a supporter of traditional, or aristocratic, civic humanism. Traditional humanist thinking reproaches the fanciful as the unsubstantiated outpouring of a single mind. Viewed from the civic position, fancy is a property which is corrupting and capricious, perhaps even antithetical to good taste and the public good. So that when Cooper speaks of fancy he is thinking of the affections which vicious luxury – like that enjoyed by the mob of St James's – might suggest to the unsuspecting, or to the already corrupted. Cooper's discussion of the 'Management of the Fancies' and his sense of the need to control the excesses of luxury, all point to a view of taste as something which requires careful control. Although the softer pleasures of the senses are appreciated throughout Cooper's text, they remain something which the masculine, public subject must guard against.

Cooper's discussion of the 'Management of the Fancies' and his sense of the need to control the excesses of luxury, all point to a view of taste as something which requires careful control. Although the softer pleasures of the senses are appreciated throughout Cooper's text they remain something which the masculine, public subject must guard against.

Cooper's overall address to the relationship between taste, femininity and desire is both vexed and uneven. He allows great prominence to women to instruct and socialise men. When describing Euphemius' excellences, the author attributes the sweetness and volubility of his friend's discourse to that 'grace' which conversation with 'these fair preceptors' gives to men. In closing the letter addressed to Eugenio, he recommends himself to the 'Ladies' of that household and wishes (as ever) to reside 'where they *reign* which such unlimited Power'.[159] His letters are furthermore replete with marital advice urging Leonora not only to comfort and soothe her husband, but also to '*Never lose the Mistress in the Wife*'.[160] His own ambiguous remarks about 'AMELIA' (a woman he seeks to court), and his desire for her approval, suggests a network of desire potentially at odds with a strictly male or civic virtue.[161] Indeed in thinking about the success and refinement of Raphael, whom Cooper takes to be a man of the most exquisite taste and genius, he writes:

I cannot help observing in this place, and I hope it is not foreign to the Subject, that frequent Conversation with Women harmonizes the Souls of

Men, and gives them that enchanting Grace, which has so delighted us both in the Address of several of our Acquaintance, not very eminent for their Virtues or Understanding. I am of the Opinion, it is this constant Idea of Delicacy and Softness, collected, from a habitual Intercourse with these fair Polishers of our Sex, and united into one complicated Form of Beauty, which, playing perpetually into the Soul of RAPHAEL, diffus'd itself thro' his look, Deportment, and Tongue, over all his words and Actions.[162]

Two points strike me here: the notion of an 'enchanting Grace' which those without genius may possess, and the more beguiling idea of 'one complicated Form of Beauty'. The first idea is perhaps indicative of those qualities represented by Euphemius, which, alongside their many talents, makes them social. In describing Euphemius, Cooper instances his gracious refinement and taste as a particularly appealing (hence beautiful) moment of culture. It is the polish which he has gained from discourse with women that makes him truly cultured and polite. This acquisition of social grace also appears to be the cause of beauty's complication. It is difficult to say whether the form of beauty (that which Raphael painted) *is* woman – about whom Cooper has a number of high flown and rather patronising ideas – or some notion of socialised taste, one which is itself a cohesion of subject and object.[163]

Upon the latter reading it is, however, feminine beauties and graces which would make Raphael truly cultured in the broadest sense. It is only by having associated with women that Raphael acquired sufficient taste to enable him to express civic values of the highest order. It is also this 'beauty' (the beauty of women) which defines and embodies that which Raphael will paint. Women, Cooper finally seems to be saying, in contradiction to effeminising luxury, provide the location (in their bodies and in their homes) for, and the manner of, true taste. The social function of women is also to provide that social sense which will enable the 'right Management of our Fancies' and so forestall the capriciousness of individual taste. Tragically, not least for Raphael, women are also corrupting; abandoning yourself to their charms leads to disease, and then to death.[164] The relation of beauty to the social becomes complex and unstable, as beauty appears as both that which will seduce the gentleman into a luxuriant effeminacy and the premise upon which any form of social life may emerge. Cooper's account unites the idea of *being* beautiful with the ability to *see* beauty; it is by endowing the viewer, in this instance Raphael, with the attributes of beauty –

grace, elevation, morals – that the beautiful is itself defined. Although Cooper's concentration of the argument in this passage can sound like half-baked Neoplatonism, with love emerging from desire as the final fruition of beauty, it is, more pertinently, testimony of the growing separation in the mid-century between the discourses which articulated public morality and those which described polite taste. In this sense, the pleasures of the individual subject have superseded the central act of deferred or declined gratification which forms the heart of civic humanism. What emerged in its stead was a concept of taste based on consuming, and, perhaps, on being consumed.

'THE SPIRITS OF THE SENSE': GENDER, FEELING AND THE TRANSFORMATION OF TASTE

A reappraisal of judgement on the scale offered by Cooper (and indeed by Hogarth and Burke) was undoubtedly a departure from earlier critical models. For Shaftesbury the physical form of beauty was thought to disrupt the pristine disavowals upon which civic humanism rested its account of masculinity. From a civic-humanist position, the physical attractiveness of beautiful women represented a dangerously sensual and effeminate presence to be repudiated with stern and unequivocal virtue. This is not quite the issue here; and while the definition of beauty clearly demanded policing to censure the immoral and to license the pleasurable, there is little sense of a form of masculinity which requires men to forgo the social (and sexual) pleasures of the fair sex. The status of feeling is crucial in this context. Prior to the 1740s, feeling tended to be thought of as either a preliminary stage, that which the man of taste went beyond, or something that was merely sexual. On the basis of this assumption, civic humanists rejected feeling as little more than a necessarily instinctual response, one which was likely, moreover, to degenerate rapidly into vice. By the mid-century, however, feeling and pleasure have become the foundations of judgement. Cooper made this commitment because he wanted to be able to argue that, as an instantaneous almost instinctual response, feeling was free from the taints of custom and prejudice. His commitment to this ideal meant that he was prepared, in certain circumstances, to allow feelings that were sensual to be virtuous.

In this respect, the importance of ideas of taste, luxury and femininity cannot be overstated, though they remain ambivalent ideological counters. Critically, the extent to which the use of these ideas resolves the tensions generated by Cooper's or Kames's dismay at, and yet partial acceptance of, modern culture, must be weighed against the distinct problems which their use raises. In the case of *Letters Concerning Taste*, it is possible to suggest that taste, as a mode of judgement, is overpowered by the excesses which the use of images of feeling and femininity generate. Indeed the use of the two latter categories as the mainstay of Cooper's argument occurs in ways which are distinctly ambiguous. It is this ambiguity which leads the text towards a more modern attitude to beauty, for while Cooper consistently advocates the necessity of a private, aristocratic retreat – much in the manner of Shaftesbury – he frames it in language which can be taken as relatively new: the language of sympathy in which the expression of sensibility is a prized commodity.[165] In these terms, a feeling for beauty becomes a means of private gratification, rather than the means through which the universal good is apprehended. This realignment was possible because the audience addressed by Cooper were not aristocratic males intended for the public and political forums envisaged by Shaftesbury. The tribulations of an over-polished Cicero do not therefore present themselves to Cooper as they had done to Shaftesbury.[166] Cooper, in fact, counsels Eugenio against participation in a public environment: 'if *fancy* has dress'd up *domestic* HAPPINESS in the Robes of Office, believe me she plays the *Spirits of the Sense* very false'.[167] Cooper later admits however, that with the death of his own wife, 'Eudocia', he is more inclined to the pursuit of 'wealth and fortune'. Public life is, then, only preferable in the absence of the more comforting and refined company of women.

Cooper's position was one of some complexity, but it is also prompted by complexity, and in particular the elaborate connections which he thought constitutive of social living. For Bishop Berkeley, writing in the wake of the South Sea Bubble, 'frugality of manners is the nourishment and strength of bodies politic'.[168] His vision of society and of morality was, therefore, one in which simplicity – of manners, dress, and social organisation – was advanced as both the virtue and the guardian of the state and the individual. By the 1750s Berkeley's sense of the need for 'plainness and good sense' no longer seemed a plausible or attractive model of the social.[169] It was not, as Cooper's remarks on the tastes of the 'Mob of St. James' illustrates, that the relationship between virtue and vice (represented via the opposition of taste and luxuriant commerce) was disregarded or downgraded as a mode of effective critique; John Brown and others were to continue to insist on the categories of civic polemic well into the 1780s. Rather it is that 'frugality' and 'simplicity' were no longer regarded as necessary guarantors of virtue; austerity and abstinence do not, as Hogarth might have suggested, guarantee virtue, only going without. Significantly, it is through such revisionist discourse, which could be elaborated into an ideology of possession, that private acquisitions began to have a social, and sociable, meaning. In order to achieve this reformulation of virtue it was necessary to simultaneously redefine what it meant to be social.

The most expansive reformulation of social interaction was put forward by Smith in *The Theory of Moral Sentiments*. According to Smith, society rested upon the relations expressed by mutual feeling (defined as 'sympathy') which existed between individuals who both needed, and yet remained in competition with, each other.[170] Smith's position, though, gained considerable currency as the century progressed, including popular endorsement as part of the 'cult' or 'culture' of sensibility.[171] In many respects Smith's theory constituted an extensive change in the forms of social affiliation and cultural personality which are expected from those possessed of a refined and correct taste. Within middle-class theories of society the subject was defined, and then judged, according to the kinds of social affiliations and relations he (or she) was capable of maintaining. That fact that these relations were multiform, and could encompass marital and commercial transactions, meant that the ideal of a stoic allegiance to the state as representative of universal good was disregarded, or at least reworked. Cooper and his contemporaries imagine not, as Berkeley would have wished, a state of simple and restricted manners, but a polite world of complicated and complicating social forms. Much of this intricacy, to use Hogarth's word, stems from the introduction of the sensual into the practices of judgement and from the acceptance, even encouragement, of women as part of the audience for that debate. Masculinity no longer existed solely in opposition to the degradations of the effeminate, but negotiated, instead, a relationship with the feminine. Crucially, while femininity is never imagined to be coincident with male identity, it is no longer repudiated as an unpleasant other. This was largely because ideas of femininity had become an important part of the social fabric in which maleness sought to constitute itself.[172] Women were, if only to a degree, to be consulted on certain matters, of which questions of beauty was one. This is an important change in the nature of debates about taste in the eighteenth century. One which both enshrines and vilifies the place of woman and the feminine. As such, femininity is at once the object in discourses attacking commerce, and yet frequently the subject with which the commercial community sought to justify itself.

CHAPTER TWO

'The Art of Being Pretty': polite taste and the judgement of women

Eighteenth-century periodicals rarely felt inhibited when it came to giving advice, and the eighty-second issue of the *Adventurer*, first published in August, 1753, was no exception. Beginning what is unquestionably an address to a middle-class readership assumed to contain a high proportion of women, the essayist soon warms to his task and announces his intention of teaching all the ladies 'the art of being PRETTY'.[1] The elegantly fashioned and gently admonishing argument strolls through a familiar terrain of condemnation and praise. The writer by turns decries folly, expresses pleasure in the dimples of a smiling girl, and questions the ineffable nature of love, before settling upon the premise that beauty resides more in the passions than in a 'smear of paint'.[2] Beauty, because it 'depends principally on the mind' that is to say, not on looks but on 'SENTIMENTS and MANNERS', may be considered a moral good. The *Adventurer's* intention is to counter the idea that the sight of beauty necessarily leads to vice. Accordingly it is asserted that:

Beauty which depends upon temper [does not] endanger the possessor; 'it is', to use an eastern metaphor 'like the towers of a city, not only an ornament but a defence': if it excites desire, it at once controuls and refines it; it represses with awe, it softens with delicacy, and it wins to imitation. The love of reason and virtue is mingled with the love of beauty; because this beauty is little more than the emanation of intellectual excellence, which is not an object of corporeal appetite. As it excites a purer passion, it also more forcibly engages to fidelity: Everyman finds himself more powerfully restrained from giving pain to goodness, than to beauty; and every look of a countenance in which they are blended, in which beauty is the expression of goodness, is a silent reproach of the irregular wish.[3]

A woman's beauty is presented here as a figure of constancy and virtue. Her true beauty embodies the virtuous form of woman; a vision which 'excites the purer passion'. Hers is an appearance which charms without dissembling, and provides a spectacle while remaining chaste and modest.

With this image in place, the writer finds it comparatively easy to assert that 'those who wish to be LOVELY, must learn early to be GOOD'.[4] Despite earlier assurances that beauty could and would be defended, what is occurring in this passage is a subtle manipulation of the terms of the argument. Throughout the essay, the beauty of women is kept as a questionable property unless it is allied with proper moral sentiments; with a propriety which chastens the desires beauty might otherwise be thought to evoke. Certainly the society ladies or 'Beauties' to which the essay refers are assumed to be less than virtuous, representing merely the vain appearance of good looks combined with tasteless coquetry. Their appearance is described as a 'wretched . . . substitute for the expression of sentiment'.[5] That 'Beauty' and prettiness are distinguished by the writer of this essay is indicative of a telling alteration in the way in which the debate on the beautiful is articulated by mid-century. Texts written in this period repeatedly effect the transposition of the beautiful into the polite or familiar discourse which marks the *Adventurer*'s advice. Once moved, the term becomes a prescriptive, as well as a descriptive appraisal of women. It is here that the writer hopes both to frustrate the power-play of the 'factitious beauty' and to teach female readers, 'an art by which their predominant passion may be gratified, and their conquests not only extended, but secured'.[6]

The persuasive rhetoric of the *Adventurer* is a cogent reminder that, if the eighteenth century was a period in which the forms of aesthetic judgement were revolutionised, it was also a period in which the cultural role of women was radically altered. Women, as was averred by many eighteenth-century writers, were thought to be necessary to the formation of a truly polite and civilised culture.[7] This is a compelling conjunction, and one which is inscribed into the texts themselves; Burke's *Enquiry* is only the most notorious example of how the beautiful and the feminine came to be regarded as identical. Hogarth, for example, sought to define beauty in terms which made explicit reference to the attractions and conduct of women.[8] In describing these connections, discourses on beauty adopted new and specific functions. In the forthcoming discussion I shall argue that the concept of beauty was not restricted to the judgements of connoisseurs, but was instead the organising term for a variety of discourses and social practices and, most particularly, those concerned with the conduct of women. Although consideration of the objects of taste, and how judgements are formed and evaluated, never ceases to be of importance, the discussion of the beautiful emerges in the mid-century as connected with, or as actually inhabiting, a discourse concerned with social codes and, in particular, the conduct of polite society. Hawkesworth had such an inquiry in mind when he referred to a pretty face as the 'expression of goodness' and as a 'reproach to the irregular wish'.[9] To employ a discussion of beauty as a means of distinguishing between proper and improper social and sexual conduct is not only to transform its meaning, but also to alter its social co-ordinates. In a text such as the *Adventurer*, there is little concern with the idea of beauty or the place of women within a social body conceived in terms of the kind of political republic found in Shaftesbury's criticism; but rather a consideration of how women are represented both in the private sphere of the drawing-room, and in the public world of ballrooms and society assemblies.

The discourse which emerges from such discussions is one that represents beauty as the moment of a woman's social visibility; one which declares her moral and sexual, as well as visual, presence. In many cases, the transformation of the terms 'beauty' and 'beautiful' into a vocabulary for marking out the proper or the obscene nature of feminine display provided the impetus for new accounts of taste, accounts which stressed the social, rather than the directly political, significance of judging right. Such a shift in emphasis represented an important change in the discourses through which taste and judgement were articulated during the eighteenth century. An example of this investment has already been witnessed via a consideration of Joseph Spence's representation of the 'English Lady at Florence' and his sense of the disjunction between taste and fashion which she embodied. Although Spence rehearsed the basic tenets of a civic-humanist account of the arts, what distinguished his work from that of previous theorists was his combination of a general investigation into the nature of beauty and an attention to conduct, principally the conduct of women. Furthermore, a reading of John Gilbert Cooper's work also indicated how a concern with femininity and sensibility came to underlie conceptions of beauty in the mid-eighteenth century. Both Spence and Cooper, together with the *Adventurer* article, realign the debate about beauty so that its more public, Shaftesburian elements are downplayed in favour of an emergent stress on private moral judgements. Arguably this shift accelerated as the century progressed, indeed the modes of critical judgement found within mid-century texts such as the *Adventurer* and *Polymetis* resulted in a new discourse in which femininity became the principal object of analysis. This chapter explores that investment and seeks to connect it to more general developments within eighteenth-century culture.

THE CONVERSIBLE REALM: WOMEN AND THE PUBLIC SPHERE OF LETTERS

In many respects the movement of beauty from political sign to social function discloses the forms of translation and mutation, which, according to Michel Foucault, necessarily attend a discourse when it is transposed from its location and function in one institution to a habitation in another. Foucault argues, that if the conditions in which a discourse is employed are radically transformed, then its meaning too will alter, so that 'a new statement must be recognised'.[10] Foucault's historicist account of discursive change provides a means for thinking about how analysis of the perceived beauties of women altered the social and cultural location in which discussions of the beautiful were undertaken; and how, in turn, this shift transformed what was written about beauty from the mid-century onwards. Crucially, the changes which occurred within the discussion of taste were a part of the growth of cultural debate defined by Jurgen Habermas as the emergence of the bourgeois public sphere. In Habermas's terms the public sphere of letters was greatly expanded by middle-class intellectuals as a means through which their aspirations, then stifled in the sphere of politics, could find expression and force. In the context of Britain he cites the periodical presses and the fiction of Samuel Richardson as the prime examples of this process. It was through such texts, according to Habermas, that the middle classes consolidated their claims to cultural authority. The debate about taste and its relation to women's beauty is another such investment, indeed the appropriation of the discourse on beauty by middle-class writers manifested nothing less than an attempt to reconcile the practice of their own social environs with a language which had initially evolved as the means of instating aristocratic prestige.[11]

The extent to which the discussion of beauty becomes a means of consolidating middle-class opinion as well as thinking about women will emerge as my account proceeds, however, a reading of David Hume's 'Of Essay Writing' will indicate what I have in mind. Hume begins his short essay by proposing a split in the 'elegant part of mankind' between the *learned* and the *conversible*.[12] These two group-ings are taken to represent, on the one hand, the solitary and intellectual domain of the philosopher and, on the other hand, the social world, which includes the talk and gossip of polite life. As Hume elaborates his idea it becomes clear, for Hume is playful in his advertisement of this position, that this is a finely wrought model of gender and social difference. It is at the point where Hume denotes the *conversible* realm as the province of the 'Fair Sex', noting that women are the 'sovereigns of the Empire of Conversation', that this becomes explicit. It is the relationship between these two areas of learned and polite society on which Hume's essay focuses.[13]

Hume shows no reserve in claiming for himself a position of pre-eminence in this scheme and soon installs himself as 'Ambassador from the Dominions of Learning to those of Conversation'. He suggests somewhat flirtatiously that were it in his power to yield his country to the fair sovereigns of the conversible world, he would perhaps do so; or perhaps not. All that is in his power is to recommend that a 'league' be established against the 'enemies of beauty and reason'. Of this alliance, Hume suggests there need be no fear:

The Balance of Trade we need not be jealous of, nor will there be any Difficulty to preserve it on both Sides. The Materials of this Commerce must chiefly be furnish'd by Conversation and common Life: The manufacturing of them alone belongs to Learning.[14]

While this statement implies a notional equity, there is something more subtle at work here. The conversible realm merely produces the 'Materials' for this trade, providing only the raw goods from which the learned will fashion more refined products. However, although the production of the objects of discourse lies wholly within the domain of learning, the valuation of the product lies beyond the learned, who are its producers. Consequently, while philosophers may produce learned treatises upon whatever subject, they cannot, within their own world, evaluate or legitimate the position of philosophy. They must leave their state of mopey reclusiveness – a kind of dull impotence – to seek approval in the outside world, which turns out to mean the approval of women:

I am of the Opinion, that Women, that is Women of Sense and Education (for to such alone do I address myself) are much better Judges of all polite Writing than Men of the same Degree of Understanding.[15]

Hume is not very clear about why women are more suited to the judging of philosophy than men, though he may be relying on the assumption, common in the eighteenth century, that women possessed a disinterested as well as a natural gentility. This commitment is in line with Hume's more general position that philosophy needed to become a properly polite activity, and hence not inimical to the tastes or experience of women, if it was to prosper in the modern world.[16]

Given the significance of these connections, the issue which most confronts Hume is that of deciding upon what grounds this approval is to be granted. Despite reservations concerning the susceptibility of women to the showy excesses of gallantry and religious enthusiasm Hume seems confident that the 'Fair Sex' will give praise and award merit wherever it is due:

Let them accustom themselves a little more to Books of all Kinds: Let them give Encouragement to Men of Sense and Knowledge to frequent their Company: And finally, let them heartily concur in that Union I have projected betwixt the learned and the conversible Worlds. They may perhaps, meet with more Complaisance from their usual Followers than from Men of Learning; but they cannot reasonably expect so sincere an Affection: And, I hope, they will never be guilty of so wrong a Choice, as to sacrifice the Substance to the Shadow.[17]

A reformation of female manners and education would then secure the process, improving both the genteel and the philosophical worlds. The point Hume is making is that while women, as the foundations of the social, are the final arbiters of taste, it is an arbitration which needs careful scrutiny. Women are represented by Hume as both the agents of tasteful appreciation and as objects of scrutiny, policed lest they mistake the 'substance for the shadow'. Women are, therefore, placed in an unpleasantly doubled position, in a role which forces them to act as both the surveyors and the surveyed.

Hume's essay makes clear the importance of polite sociability within the middle-class led culture of the mid-century.[18] As Lawrence Klein has argued, the emergence of politeness was one of the foremost changes to occur in British society during the eighteenth century: 'it became a key word, a point of verbal intersection among different areas of human experience, providing a unifying rubric for greatly diverse activities'. Klein's reading of the early eighteenth-century debate further suggests that the protocols of politeness emerged from within a culture which had a profoundly ambivalent attitude to commerce, indeed polite discourse was an attempt to reconcile interest with virtue.[19] This was an endeavour which was only distantly connected to the political public framed by civic-humanist discourse. Indeed Hume, along with Addison and Steele, distanced himself from the priorities of Shaftesbury in order to fashion a social realm which included not only new readers, but also new ideas. The transposition of the account of knowledge and learning to a new site on what de Bolla has termed the 'discursive network' which articulated eighteenth-century culture enabled a particular staging of discourses around the beautiful. Most significantly, there was a willingness, from about 1740 onwards, to unite a previously problematic group of ideas – namely, feeling, taste and femininity – within the newly defined space of polite discourse. It is the contiguity which exists between these terms that determines the direction of mid-century accounts of taste. What these diverse investments suggest, as a close reading of the texts confirms, is the existence of a discourse which either described taste and beauty in relation to how women appear, and how women act, or described the apprehension of beautiful forms in terms which require the male viewer to respond as if he were looking at a woman. Significantly, the two options were far from being mutually exclusive. For example, in his scholarly An Essay on Taste, Alexander Gerard argued that women, because they possessed more 'lively passions' than men, were capable of a greater 'sensibility of Taste'.[20] In the most extreme cases, when women were heralded as the most sensitive of connoisseurs, this connection could amount to a request that the male connoisseur respond as if he were in fact a woman; sensitive, impressionable and yet quietly discerning.

'THAT MAGDALEN LOOK': REAL PERSONAL BEAUTY AND THE FEMINISATION OF TASTE

The text which best exemplifies the changed nature of the discourse of taste at mid-century is Joseph Spence's *Crito; or A Dialogue on Beauty*, a text written half a decade after *Polymetis* and read with a mixture of enthusiasm and polite good humour throughout the remainder of the century. What made Spence's argument distinctive was its explict formulation of beauty as sensuous and virtuous femininity. This was a claim bold enough to ensure that *Crito* acquired, if not a degree of influence, then at least a measure of currency within debates about the nature of taste. Allan Ramsay, for example, although he mocked what he saw as Spence's affinity with women, took Spence seriously enough for his theories to be the subject of debate between his creations, Colonel Freeman and Lord Modish. In recent years, connections have also been made between Spence's text and the work of Hogarth and Reynolds.[21] Perhaps most impressive is the fact that when Daniel Webb dedicated *An Inquiry into the Beauties of Painting*, to Spence, he announced that, 'It was natural for me . . . to address my observations on Painting to the author of CRITO.'[22] The dedication to Spence is perhaps not surprising (Webb subscribed to the first edition of *Polymetis*), but that it is to him as the author of *Crito*, and not of *Polymetis*, is intriguing, the more so as a reading of *Crito* reveals that Spence's intention was to relocate the appreciation of the beautiful, half in the realm of conduct literature and half within the kinds of anguished tableaux characteristic of the sentimental novel. In both instances women, or at least conceptions of femininity, were given a more decisive role than had previously been imagined for them within the sphere of tasteful contemplation.[23]

The centrality of ideas of femininity and of discourses about women to the analysis of taste can be made evident by a consideration of how *Crito* begins and by an examination of the occasion of the debate. Beginning as a convivial and gentlemanly dialogue, *Crito* represents a rural scene in which gentlemen have gathered to discourse on the nature of beauty, and upon the attractions of the fair sex. In these terms, the point of origin, the location which the text describes, is positioned as feminised or leisured, most obviously in opposition to the implicitly masculinised 'Noise and Bustle of the Town'.[24] The figure of woman emerges as the major trope of the narrative, and, perhaps more pertinently, as the enigma the text seeks to resolve. Asked to define his sense of beauty, Crito describes a scene of particularly affecting distress. The story he tells concerns Mrs B***, a beautiful woman of the neighbourhood, who endures the double misfortune of being possessed of a 'brute' of a husband, and grieving the loss of her only son. On the single day which comprises the whole action of *Crito*, Crito disturbs Mrs B*** weeping over the lost boy, whose birthday it would have been. Crito has stolen in upon her, and finds her in the full flow of her grief:

I walked toward the Room; and found the Door only just open enough, to let me see her leaning on a Couch, with her Head rested negligently on the one Hand, whilst with the other she was wiping away a Tear, that stole silently down her Cheek. The Distress in her Countenance, and the little Confusion that appeared about her Eyes, on her first discovering me (just as I was doubting whether I should retire or not), added so much to the other Beauties of her Face, that I think I never saw her look so charming in my Life.[25]

Her easy pose, worthy maternal emotions and the beauty of her features give Mrs B*** an irresistible charm. Crito, a man of feeling, is instantly struck both by her virtue and by her visible, physical beauty. For Crito, Mrs B***'s tears have lent her what he will later describe as the particular and principal beauty of weeping women: 'that Magdalen look'.[26] With the occasion of his disquiet now revealed, and disapprobation of the husband and encomiums on the wife made general, Crito is subjected to a closer form of questioning, which will form the basis of the conversation. Immediately, he is asked 'but, pray, how come you to think, that her Sufferings should add to her Charms? Or that a Distress, like hers, could ever be pleasing to the Eye?'[27] It is in response to this question that Crito launches into an exegesis on the nature of the beautiful which positions women as both the signs of taste and as the guarantors of male virtue.

Before coming to the details of Crito's argument, I want to pause to consider the role of the silent, weeping Mrs B***, who is referred to on two further occasions in the course of the text: when she scores top marks with 73 points in Crito's grotesque revision of du Piles's critical method, and when she is represented as the right choice for a modern Hercules.[28] What is important about Mrs B*** is not the extent of her attractiveness, though this is itself impressive – as she only loses to the *Venus di Medici* by a slender margin – but the fact of her beauty as the occasion for a particular discourse on beauty, which is focused on the bodies of women. It is her beauty which is the fountain-head of Crito's argument; without the beautiful Mrs B***, there would be no enigma to resolve, no dialogue needed. The tableau of her charms – the agony of the object mixing with the ecstasy of the subject – provides the material which Crito will attempt to explain. In this sense, the narrative focuses on an image of womanhood and an ideal of femininity which it represents as exemplary. The role which may be ascribed to women within the field of aesthetic evaluation has already been explored in relation to Cooper's *Letters Concerning Taste*. In this instance, the inflection is different; women do not so much represent an authority to which it is possible to defer as a problem to be solved. The questions asked by the text might be articulated as follows: why are women more or less attractive to men, and what motivates and guides that attraction? Crito will investigate whether there is some physical or moral quality that guarantees the worth of a particular body, or person. Ultimately, however, he is seeking to account for women's place both as objects within the field of male vision, and as moral subjects active within society.

The significance of polite femininity will emerge repeatedly during the course of *Crito,* for it determines the objects chosen for analysis and the terms which constitute the framework of that approach. Crito's central object of study, what he terms 'Real Personal Beauty' is a case in point. Like all writers who sought to explain the beautiful, Crito must define the object of his study. Given the ambiguous nature of his inquiry, this requires a judicious confession of the immensity of the task, and a due attempt to reduce the object field:

Every Object that is pleasing to the Eye when looked upon, or delightful to the Mind in Recollection, may be called beautiful; so that Beauty, in general, may stretch as wide as visible Creation, or even as far as the Imagination can go; which is a sort of new or Secondary Creation. Thus we speak not only of the Beauties of an engaging Prospect, of the rising or setting Sun, or of a fine starry Heaven; but of those of a Picture, Statue, or Building; and even of the Actions, Characters, or Thoughts of Men. In the greater Part of these, there may be almost as many false Beauties as there are real; according to the different Tastes of Nations, and Men; so that if any one was to consider Beauty in its fullest Extent, it could not be done without the greatest Confusion.[29]

Crito first of all delimits a 'Beauty, in general' which is formed on the basis of a pleasingness to the eye, or to the imagination. The prospect of this definition stretches far and wide; it is too large and wholly unworkable, and moreover largely false. Crito then tries to purge his account of these specious beauties. He continues in a

manner which would be familiar to Reynolds, and broadly consistent
with civic demands upon criticism:

I shall therefore confine my Subject to visible Beauty; and of that, to such
only as may be called personal, or human Beauty; and that, again, to such
as is natural or real, and not such as is only national or customary; for I
would not have you imagine, that I would have anything to do with the
beautiful thick Lips of the good People of *Bantam,* or the excessive small feet
of the Ladies of Quality in *China.*

Only that which is 'natural and real' may be included, for the rest
is merely 'national or customary'. The decision to exclude the
'beautiful thick Lips of the good People of *Bantam*' may be profitably
compared with many of Reynolds's injunctions to the readers of the
eighty-second number of the *Idler* in 1759, in which he exhorted
artists to expel from their work all that was accidental, customary or
motivated by habit alone.[30] According to Reynolds, the painter's art
required the separation of the varied and unruly 'second nature'
from the 'ideal nature' which lay beneath the surface. Spence
appears to be making a similar point here.

Close analysis of *Crito* reveals that there are a number of different
definitions of the beautiful in circulation within Spence's text. Firstly
there is the general beauty of everything which pleases, a conception
which is rapidly disregarded – officially at least. Secondly, there is a
beauty of a more rarefied and restricted nature; in short *real* beauty,
untainted by custom or national taste. Finally, there is Crito's chosen
object, 'Real Personal Beauty', which claims similar differentiation
from custom and habit, but which ultimately takes the passions,
rather than the mind, as its justification. This is a definition of
beauty which, because it excludes the customary – the forms of the
Bantam or Chinese Beauties – is consistent with the high ideals of
civic art as outlined by Reynolds. However, it is distinctive in the
calculated centrality of the 'personal', and the role which is ascribed
to that figure. It is hard to reconcile the avowed *personality* of the
beauties under discussion, such as Mrs B*** or any other fair
creature, with the generalising and universalising impulse of civic-
humanist theory which seeks not the person, but the grand historical
expression.[31]

Spence's concentration upon the 'personal' nature of beauty
positions 'Real Personal Beauty' at some distance from straightforwardly civic conceptions of the taste. Significantly, the emphasis on
the beauty of women prevents the easy exclusion of the passions

made in Reynolds's *Idler* article: 'It is absurd to say, that beauty is possessed of attractive powers, which irresistibly seize the corresponding mind with love and admiration.'[32] For Reynolds, defining beauty merely by saying that it pleases signifies an inability to come to terms with the impact of custom in forming taste. More strikingly, the notion of 'attractive powers' suggests the action of the passions rather than the calculus of virtue. The discourse of ideal beauty is, then, only partially unfolded by Crito; gathered around its margins there is an index of values which depend less on real discernment, than on the inclinations of the passions. Desire, in the shape of the passions, and not custom, as in the case of Reynolds, becomes the central concern.[33]

The emphasis on the sensible qualites of the beautiful and the sensibilty which is required to apprehend it determines the remainder of Crito's argument. Although, Crito delimits what he terms the 'four heads' of beauty, which are 'Color, Form, Expression, and Grace', he makes it clear that it is the last two terms which constitute the 'Soul of Beauty'.[34] Accordingly, his reflections on form and colour are far from remarkable. For the most part, Crito is content to point out the value of variety and liveliness (here representing good health as much as vivacity). Crito argues that the 'general Cause of Beauty in the Form or Shape is a Proportion, or an Union and Harmony, in all Parts of the Body'.[35] Significantly, different bodily forms are appropriate to each sex. The qualities Crito desires in the bodies of women fulfil a well-established agenda, one that aims to provide simple and irrecoverable sexual differentiation. He seeks delicacy, softness, smallness and whiteness of skin; in short the signs of a body which has abstained from labour. In contradistinction, the bodies of men ought to exhibit 'apparent Strength or Agility'.[36]

Distinctions of gender also determine Crito's discussion of the 'Beauties of the Soul', defined as 'Expression' and 'Grace'. The discussion of 'Expression' is primarily concerned with the due representation of the emotions in the face and body; more particularly, the 'Expression of the Passions; the Turns and Changes of the Mind, so far as they are visible to the Eye, by our Looks or Gestures'.[37] Pleasing passions, moreover, add something to the appearance, and to the face in particular. Significantly, the forms of expression appropriate for the face are explicitly feminised:

The finest Union of Passions, that I have ever observed in any Face, constituted a just Mixture of Modesty, Sensibility and Sweetness; each of which when taken singly, is very pleasing; but when they are all blended together, in such a manner as either to enliven or correct each other, they give almost as much Attraction, as the Passions are capable of adding to a very pretty Face.[38]

These are exemplary feminine virtues, attributes of a largely passive and confined identity. Burke, of course, similarly proposes compliant and retiring charms as the source of feminine beauty.[39] According to Spence, it is through such charms beauty increases, as does the pleasure offered to the observer:

It is owing to the great Force of Pleasingness which attends all the kinder Passions; 'That Lovers do not only seem, but are really more beautiful to each other, than they are to the rest of the World'; because, when they are together, the most pleasing Passions are more frequently exerted in each of their Faces, than they are in either before the rest of the World.[40]

It is the emphasis on 'pleasing' that should detain us here. For it is the relationship between beauty and pleasure, variously conceived, which determines the course of the argument put forward by Spence. Indeed as the account proceeds Crito increasingly substitutes 'pleasingness' for 'beauty' as the appropriate term for describing the effect of particular forms and expressions. Crito suggests:

That a Face without any good Feature in it, and with a very indifferent Complexion, shall have a very taking Air; from the Sensibility of the Eyes, the general good-humoured Turn of the Look, and perhaps a little agreeable Smile about the Mouth. And these Three Things, I believe, would go a great way toward accounting for the *je ne scai quoi* or that inexpressible Pleasingness of the Face (as they chuse to call it), which is often talked of, and so little understood; as the greater Part, and perhaps all the rest of it, would fall under the last Article, that of Grace.[41]

Here pleasure occupies the space left by the absence of any real (in the sense of tangible) qualities. A movement away from visible qualities – form and colour – is being made throughout the passage, and even grace is constructed largely in terms of the pleasure it gives.

The consequences of this investment need to be considered in some detail. On the one hand, 'pleasingness' could merely signify an attempt to describe, within an emotional register, the effects of real personal beauty upon the discerning observer. Conversely, the term could herald a further shift away from a scheme seeking to solicit the

true, natural and 'real' causes of the beautiful to an analytic resting
solely upon individual approbation. Nowhere is this change more
apparent than in the discussion of the last of Crito's 'four heads' of
beauty, Grace. Grace is, Crito announces, the most stunning
element, and the 'chief of all the constituent parts', of beauty; 'pretty
women', Crito claims, are always capable of grace.[42] Grace is,
furthermore, rare and always pleasing, representing something
which rises 'above' the taste for blonde or brown hair. Curiously,
Crito announces that Grace can manifest itself as a 'certain Deli-
ciousness that almost lies about the mouth', indicating, perhaps, an
'Approach towards a Smile'.[43] There is something faintly lascivious
about this flickering image, which makes the graceful look more like
a specious bashfulness than a genuine moral quality. Indeed, as
Crito acknowledges, although 'Grace is pleasingness itself' there
'seems to be something else, what I cannot explain, and what I do
not know that ever anybody has explained, that goes to the
Composition; and which possibly may give it its Force and Pleasingness'.[44] At this point in the text, defining what constitutes 'pleasingness' becomes the overriding concern. The issue cannot
convincingly be resolved by either Crito or his interlocutors; as the
question of what pleases is both too ineffable and too personal. In a
brief pause in Crito's disquisition, the friends offer nothing more
telling than the fact that pleasure and true taste are coincident, a
point attested to by the gratification of eating fresh fruit. Pursuing
the debate further, they agree that a pineapple has its various
seasons each improving or ruinous to its taste. This is a cycle of
rising and falling excellence which is also detectable, so they claim,
in the bodies of women. By allowing the word 'taste' to shift its
meaning from food to women, and finally to 'Taste' in general, Crito
and his company hope to endow aesthetic appreciation with a
physical quality which would make it more readily apprehensible:
excellence in philosophy would become analagous to 'ripeness' of
food, and (more shamefully) women.

Following this far from convincing attempt to postulate efficient
causes for the beautiful, Crito and company engage in an attempt to
fashion their own 'mathematical style'. This 'calculation', borrowed
from du Piles's analysis of art, involves the awarding of a score to
various women of their acquaintance. The enterprise is warmly
entered into and scores are posted ranging from Mrs B***'s 73 to
poor Mrs P***'s −45.[45] However, Mrs B***'s success at the polls is

not reliant upon the extent of her physical beauty, as in terms of colour she is eclipsed by both Lady R*** and Lady S***. Mrs B*** wins her laurels on the unconquerable status of her grace, for which she gains an impressive thirty points from the munificent Crito. Despite the unabashed ease with which this task has been completed, the judging of 'proportional excellence' is, as Crito concedes, open to the intrusion of 'false byas'. The cause of such failures of taste are numerous and include custom, occupation and habit; Crito, however, candidly vouchsafes the superlative excellence of English beauties.[46] Rather archly, Crito claims that this is a most fortunate occurrence, as without diversity of tastes the competition amongst men for the few women agreed to be universally beautiful would lead inevitably to a 'Scene of Blood and Misery':

> But now that Fancy has perhaps more to do with Beauty than Judgement, there is an Infinity of Tastes, and consequently an Infinity of Beauty; for, to the Mind of the Lover, supposed Beauty is as full good as real.[47]

The statement that 'supposed Beauty is as full good as real' marks something of a climb down for Crito, for he appears to have abandoned the reality of 'personal beauty' with which he began his inquiry. Instead the role of fancy secures the fact that different beauties will appeal to different groups of men, so that 'everybody may be beautiful in the imagination of some one or other'; which is convenient, if nothing else. There is, then, a variety of beauties which may be pleasing, particularly where form and colour are concerned, so that 'false grace has all the effects of the true'.[48] The difference between true Grace and particular pleasingness would, therefore, appear to be abstract or merely theoretical, and not the immediate, sensual and practical experience which is the function of the Fancy, and of the lover. Men, according to this account, cannot differentiate between 'supposed beauty' and the real thing, and there seems little reason why they should.

In making this claim Crito effectively abolishes the proposition with which he began; namely, that there is a quantifiable method for judging beauty. Unlike Ramsay, who was prepared to define beauty as the consequence of personal inclination, even suggesting that a uniformity of taste ran counter to 'all hitherto known principals of nature', Spence remained unwilling to allow beauty to elude a general definition.[49] This theoretical problem determines the move ultimately made to invoke 'Virtue' as the chief cause of beauty.

Indeed, Crito claims explicitly that 'the Beauty of Virtue or Goodness exceeds all other Beauty, as much as the Soul does the Body'.[50] With this in mind, he concludes his argument by extolling the fact that:

> If Virtue be the chief Beauty, People, to be beautiful, should endeavour to be virtuous; and should avoid Vice, and all the worst Sort of Passions, as they would shy Deformity. I wish the more beautiful Half of the human Creation, in particular, were thoroughly sensible of this great Truth; 'That the readiest way to be beautiful, is to be good'; and such of them as are more solicitous about choosing and adjusting what they wear, and how they appear, than about forming their Minds, and regulating their disagreeable Passions, will really fall under the Censure I mentioned before, from one of the *Latin* Poets; and show too plainly to all the World, that they, in their own Hearts, consider their dress as the better part of themselves.[51]

The excesses of an over-dressed femininity are central to this conclusion, as such extravagance entails an unwillingness to act in accordance with the dictates of prudence and propriety. Crito's point, though, is not visual disappointment, but rather moral condemnation. Too great a consideration of appearances indicates a vice which can only leave the individual (and those who look at her) morally deformed and unsightly.

By making these connections function as the guarantors of beauty, Spence discloses, as the *Adventurer* had done, his intention to seek a reformation of female manners via an appeal to the discourse of taste. Unlike Pope's *Epistle to a Lady*, Spence sought to accomplish this by stressing the femininity of women.[52] Whereas Pope offers the masculinised hybridity of the 'softer Man' as the ideal to which Martha Blount may successfully aim, it is an idea of pleasing feminine prettiness which prompts Timanthes to close *Crito* by urging his friend to publish his reflections 'for the benefit of the fair sex in general'.[53] By this point, however, Crito has admitted into his discussion more or less every form of beauty which he had originally sought to exclude: the fanciful, the merely pleasing and the national. It would seem, furthermore, that it is the emphasis on *personality* upon which his theory rests that has made this inevitable, as the emphasis on the individual body form, and the singular moment of approbation, excludes any stability of judgement. The fact that he later has to change discourses from that which first articulated real personal beauty – a discourse which still relied in part on civic-humanist terminology – to a discourse which can be thought of as a discourse of domestic or feminine beauty represents a considerable shift in his position, one which is indicative of greater changes within the discourse of taste at mid-century.

What is so crucial about Spence's reformulation of the discourse on taste in *Crito* is that he establishes that beauty can be argued for by analogy with a desire *for women*, rather than (as in Burke's *Enquiry*) in terms of a mere description of women. Burke, as we have seen, tried to maintain a distinction between desire for women and a more generalised social love. Shaftesbury, similarly, only countenanced women's beauty as an inferior form of a properly public object. In *Crito*, the desire for women is established, by contrast, as the definition of beauty itself. The beauty of women as the object of male desire, is legitimated by Spence because he is able to make it not solely a figure of sexuality, but instead a means of social address. In many respects it is Spence's advocacy of the beauties of women, and the pleasures of their society, which made *Crito* innovative. While Spence's earlier *Polymetis* can appear playful in its address to sexuality and to the issue of gender in general, women are not given the space or the centrality which they receive in *Crito*. True, the *Venus di Medici* was discussed by Polymetis and his companions, but it was in no sense the principal object of inquiry. As a result, the statue is represented as the site of potential luxury or folly against which Spence's male, connoisseurial gaze was defined.[54] Similarly, when Spence introduced the 'Lady at Florence', she was assumed to be so restricted in her capacity to judge the *Venus di Medici*, as to be only able to do so with reference to either fashion or narcissistic self-congratulation. Throughout *Crito*, by contrast, Spence alters the terms of the discourse on beauty and grants women a less negative role in the production of tasteful discourse; women remain, however, the objects and not the subjects of the account.

The manner by which the discourse on taste is established in a position away from the demands of aristocratic politics is, therefore, exactly in proportion to the degree to which it is transformed into a means of evaluating women. This is the meaning, finally, of Mrs B***; a critical moment which encompasses the imposition of moral requirements upon a supposedly philosophic discourse. Such connections were not uncommon in mid-century accounts of taste or beauty; Kames, for example, also employed an image of distressed femininity as part of his definition of beauty in the *Elements of Criticism*:

Pity interests us in this object, and recommends all its virtuous qualities. For this reason, female beauty shows best in distress, and is more apt to inspire love, than upon ordinary occasions.[55]

According to Kames, pity warms and melts the spectator, thus preparing him 'for the reception of other tender affections'. Spence's Mrs B*** could also be described as a spectacle wherein 'admiration concurred with pity to produce love'.[56] David Solkin has argued that Kames's account provided the eighteenth-century art world with the vocabulary with which to engage with the nature of modern taste in a manner consistent with civic virtue.[57] However, it was also a means of formulating a response to the presence of women within polite society. This was a crucial endeavour in mid-century culture because it was the conduct of women which was most often regarded as the embodiment of the culture's moral standards. In the remainder of this chapter I want to explore how the two aims of defining taste and regulating social interaction interpellated one another across a range of texts. In the first instance Daniel Webb's *An Inquiry into the Beauties of Painting* is examined. Latterly, James Usher's account of taste is studied on the basis of his book, *Clio; or, a Discourse on Taste*. The account of both texts is intended to prepare the ground for the discussion of portraiture and the novel which occupies the final chapters of this book.

'CERTAIN PLEASING SENSATIONS': A DIALOGUE ON PAINTING

Published in 1760, Daniel Webb's *Beauties of Painting* adapted the dialogue form in order to provide a leisured, as well as polite, introduction to the intricacies of painting.[58] Like Hogarth's *Analysis of Beauty* and Kames's *Elements of Criticism*, Webb began his text with the aim of correcting taste by outlining the aesthetic and psychological effects of beauty. More specifically, Webb wished to define the '*Capacity to Judge of* Painting' and to explain how best to appreciate the works of the great artists. Fortunately, Webb assured his readers that painting was, of all the arts, 'the most easily understood' and 'the most natural in its means and effects'.[59] The natural effects which underlie what Webb termed the 'science' of criticism are such that he can suggest that taste is a 'faculty in the mind to be moved by what is excellent in an art; it is a feeling of the truth. But, science is to be informed of that truth, and of the means by which its effects are produced'.[60] The difference between a 'feeling for the truth' and the foreknowledge of the 'means by which its effects are produced' is perhaps an uncertain one, particularly as the difference cannot be attributed to a knowledge of the mechanic parts of painting. Indeed, Webb argued that painters, the group most obviously possessed of such knowledge, were rarely able to 'rise to an unprejudiced and liberal contemplation of true beauty'.[61]

Webb clarified his position somewhat by suggesting that if the 'source of taste is feeling, so is it of judgement, which is nothing more than this same sensibility improved by the study of proper objects, and brought to a just point of certainty and correctness'.[62] Described in these terms, judgement comes to depend upon innate feeling, while science is figured as a sophisticated knowledge of the process by which that sensation is produced. By making these connections, Webb, like Spence in *Crito*, asserted the possibility of virtuous desire by making the aesthetic an issue of 'pleasingness' within a system of judgements which similarly relied on feeling. In this way Webb hoped to avoid the problems raised by texts such as Cooper's *Letters Concerning Taste* where feeling appeared unregulated. As we shall see in a moment, Webb, again like Spence, further justified his methodology by connecting them with a desire for women. This was arguably why Webb found it 'natural . . . to address my observations on Painting to the author of Crito', for it is by making feeling so central to judgement that Webb moves into the territory sketched out in *Crito*; in short he regards the pleasure of painting as itself a 'passion, founded on the love of what is beautiful'.[63] The statement implies, as does his account of the excitement of 'proper objects', a sense of the 'pleasingness' of beauty that is comparable with the account provided in *Crito*. It is in this sense that the art of painting, and its particular 'beauties', are easily understood, and pleasurably so, which marks the point at which Webb's debt to *Crito* becomes apparent.

The commitment to 'pleasingness' and 'feeling' are important because Webb uses such ideas to bring painting within the purview of the polite arts. According to Webb, painting can be considered as an essentially polite art, as 'it is certain, that the love of this art has been considered in every civilised nation, not only as proof of politeness, but even as the test of their humanity':

To effect this, the softer passions, and even elegant habitudes are to be employed: These only can harmonise the mind, and temper it in a sensibility of the slightest impressions, and most exquisite feelings. Hence spring attention, civility, the finest disguises of our own passions, and insinuating addresses to those of others; these fashion themselves into a system of politeness; society becomes amiable, as well as good, and we have at last, the best incitements to the practice of virtue in the agreeableness of its objects.[64]

Although Webb is ostensibly talking about the modes of 'Athenian politeness', it is clear that he intends the social qualities he describes to apply equally to the successful fruition of a modern society. Importantly, it is the delights of the Graces, and of grace in general, which are taken to be the chief pleasure of a refined society and its arts. Commenting on the wisdom of the Greek myths, it is noted that the Graces:

were made to preside over courtly, and outward charms: The assigning them this double province was happily imagined; for civility, or the desire to please, naturally produces a gracefulness of action; and spreads over the person that venustas, which is the contemplation of exterior beauty.[65]

Grace, as *Crito* indicates, became in the eighteenth century the primary means of representing appropriate social conduct, and more particularly the correct conduct of women; it was because of her grace, that Mrs B*** pleased. Similarly, Webb defines grace as 'the desire to please' and as the 'contemplation of exterior beauty'.[66] That the value of painting as an art is located in terms borrowed from a discussion of feminine grace would appear to alter the whole project. This attention to the attractions and pleasures of the beautiful (gendered as feminine) would be expected to undermine what Webb terms criticism's 'chaste eye'. Certainly the 'pleasing sensations' attributed to painting are ambivalent in this context, the more so, because the prominence they receive has the effect of reducing judgement to the effect of felt pleasure (again, this is an assumption shared with *Crito*).[67] This emphasis is crucial: throughout the *Beauties of Painting*, Webb takes a set of terms – grace, 'pleasing-ness' and feeling (sensation) – which Spence used to judge women and upholds them as keys to the arts. This move had its advantages as well as its embarrassments.

Initially, Webb's point seems to be that painting, because it is gracious and pleasing, has the ability to harmonise and to socialise, blending a sensibility which is both refined and amiable.[68] This argument is underlined by the suggestion that the progress of sociability may be summarised in terms of the gracious softening effected by the polite arts:

Thus the first motives may be said to act like the pressure of the heart or current of the blood; their operations are evident: But the latter, of a more refined nature, like the animal spirits, though they work unperceived, give life and movement to well ordered societies.[69]

In this context, the difference between an immediate, sensual response and the proprieties of a sociable gaze is a fine one. Significantly, it is a separation which not everyone can make, and many 'continue, to the last, under the influence of the same boyish and wanton imagination'.[70] Burke was similarly ambivalent when discussing the extent to which the perception of beauty could be attributed to reasoned perception or to an immediate felt, and hence non-cognitive, perception.[71] That painting, and by extension other forms of beauty, offer an exciting but socialising pleasure is a view endorsed throughout Webb's text. However, the argument is rarely able to proceed beyond the general contention that painting produces a felt sensation: 'I should say something of the pleasure we receive from it: But as this is itself a passion, founded on the love of what is beautiful, and the delight we see in having our passion moved, it is easier to affirm its existence, than explain its nature.'[72] Resistant to analysis, save as a vague identification as 'passion' the sensations which both enliven and soften appear curiously undefined throughout Webb's text.

It is possible to explore further the connection between feeling and judgement by examining Webb's discussion of Correggio, focusing on its specifically gendered implications. Correggio's work is frequently commented upon, and often praised for its painterly beauty and grace.[73] As part of a discussion of Correggio's success in the practice of the 'clear obscure', for example, it is suggested that:

It is easy to conceive, what advantages, an uncommon genius, and elegant imagination, must draw from such resources as these; hence springs that warmth, that variety, that magic, which enchants the eye, and prepossesses the understanding . . . This seduction is no small merit in a painter; it is an union of the mechanic and the ideal; it is the power of realising his conceptions; from which, however, we should receive little pleasure, were not those conceptions in themselves pleasing.[74]

The final clause marks a retrenchment around scholarly judgement. Certainly it does not fit in with the notion of the eye being enchanted or the mind prepossessed; two points which combine to ensure that 'we do not judge of Correggio as of other painters'. The difference arises because Correggio is too pleasing 'we view his work with a predilection, which doubles his beauties and blinds us to his errors'. Such was Correggio's desire to 'gain his end, which is to please', that he was sometimes guilty of substituting 'affectation for grace'. In these terms, while Correggio has striven to please, he has neglected the true object of art, which is great beauty.[75]

The terms used by Webb to describe Correggio are similar to those offered by Reynolds in his fourth Discourse, first delivered to the Royal Academy in December 1771. Correggio, Reynolds claims, is 'foremost' amongst those who have attempted the 'composite style':

His style is founded upon modern grace and elegance, to which is super-added something of the simplicity of the grand style. A breadth of light and colour, the general ideas of the drapery, an uninterrupted flow of outline, all conspire to this effect. Next to him (perhaps equal to him) Parmegiano has dignified the genteelness of modern effeminacy, by uniting it with the simplicity of the ancients. It must be confessed, however, that these two extraordinary men, by endeavouring to give the utmost degree of grace, have exceeded its boundaries, and have fallen into the most hateful of all hateful qualities, affectation.

The twice hateful affectation, the debility of the modern, is located for Reynolds in the figure of the feminine. It is, he says, quoting Pope's *Epistle to a Lady*, 'the brink of all we hate'. Reynolds's position is quite clear: he can tolerate a measure of grace and elegance, but too much reaches 'the very verge of ridicule'. For Reynolds, the masculinity of both the painter and the critic is threatened by the dangerous and excessive softening enacted by an overly-polished art.[76]

Webb remains more ambivalent, and although, like Reynolds, he endorses the superlative excellence of ancient art's 'one great expression' – the great force of a single, beautiful idea resolutely expressed – he opposes to this the winning delicacy and refinement of the moderns.[77] However, the problem of distinguishing between the delicate refinement of modernity and a more unseemly 'modern effeminacy' remains. The need to further define taste is implied in Webb's text when it is asked:

Though what you have offered, be applied only to painting, may we not extend it into common life; and account, from hence, for the differences of our opinions, concerning the beauty of women; each man esteeming her most beautiful, who most readily excites in him those sensations, which are the ENDS OF BEAUTY?[78]

Despite the virility implied by the 'ENDS OF BEAUTY', it is difficult to see how the analogy could function if the paintings to which the text refers are imagined to be history paintings, or indeed any genre containing a narrative structure. The appreciation of women, as *Crito* has indicated and Burke agreed, is a private matter; an issue of *personal* rather than *civic* ideas. One cannot grasp the meaning of the *Judgement of Hercules* as if one were appreciating women at Vauxhall gardens, or the viewer would have failed to grasp the public and general terms which the image was designed to convey. The argument can only make sense about images from the lower genres of the art, the kind of paintings Webb would rather his readers ignored. It is for this reason that Shaftesbury, though he makes the appreciation of beautiful women *like* pleasure in more elevated kinds of beauty, is repeatedly strict in his insistence that, in order to be manly, it is necessary to move on from these idle gallantries.[79]

In many respects an unfinished debate about the relative merits of ancient and modern art proves to be the issue underlying Webb's theoretical agenda. Critically, Webb's attitude is somewhat bifurcated, while he certainly holds forth on the virtue of classical art, the claims of modern painting to be considered worthy are not represented as wholly unreasonable. Indeed, there is much to be said in defence of the modern taste; when ancient and modern art are compared it is noted that 'the former drew the passions to a point, collecting the powers of painting to one single and favourable expression; whilst the genius of Raphael, more placid and diffused, illumines and is reflected by numberless objects'.[80] The difference proposed between ancient and modern composition is informed by this paradigmatic attention to the nature of the feeling produced by works of art. The ancients, it is argued, brought their compositions to one singular point of great beauty or moral truthfulness. Accordingly, their achievement was unique, one which was elevated above the natural order. Modern painters, and Raphael is the main example, have produced more diverse and, hence, more pleasing images. For although modern painting is weakened by the lack of the sublime sources and models, which benefited ancient art, it can gain by adopting the delicacy and manner of the mixed composition.[81] Both Milton and Raphael are discussed to support this claim; more substantively, the notion of a 'more placid and diffused' image coincides with contemporary representations of eighteenth-century culture. And, to a degree, this seems to be Webb's point; however, he does not want wholly to abandon the idea that modern placidity can incorporate the over-refinement found in Correggio. The ambiguity of this position is reflected in the singular way in which Webb seeks to counter the suggestion that modern art works by a process of accumulation:

This progress is just inverted in painting; the whole production is at once more on us; our attention is immediately fixed on the most interesting expression; when we have studied and felt the powers of this, we then, and not till then, descend to the examination of inferior movements.[82]

In these terms, the contemplation of great art remains a mode of lofty contemplation. All would appear to be stable at this point, as effeminacy and any undue effect on the passions are excluded. However, Webb continues his refutation with what is a telling, if unfortunate, analogy:

Thus when we enter into the assembly of women, should there be one amongst them of distinguished beauty, the eye dwells with constancy on her; and having taken in all her advantages, passes to a careless observation of the rest. It is evident, in both these cases, that the superior acts with intrinsic, and not relative force.[83]

Like beautiful women, great paintings possess a unique force by which the viewer is automatically 'seized' by the 'impression of the instant'.[84] Once again, the comparison is not distinguished by being overly high-minded; though it is a pertinent reminder of the degree to which theories of art have consistently expropriated images of women for their key tropes.[85] Equally important is the fact that while Webb is suggesting that, as with Crito's definition of beauty, true taste relies on male susceptibility to the femininity of the object in question, he also indicates that it is necessary to guard against the excesses of these 'softer passions' (often dangerously close to effeminacy) by reasserting maleness as a form of acquisitive desire. Webb is, therefore, producing an account of painting which, although it relies upon the assumption that painting produces a beneficial polishing and refining of the male connoisseur, also reasserts the active aspect of masculine responsiveness.

Conceived in terms of a complex formation of desire, Webb's account of painting increasingly relies on the responsiveness of innate feeling as the key to appreciation, while judgement is downplayed as a sophisticated knowledge of the process by which that sensation is received. Webb's position might be contrasted with that

of George Turnbull who, in his *Treatise on Ancient Painting*, differenti-
ates between the 'Learned and the Vulgar', on the basis that: 'the
latter are not able to apply Rules and Maxims, but judge merely
from what they feel; whereas the former can reason about their
feelings from the Principles of Science and Art'.[86] Although Turnbull
conceded that 'the Unlearned are seldom wrong in their judgement
about what is good or bad in any of the Arts', he was far from
imagining that the 'Vulgar' were really capable of judging right with
any consistency. Turnbull's argument turned on the assumption that
feeling was either a preliminary stage, that which the man of taste
went beyond, or something that was merely sexual or hopelessly
uncultured. In making this claim Turnbull was in agreement with a
large part of the civic tradition which regarded feeling or passion as
little more than instinctual response, one which was likely moreover
to degenerate rapidly into vice. Webb, like Cooper and Spence,
however, regarded feeling as the foundation of taste. He did so
because he was able to argue that as an instantaneous, almost
instinctual, response, feeling was free from the taints of custom and
prejudice and the insipidity of luxury.

Webb's reappraisal of the modes and motivations of judgement
represents a departure from earlier critical models. Within civic-
humanist criticism the physical form of beauty was thought to
disrupt the pristine disavowals upon which civic tradition rested its
account of masculinity. This was not, however, the issue for Webb;
and while the situation is clearly one which demands policing to
censure the immoral and to license the pleasurable there is little
sense of a form of masculinity which requires men to forgo the social
(and sexual) pleasures of the fair sex. The crucial point, I think, is
that, despite the advocacy of ancient art and the chastity of taste,
Webb is endeavouring to describe, not general, but particular
relations. Unlike Shaftesbury's attempt to formulate an account of
taste which rose above individual interest (a conception which
Shaftesbury called the 'universal good'), Webb's argument in *The
Beauties of Painting* is an attempt to define taste on the basis of
precisely those specific interests – politeness, modern refinement, the
'ENDS OF BEAUTY' – rejected in the *Characteristics*. Indeed, particular
desire safeguards the general condition of refined taste from the
charge of effeminacy. This taste is secured by employing a notion of
male desire as a guarantee of the clarity and untainted nature of a
socialised taste. It was such sexual focus that Burke had in mind

when he argued that men were 'attached to particulars' in questions of taste; again, women were the objects under analysis.[87] Indeed Webb's argument in *Beauties of Painting* serves to give further indication of the highly gendered way in which eighteenth-century theorists undertook the analysis of taste and the arts.

'THE SHAPE OF LEARNING': THE JUDGEMENT OF WOMEN AND
THE DEFINITION OF TASTE

James Usher's *Clio; or a Discourse on Taste* similarly takes femininity and its relationship to feeling to be the key to understanding beauty. However, while the dialogues written by Spence and Webb were located in closed male social gatherings, Usher's text is somewhat different, and takes the form of an address to a woman. Its intended audience was not to be found in the male space of the pavilion, but in the mixed society of the drawing room:

MADAM, When I had the pleasure of drinking tea with you a few days ago, and occasionally read to you Rollin's General Reflections upon what is called Good Taste, some observations you made brought on a lively and pleasing conversation, in which you opened so many new prospects to me upon our subject, that I had thoughts of reducing my ideas to writing while they continued fresh in my memory, and you were pleased to approve my design.[88]

Usher immediately acknowledges that it is the familiar and elegant conversation of the lady that has rendered his enterprise possible. The text which follows is the product of conversation, just as the texts by Spence sought to dramatise or reproduce that style. It is possible to see, in all of these texts, the translation of critical debate from learned treatise to sociable conversation, a move which represents the accommodation of philosophic discussion into the pleasantries of English life. There is an important difference, however, between this form of representation and that found in Shaftesbury's more elevated dialogues. The textual shifts evident in texts by Spence and Usher represent a process of familiarisation in which the terms of an aesthetic inquiry are transposed into the discourse of domestic manners. This had, of course, been signalled earlier in the century, when Addison expressed the hope that he had 'brought Philosophy out of Closets and Libraries' to reside at 'Tea-Tables, and in Coffee-Houses'; and it is possible to see the works under discussion here as participating in a similar project.[89]

More particularly, Usher's text uses the idea that it is addressed to a polite young woman in order to provide an image with which the text's actual readership can seek to identify, or desire to be. It is in these insinuating terms that *Clio* proposes an account of femininity as central to any analysis of taste and morals. The text's full title gives a strong indication of its final orientation: for in *Clio; Or, a Dialogue on Taste addressed to a Young Lady*, the general addressee is merged with the more specific identity, that of a *'Young Lady'*, to produce an account of beauty which appropriates the sign of *Clio* (the muse of epic poetry) as an organising metaphor for the relation between polite society and refined taste. She is a woman, moreover, who, along with Sir Harry Beaumont, is the 'bright original' who inspired and instructed the writer.[90] Recollecting a point in their discourse where they debated the proposition that the 'graceful and the becoming are never found separated from nature and propriety', Usher reminds his lady that:

you made an objection, that obliged me in order to answer it, to make some reflections, which lead me to approach nearer the origin of elegance than I expected. Your objection madam, was this: 'if elegance be inseparable from propriety and nature, why are not the common people, who are without education, just as nature made them, the most graceful? and why does elegance reside only amongst those who are formed by art?' I could not pass over this ingenious question without an answer, and it led me to the following observations.[91]

Usher responds to his fair interlocutor by claiming that, because 'labour requires harsh, forced, and violent motions', it produces an 'ungenerosity of disposition', in effect a subject incapable of tasteful speculation.[92] Moreover, the lady's ingenuity, her engaging sallies, have pricked the pedantic aesthete into action, as he confesses earlier in the text, remembering that 'you stopped me with a very subtile and confounding objection, which became stronger by your sprightly manner of supporting it'.[93]

It is in this manner that the form and the function of the addressee's bright originality is made central to the development of the text, providing 'that picture from which I borrowed my ideas of elegance'.[94] The lady, however, is more than the docile recipient of the narrator's advice and pedagogic flirtatiousness. She is, in fact, his inspiration, a figure who supplies the place of his muse. Usher wants to suggest that it is to the lady that he owes his realisation of the possibility of a 'transition' from the 'beauties of writing to the elegance and propriety displayed in polished life'. This is a realisation entirely owing to her 'simple original principals of taste'.[95] The moment, however, is not without an insistent level of condescension: 'I have dwelt on personal elegance, because the ideas and principals in this part of good taste are more familiar to you'.[96] Usher has focused on the subject of personal elegance – the morality of polite behaviour and social grace – because this is what he feels women understand best. Discussion of these topics is held to be the best way to introduce the more complicated areas of thought to ladies. By 'fair sexing' it in this way, deferring always to the authority of women, Usher's text might be seen as productive of a domesticated landscape familiar to readers of The *Tatler* and The *Spectator* earlier in the century. But it is the 'Lady' as motivator, and metaphor, of moments of cultural transmission that is most striking in Usher's text. It is women, or more broadly conceived notions of femininity, which in Spence and Usher provide the means of moving between discourses which describe society, polite culture and the conventions of taste. They do so by encoding the address and form of the debate within the particular setting of private domesticity and social familiarity, thereby uniting a diverse discursive network rapidly around a central topos of feminine, personal beauty. The elegance and natural refinement of Usher's young lady represent the unity of both genteel social living and complaisant good taste. It is a movement between public and private which, as in Spence and Webb, undertaken with reference to the presence of a woman who is conceived of in terms of the production of a range of socialised pleasures. This is a gratification which is established within distinctly masculine codes of taste and 'pleasingness'.

The manipulation of the audience's response is an important rhetorical move within the ideological structure of these texts, and is comparable to the strategies employed by the periodicals published in the same period. In her analysis of early eighteenth-century periodical literature Kathryn Shevelow has written of the 'programmatic representation of reader complicity' and of an 'appearance of dialogue' in the style and form of journals such as the *Athenian Mercury* and the *Spectator*.[97] These devices, which Shevelow sees as operating within a 'dialectic' between society and genre, manipulate and position the reader and his or her desires. The audience's composition, and, in particular, its idea of itself, becomes a *textual* product, and one which is created by the journals themselves, so that the composition of their readership 'cannot be understood by statistical or descriptive investigation alone'. Shevelow argues that the 'community of the text, a construction of writing, was a figure imposed by the periodical distinct from, though engaged in inter-action with, the forms of social organisation actually lived by its audience'. To read periodical literature becomes, on this account, a realisation not only that it is possible to participate in such discourse, but that it is necessary for a polite subject to be able to do so. By offering the reader the possibility of intervention, the text becomes part of the 'vicarious leisure' offered by polite literature, the audience for which would have included a high proportion of women. The presence of women, or at least representations of women, in so many accounts of taste and in particular those addressed to a middle-class audience is therefore far from being merely contingent or coincidental. Crucially, it enables these texts to occupy a dual role, whereby they at once define taste – exploiting the bodies and sensibilites of women to do so – and yet also seek to provide models against which their readers can measures themselves or their acquaintances.[98]

The dual position of women, as the judging and the judged, can be found throughout Usher's text. In common with *Crito*, the argument of *Clio* is conducted at one remove from the general or philosophic discussions of taste found in the work of, for example, Hutcheson or Kames. The focus of Usher's argument is close to that of Spence, concentrating upon what Usher terms 'personal ele-gance', in particular, the elegance of domesticated beauties. However, Usher's account remains more broadly conceived than those advanced in *Crito*, and does provide a general discussion of taste. Throughout, taste is defined conventionally enough as 'a clear sense of the noble, the beautiful, and the affecting, through nature and art. It distinguishes and selects, with unerring Judgement, what is fine and graceful from the mean and disgusting.' Moreover, taste is separated from the whims of 'mode' and its existence is 'testified [to] by the voice of nature', which Usher vouchsafes by citing the real and intrinsic value of objects.[99] Despite these assurances, numerous problems recur throughout the text. Although Usher is able to propose universal beauty as a quality inherent in particular forms, he is less able to say which objects should be so lauded. It is on precisely this point that Usher comes unstuck. He continues:

The general opinion is, that this most conspicuous part of beauty, that is perceived and acknowledged by everybody, is yet utterly inexplicable, and retires from our search when we would discover what it is. Where shall I find the secret retreat of the graces, to explain to me the elegance they dictate, and to paint in visible colours the fugitive and varying enchantment that hovers round a graceful person, yet leaves us for ever in agreeable suspense and confusion? I need not seek for them, madam; the graces are but the emblems of the human mind, in its loveliest appearances; and while I write for you it is impossible not to feel their influence.[100]

The language of 'suspense and confusion' indicates the presence of something like sexual desire, with all the problems for a conception of masculinity which it possessed in the work of Shaftesbury and Burke. Beauty is constructed as the hidden *je ne sais quoi* of an ambiguously philosophical discourse, as such it is regarded as inexplicable, retiring and fugitive in ways which render it forever indefinable. This account of the beautiful is a much more coy rendition of pleasure and its indefinability than even Addison's secret pleasures. Such a moment is furthermore, bound up in the flirtatious tone of the passage, which is personal and conversational, a passage apparently at ease with itself and its intended readers, which creates a situation which allows the object of analysis and the 'Lady'-reader to become one and the same. Beauty, transposed through the Graces, becomes the addressee of the discourse.

Despite these refinements, however, beauty remains essentially indefinable in objective empirical terms. Beauty, as Usher points out, is a 'waving flame', ever insubstantial and in retreat. Perhaps because of this indeterminacy, the concept retains an allure as an object of desire:

The curious eye with eagerness pursues the wandering beauty, which it sees with surprize at every turn, but is never able to overtake. It is a waving flame, that like the reflection of the sun from water never settles; it glances on you in every motion and disposition of the body; its different powers through attitude and motion seem to be collected in dancing, where it plays on the arms, the legs, the breast, the cheek, and in short the whole frame.[101]

There is some confusion here, largely centred on the apparently mobile 'it' of the passage. Precisely what the pronoun of the passage refers to is unclear; beauty begins as an abstract principle, but appears to move through an objectified corporeality, perhaps even becoming a subject in its own right. The vague nature of Usher's

prose leaves it uncertain as to whether 'glances' denotes the eye of
the spectator or the object which is being described. The ambivalence is such that beauty fails to become a properly realised object. A
similar point is made when Usher asserts that musical beauty is so
'shadowy' that, while it may be 'sufficiently perceivable to fire the
imagination', it is not 'clear enough to become an object of
knowledge'.[102]

The problems associated with the unreachableness of beauty and
its efficient causes are overcome by turning women into the objects
of analysis and debate. In the first instance, Usher achieves this by
changing his focus away from beauty and towards what he terms
'Personal Elegance'. Usher writes that personal elegance is a combination of a 'lofty consciousness of worth or virtue' and 'Good-
nature approaching to affection, of gentle affability, and, in general
of the pleasing passions'.[103] By uniting these qualities, elegance
appears, according to Usher, 'like a reserved and virgin kindness'.
Throughout, the elegant is returned to the domain of the pleasing
and the amiable:

In short, complaisance gives an agreeableness to the whole person, and
creates a beauty, that nature gave not to the features; it submits, it
promises, it applauds in the countenance; the heart lays itself in smiles at
your feet, and a voice which is indulgent and tender, is always heard with
pleasure.[104]

In these terms, personal elegance is a question of submission and
acquiescence; at once docile and yet beguiling, elegance pleases in a
way which is thoroughly feminised. Usher's 'power of pleasing',
moreover, is wholly domesticated; this is a vision of daughterly or
wifely obedience, in which the sexually ambiguous language of
'suspense and confusion' is subsumed to a moment of passive
obedience.

However, as Usher's account progresses he begins to talk of the
'secret joy' and 'suggestive lustre' of elegance, the appearance of
which is associated with a 'pleasing delusion'. While it would appear
that personal elegance has a certain seductive quality, Usher is
insistent that the image entails, not desire, but the reformist empire
of true beauty:

Elegance assumes to itself an empire equal to that of the soul; it rules and
inspires every part of the body, and makes use of all the human powers; but
it particularly takes the passions under its charge and direction, and turns
them into a kind of Artillery, with which it does infinite execution.[105]

As this extract makes clear, personal elegance inhabits the bodies of the virtuous, making them still more lovely by making them pure and chaste. It is an image of active refinement; once it has taken hold, the whole body is reorganised under elegance's spreading empire. In common with the *Adventurer*'s 'eastern metaphor' of the fortified city, 'personal Elegance' is a figure of propriety designed to improve its readers. It is striking, in this context, that a discussion of taste has begun to inhabit the vocabulary which is conventionally associated with conduct literature. Certainly, the rhetoric of empires and fortifications is reminiscent of numerous injunctions addressed to young women during the eighteenth century.[106]

In line with these strictures, Usher's notion of beauty, while it renders the elegant subject attractive, chastens and rebukes unwanted attentions with an artillery of virtuous passions. Given this profoundly regulatory position, it is no surprise that elegance is made to represent a perfect and internalised taste. Usher writes that 'Good taste, like the moving beam, paints in their different colours all the objects of our view, and informs us of what is beautiful and engaging. It is the inward light of universal beauty.'[107] Such a definition is less straightforward than it might first appear: the phrase 'inward light' has two possible interpretations. The phrase could entail a stream of worth entering the soul at the sight of a beautiful object; alternatively, it could be a description of rays given off by the woman of taste, who is herself a manifestation of 'universal beauty'. This image, Usher tells his readers, may be defined as the 'reflection of the grandeur and beauty of the invisible soul. Grandeur and beauty in the soul itself, are not objects of sense; colours cannot paint them, but they diffuse inexpressible loveliness over the person.'[108]

In common with Spence's discussion of 'Real Personal Beauty', Usher's definition of personal elegance seems to fulfil two functions; first, it helps to define an otherwise baffling idea of beauty; and, secondly, it installs a reformist discourse on female manners. On this reading, beauty, taste and elegance coalesce within an image of the refined femininity. It is a move which short-circuits much of Usher's original dilemma. The relationship between taste and the subject – and of these ideas to beauty or elegance – is therefore decisive. Importantly, elegance is not beauty but 'the effect of a delicate and awakened taste'.[109] Conventionally, it might be assumed that the beautiful was the object apprehended by the tasteful gaze; in this sense, beauty is exterior to the viewing subject, and objectified by his or her gaze. To an extent, Usher seems to depart from this practice, effectively circumventing the indefinable nature of beauty by placing it not outside but within the subject. This, however, is achieved at the expense of making his text into a conduct book in which taste is closely allied to etiquette. As I have already argued, this realignment is centred upon women and their capacity for judging and for facilitating judgement. In this context, the manipulation of terms effected by Usher's text – in particular the confusion of the relationship between subject and object – has a broader and more complex referent than mere philosophic waywardness. Usher's argument appears to indicate that, unlike the expansive discursive formations Peter de Bolla has detected at work within the discussion of the sublime, the beautiful more often leads to the production of smaller, more localised concepts.[110] The process would seem to be in line with that described by Paul de Man when he writes that 'if the condition of the existence of an entity is itself pragmatically critical, then the theory of this entity is bound to fall back into the pragmatic'.[111] The practice in this instance is the control of feminine propriety and display within polite society.

It will be necessary, in a moment, to elaborate the degree to which Usher's text, like Spence's, overlaps with conduct literature. However, it is first worth examining Usher's treatment of female taste in more detail, as it is particularly to women's achievements and values that he directs his inquiry. The superlative excellence of women is further attested to when Usher announces that:

When you except a few men of distinguished talents, ladies both write and speak better than scholars. If you ask me the reason for this, I must inform you, that the easy and natural excursions of the imagination are seldom checked in ladies.[112]

This refinement, Usher believes, is owing to the 'nauseous draft of learning' which is foisted on young men during their education. The 'unaffected grace' and 'easy spirit of . . . words' which forms the style of women's letter-writing, therefore, excels over the schooled drudgery of male discourse. Thus, while taste is universal, it is, further Usher confesses, 'communicated to different persons with such different degrees of light and clearness' that some remain laboriously ignorant, while others see beauty with an easy and instant 'warmth'.[113] There are, then, different degrees and classes of taste, a fact which, for Usher, devolves a particular responsibility to those who are tasteful. It requires them to preserve and extend the influence of good taste throughout society, and this would seem to be the role of women in Usher's view of polite culture. However, this position is far from being emancipatory. Usher believes that learning 'fits' as awkwardly on a woman as would 'her grandfather's large spectacles'. This image of bodily incongruity provides Usher with a means of restricting women's involvement in the very sphere in which they are the supposed exemplars, and thus he writes of a woman's education:

She should have an acquaintance with the fine arts, because they enrich and beautify the imagination; but she should carefully keep them out of view in the shape of learning, and let them run through the easy happy vein of unpremeditated thought: for this reason she should never use nor even understand the terms of art: the gentleman will occasionally explain them to her.[114]

The 'shape of learning' is an ambiguous figure here. In the context of an account which moves between abstractions and an account of women's bodies, such an image has a complex referent. It refers, partly, to the body of the woman and to her capacity for judgement, a talent which, like her flesh, ought to be gracefully disguised beneath the eloquence and adornment of imagination and politeness. There is a sense, here, of having come full circle. Usher's logic runs as follows: beauty is not an object of knowledge, and is therefore, feminine in character; yet, to be truly feminine a woman must never display the ownership of any studied knowledge. Women can facilitate culture, providing the gentility necessary for its development, but they cannot, for Usher, intervene in its production without sacrificing the very quality – femininity – which has permitted their inclusion.

In the context of eighteenth-century ideas about women, there is nothing very unusual about the kinds of assumption Usher is making in his book about taste. Comparable attitudes to the intellectual capacity of women can be found, for example, in *The Polite Arts, Dedicated to the Ladies*, by Cosmetti. The prose of this piece is commonsensical enough: 'the bigness of a column implies the measure of its diameter'.[115] Simple prose is central to Cosmetti's aim; indeed, he makes clear his 'intention to avoid prolixity by descending to particulars'.[116] The choice of style conveys more than a caution against being verbose, as it marks an assumption underlying the book that anything but the most empirically obvious will be either too dull, or too complex for his readers. This accounts for Cosmetti's decision to describe the art of painting almost entirely in relation to the mimetic capacities of landscape and portraiture. History painting is scarcely mentioned. Cosmetti does not, however, restrict himself to the higher arts alone; his text is broad-ranging in this respect, and includes references to copper-plate engraving as well as to mosaic and the plastic arts.[117] There is in this emphasis more than a suggestion that the audience to whom the book is directed is composed of those who seek to furnish their home politely (there is advice on how to hang pictures, for example), and to be easy in conversation.[118] It is an estimation of female education entirely in line with the restriction proposed by Usher in the course of *Clio*, a point underlined by the largely feminised vocabulary of the text, which uses words such as 'charming', 'affection' and 'lovely' to describe the arts under discussion.

Cosmetti's readers, unlike Webb's more cultured audience, were almost wholly concerned with the domesticated space of genteel consumption, a sphere in which women are required to arrange fashionable commodities rather than to appraise history painting. Significantly, Cosmetti's account is consistent with the modes of middle-class sensibility evident throughout *Crito* and *Clio*. All three texts place the discussion of taste within a domestic setting which they take to be appropriately feminine. Given the extent of the interchange between different kinds of text on taste in the eighteenth century, it is important to be clear about the cultural implications of the 'beauties' which have been discussed in this chapter. Certainly, Spence and Usher use the word frequently and offer the usual repertoire of terms and phrases necessary for discussions of taste and pleasure. But, while they describe the effects of the beautiful, the qualities which they ascribe to it (modesty, pleasingness, grace), and the place where they locate it in the physical world (the bodies of women), suggest a different agenda.

BEAUTY AND THE SPECTACLE OF CONDUCT

Investments of the kind which have been attributed to Spence and Usher were not uncommon in the eighteenth century. The remainder of the argument of this book will be taken up with exploring the impact of the notion that the beauties of women could express moral as well as physical qualities. At this juncture, it is merely necessary to note that there is a considerable interplay between the account of women provided in treatises on taste and the strictures of conduct books; and, indeed, between accounts of beauty and the presentation of virtuous femininity in the literature of the period more generally. Pope's opinions, as expressed in the *Epistle to a Lady*, have already been noted, but the more germane comparisons are with texts by Richardson and Fielding and with the plethora of improving literature aimed at the young men and women of the middle classes. Texts such as *Pamela* and *Amelia*, along with works by John Brown and James Fordyce, promote accounts of feminine virtue and female beauty which focus upon the question of a woman's social and sexual desirability.[119] The titles of many conduct books reveal this investment clearly: *The Economy of Beauty*, for example, anatomises the role of women and their expected conduct;[120] while Marriot's *Female Conduct: Being an Essay on the Art of Pleasing*, published in 1759 is a lengthy poem in a similar vein.[121] Both of these texts, along with their numerous contemporaries, sought to provide an image of beautiful conduct to which their readers might reasonably aspire.

Working within this changed situation, writers on taste in the mid-century connected the definition of beauty to an account of female manners or feminine morality. Such a change of intention and address reveals the shifting gender politics which underlie the polite discourse on taste during the eighteenth century. Those who were, in Usher's phrase, 'formed by Art', achieve perfection by participating in polite and sociable interaction and by signalling their complaisant good nature.[122] Rather than a grand ideal of beauty suited to the expression of public virtue, what is offered by theorists such as Usher is a discourse on taste ideally suited to the assemblies, publications (novels and journals) and the pleasure grounds of classes as yet without political power, but of considerable cultural influence: the lower gentry and the commercial classes of the middling sort.

The definiton of beauty which interests Spence and Usher is, therefore, fundamentally different from that calling forth the grand public gesture in either Akenside's *Pleasures of the Imagination* or Shaftesbury's *Characteristics*. It is a form of beauty which is concerned with the social conduct of the individual – viewed as a private citizen lacking in public capacities and expectations – rather than the public body as a whole. What Spence and Usher have advanced is an account of beauty wherein that category is conspicuously an appeal, not for the regulation of the public, but for a reformation of female manners. What seems to be happening in these texts is that the femininity of beauty, the founding category of polite taste, provided not only the most plausible and accessible vocabulary theorists had to offer, but also provided the major social problem which criticism sought to address. To base an account on the perceived relationship between femininity and beauty meant that it was necessary to suggest that women were capable of virtue. This assumption was required because once taste had endorsed so much of the sensual (as it did for Burke and Hogarth) it would appear lascivious if it were not also possible to say something in defence of the object so viewed. Without such a commitment, programmes of the kind found in *Crito* and *Clio* would become essays in irrational gratification. The explicit formulation of this problem, as in the sermons of Fordyce and Brown, indicates the degree to which the category of taste reformulated in the mid-century could become at once adapted to the purposes of commercial society and capable of effecting its reform.

This discourse, characteristic of the 1750s and 1760s, represents an articulation of both gender and class roles which is productive of a new form of sociability, which, though it originates in the plenitudes of polite conversation, takes as its primary symbol the spectacle of a virtuous woman. In order for this discourse to function women have to be considered carefully and their conduct viewed insistently. The *Spectator* and the *Tatler* had suggested a similar strategy already and, in many respects, the philosophical conversations envisaged within the texts I have been describing are closer in nature to the discourses which articulated literary criticism than to the visibly political discourses of civic humanism.[123] In this context femininity represents not a threat to polite discourse, rather, a quality to be moulded and remade. It is attitudes such as this which structure and yet make ambiguous this passage from The *Connoisseur*:

Some persons are (according to the strict import of the phrase itself) born Good Natured. These fortunate people are easy in themselves, and agreeable to all about them. They are, as it were, constitutionally pleasing; and can no more fail of being affable and engaging in conversation than an *Hamilton* or a *Coventry* can be beautiful or charming.[124]

Being 'Good Natured' was, along with charity and politeness, one of the qualities middle-class theorists sought to elevate to the status of morality. Addison, for example, comments that 'Good-Nature is more agreeable in Conversation than Wit, gives a certain Air to the Countenance which is more amiable than Beauty.'[125] Accordingly, the positive valuation put on being 'affable and charming' is plain enough, and represents an ability to live justly and in concord with those with whom one lives or does business. However, what this entails for the quality of being 'beautiful and charming' is less clear. It threatens to become both in Addison's text and the *Connoisseur*, not the representation of virtue, but its antithesis: folly, luxury, effeminacy. That the terms remain unstable will be brought into close focus in the next chapter, which, by examining the fortune and the presentation of Elizabeth Gunning, the Duchess of Hamilton, one of the *Connoisseur*'s chosen beauties, will reveal the ambiguities of that existence. Her presence – like that of other beautiful, often aristocratic women – will trouble the complacent plenitudes issued by Spence, Usher and Webb. For the representation of Elizabeth and Maria Gunning raises the issue, not only of beauty, but also beauty's relation to what was regarded as vicious or effeminate.

CHAPTER THREE

'Such Strange Unwonted Softness': Joshua Reynolds and the painting of beauty

Between January 1758 and the June of the following year, Elizabeth Gunning, the recently widowed Duchess of Hamilton and a former society beauty, sat to Joshua Reynolds. The commission would have been an important one for Reynolds, given the fame and status of the sitter, and this may account for some of the panache which accompanied its execution. The portrait, which resulted from a series of protracted sittings, was exhibited, along with three other works, at the Society for the Encouragement of the Arts, Manufactures and Commerce in April 1760.[1] In a culture in which the evaluation of art was undertaken within a discourse that made explicit its appeal to the senses as a guarantee of taste, Reynolds's striking and rather elegant depiction of a beautiful woman would have made for an interesting spectacle. The painting's exhibition is made all the more intriguing because of the close relation in eighteenth-century thought between the discourses describing taste and those which defined the modes of acceptable social behaviour. In these terms, the prominent display of the painting will provide another instance of the ways in which an account of beauty could be mobilised within a discourse which connected the appreciation of art with the judgement of women. In this chapter I want to explore how a consideration of this portrait would, in the 1760s, have had a set of complex social referents, as well as making an impact on contemporary appreciation of the nature and status of British art.

It is significant in this context that Reynolds's portrait of Elizabeth Gunning has consistently been awarded a high place in the appreciation of Reynolds's art, and of British portraiture in general. This is, in no small part, due to the period of the painting's production, which comes a few years after Reynolds's equally powerful *Commodore Augustus Keppel* of 1753, and coincides almost perfectly with the publication, in the *Idler*, of Reynolds's first forays in the theory of Art.

Figure 3 Sir Joshua Reynolds, *Elizabeth Gunning, Duchess of Hamilton and Argyll*, 1760

This timing has made the painting available to those who wish to propose, not only a linearity in the development of Reynolds's canon, but also a match between his theory and his practice which excludes the possibility of interpretation in a wider context. It is in this vein that Desmond Shawe-Taylor has claimed that, 'more than any of his previous works, this [painting] puts into practice Reynolds's theoretical system of aesthetics'.[2] Shawe-Taylor's account brings together an impressive array of eighteenth-century theoreticians, most notably Edmund Burke, Daniel Webb and Jonathan Richardson, in order to represent the *Duchess of Hamilton and Argyll* as the fruition of Beauty within the Grand Style. For Shawe-Taylor it is not the sitter's beauty which signifies, but the beauties of a fully realised aesthetic. His account, which sees the *Duchess of Hamilton and Argyll* as a 'demonstration piece', places the painting in the frame provided both by Reynolds's public career and by his published pronouncements on art, and in particular his *Discourses*.

Certainly the portrait was a public one, and demands an appreciation of the nature of publicity (and of public meanings) if it is to be considered more broadly. As David Mannings has observed, the *Duchess of Hamilton and Argyll* is 'one of Reynolds's earliest experiments with the full-blown exhibition picture'.[3] Mannings underlines this exceptional status when he comments that 'Reynolds would have been keen to paint this sensation of London Society because he knew it would attract attention at the exhibition.' An exhibition portrait is, by its very nature, an image which is presented for a level of judgement and appreciation beyond the private demands and expectations of its patron. Furthermore, the economy of consumption in which it participates is general and public. The nature of 'publicity' in this context is a difficult issue given the number of definitions to which the word 'public' was subject within eighteenth-century discourse: to be 'public' could have meant something different for Reynolds, his sitter, her image and indeed for the 'public' itself. There is a need therefore to look at the forms of discourse and reception which could be mobilised around this kind of portrait in the eighteenth century. In the two previous chapters the notion of the 'public' to which Francis Hutcheson, Webb and Usher referred was that of an aggregate of fashionable consumers enjoying polite contact and prudent consumption. As my discussion has illustrated, the status of this idea of the public, while gaining credence in the mid-century, did not go unchallenged. I have described how it was opposed by the contributors to the periodical press, by John Gilbert Cooper, and by those writers who attacked what they saw as the enervating luxury of modern society – all of whom used civic-humanist terminology to some extent, and shared that discourse's sense that the public should be a site of political virtue. In any discussion of Reynolds's relation to publicity, the problem of deciding which definition of the public is appropriate is particularly acute. Reynolds occupies a potentially uncomfortable position between the notion of the public conceived by the discourse of civic humanism and that produced by the day-to-day perform-ance of life in commercial Britain: he is at once the greatest champion of republican views on art in the late-century, yet remained a professional artist keen to press home his commercial advantage.[4]

The conflicting contexts suggested for the painting by the work of Shawe-Taylor and by Mannings capture this hesitation well. When Shawe-Taylor writes of the painting being a 'demonstration piece' and a 'treatise on female beauty' he is seeking to establish the painting in a close relation to Reynolds's *Discourses*, a series of lectures that were avowedly civic in their conception of what it is to be public. Shawe-Taylor quotes from the fifth Discourse of 1772, to illustrate his contention that what is being demonstrated by Rey-nolds is art in the Grand Style.[5] Mannings conversely does not have this in mind when he describes the portrait as an 'exhibition picture' executed with the intention of drawing a big crowd. Crowds do not – as Reynolds and other artists were fearfully aware – necessarily form themselves into a public; they can become mobs. The organi-sers of the Society exhibitions of the early 1760s were wary of the crowds that were drawn to their galleries, and used entrance charges and compulsory purchases to regulate their audience. Although the Society for the Encouragement of Arts, Manufactures and Com-merce initially resisted an entrance fee, one was soon introduced to restrict the entrance of undesirable lower-class visitors to the exhi-bition. Reynolds's work would seem therefore to be explicable in terms of two competing accounts of the public, the civic and the commercial, both of which attempt to find expression in the 'public exhibition'.

Once we have begun to consider this central problem of eighteenth-century discourse, to which the *Duchess of Hamilton and Argyll* both contributes and is subject, then the kind of analysis which

Shawe-Taylor offers begins to look a little foreclosed. For there is something constrictive about the form of such an inquiry despite the range of its references. It glides over very real difficulties in the relationship between the theory and practice of portraiture in the eighteenth century, and all too easily invokes Reynolds to explain or justify his own artistic production.[6] The use, common amongst art historians, of the *Discourses* to offer a commentary on Reynolds's own work requires some revision. For when he is speaking as the President of the Royal Academy, Reynolds is talking mainly, if not exclusively, about the theory of history painting. While he does offer some suggestive remarks about the practices suitable for a portrait painter, these are outside his main concern, which remains with the higher branches of the art.[7] John Barrell has argued that the primary context for, or motivation behind, Reynolds's thinking in these lectures, was the desire to cultivate a properly civic and republican theory of art; a theory which was self-consciously political and unashamedly masculine.[8] The space which might be available within this framework for either the discussion or the production of images of beautiful or fashionable women is, therefore, restricted, and remote from, if not antithetical to, the main thrust of Reynolds's design.[9]

Given the civic-humanist polemic underlying Reynolds's Academy lectures, his portraits – and particularly his portraits of women – would appear to be removed from Reynolds's more intellectual ambitions. The problem was no less apparent in the eighteenth century, as, although civic humanism could, conceivably, provide a rationale for the portrayal of men, for whom representations of heroism and public office provided a justification for self-display, women lacked access to such elevated forms.[10] Habit and prejudice often demanded that representations of women were confined to the conversation piece and the marriage portrait. More importantly, the action of looking at women could not be reconciled with the civic demand that public art should prompt worthy action; indeed, it might all too easily encourage desire. The problem of the sitter's desirability is indicative of tension which may have surrounded Reynolds's portrait when it was exhibited in the eighteenth century. For a professional artist, such as Reynolds, this problem would have manifested itself most obviously as a concern with the representation appropriate to the famously beautiful sitter. If her portrait lacked beauty the result would be insipid and uninteresting, yet, too much beauty would raise the dangerous promptings of desire. A delicate balance had then to be struck, one which allowed the display of a pleasing physical form without encouraging an improper response. These concerns which would have been very real to Reynolds and his audience make a consideration of Elizabeth Gunning's beauty central to the appraisal of the portrait, particularly in terms of the affect it might be expected to have on the viewer.[11]

Despite the complex nature of eighteenth-century discourse on female beauty, the significance of Elizabeth Gunning's legendary beauty has been down played by generations of critics. Although Elizabeth Gunning's reputation as a 'Beauty', and the stories which surround her celebrity are always referred to, art historians have often merely noted Reynolds's success in the realisation of the image or have commented solely on his shrewdness in choosing to display such an ambitious painting.[12] What is suggested in these accounts is a rather smart piece of marketing or self-promotion by Reynolds, as though he has used the Duchess's fame astutely, and she, once used, disappears behind the public façade of Reynolds's business practice. Within such an approach, her presence has no function other than that which is given to it by Reynolds. This disregard is by no means uncommon; Shawe-Taylor is after all only talking about the 'theo-retical' nature of beauty, and not its actual manifestation in the body of a woman. The beauty of the sitter becomes, in this way, merely an addendum in the historicist account surrounding the painting – similar to the way a portrait of Burke may be described in terms which make a passing reference to his literary career. This supposi-tion will not, however, hold; beauty, in this case at least, is a vastly different entity from authorship. The beautiful is both a baffling and rhetorically complex concept, and a part of a decisive matrix of values and judgements at the heart of polite discourse.

In these terms, to be beautiful is not only to possess an engaging physical presence, with all the complexities of recognition and evaluation that fact implies, but to be positioned in relation to a series of moral injunctions, which on the one hand raise and endorse women's public presence, while on the other they damn the beautiful woman as the source of enervating effeminacy. Beauty cannot be referred to casually by either Reynolds or those who examine his work. David Mannings both reveals and denies this when he refers to Reynolds's enthusiasm for painting the portrait in the first instance. For the painting to have been the crowd-puller it

was expected to be (and accounts suggest that it was), the audience
for it must have been able to recognise the person portrayed.
Although the painting's exhibition title, *A Lady, Whole Length*, would
have given no clues in this respect, the reviewer for the *Imperial
Magazine* was able to assert, 'A Lady, Whole Length, said to be the
Dutchess [*sic*] of Hamilton, but rather the Queen of all Grace and
Beauty'.[13] It is unlikely that the exhibition audience would have
seen the woman presented solely in terms of her being, in reality,
the Duchess of Hamilton. Instead, the viewer may well have been
expected to have had a sufficiently good grasp, not only of art
theory but also of contemporary gossip, to be capable of discerning
not just the Duchess's likeness, but also its relation to her looks and
'life', and to Reynolds's 'reading' of that history. It was, after all, a
life of some public notoriety. One which, as we shall see, would
make any accommodation of the sitter to civic art, at best,
uncomfortable.

With this in mind, I want to explore the means, and the problem,
of a woman's public representation in relation to both civic and
polite conceptions of the public. A careful reading of the discourses
of civic humanism – and concomitant developments in polite culture
– cannot but reveal a highly gendered social practice, one which is
preoccupied with the impact of desire and sensuality on the public
subject. Throughout the eighteenth century, women had a complex
and contested relationship with public culture. While it was women
who are called upon both to humanise the machinations of the
market, and to moderate the excesses of male social practice, it is
also women who are represented as the occasion of society's disrup-
tion and its decline into lasciviousness and scandal. John Brown,
writing within a civic-humanist discourse that was embittered
against modern society, specifically identified the increased public
visibility of women as one of the causes of the vanity and effeminacy
which he saw as draining England's national resolve.[14] Elizabeth
Gunning, who was frequently identified as a 'Beauty', would have
represented a particular form of public visible woman – close (or at
least potentially so) to the figure of the actress or the prostitute. To
be a 'Beauty' was, in the popular idiom of the period, not merely to
be a beautiful woman, but to be a figure whose existence was defined
by her publicised (and it could be very public) attractiveness. To be
sure, like any other woman, Elizabeth Gunning participates in the
social round and in the economy of the marriage market. But it is

her function as a public spectacle which is most striking. For it marks, on the one hand her commodification and loss of privacy, while on the other it endows her with the dubious empowerment appropriate to a woman of her charms.

As I have begun to argue, the *Duchess of Hamilton and Argyll* images the figure of a woman in relation to a discourse on her publicity. However, we must not neglect, while exploring the discourse on gender and sexuality which the painting mobilises, the other abiding obsession of the mid-century: commerce. Contemporary periodicals, such as the *Connoisseur*, were preoccupied with the subject of Britain's changing economic and social organisation, and in particular the expansion of trade. It was a transformation which the *Connoisseur*'s authors saw as destroying the balance of, and proper distinction between, classes. Alongside these material changes (both social and economic) the *Connoisseur* details a decline of public virtue leaving only 'modest' politeness, seen as an attention to form lacking in the substance of good-breeding.[15] With mounting frequency, this disassembling of class distinctions and proper manners was represented by a discourse on modernity which saw change as coincident with the decline in feminine virtue. the *Connoisseur* pursues a rather complicated argument (too involved to be fully worked through here) which regards both the decline of public manners and the loss of feminine modesty as in some way connected to trade. For the result of practising trade is a ubiquitous and all too explicit displaying of wares. For the *Connoisseur* the signs of this decay are plainly visible: society women parade in near nakedness; the Marriage Act only serves to ensure that 'acre marries acre'; and the distinction between a Fine Lady and a prostitute is merely a technical one, that of cash payment.[16] In this narrative, the luxury of the times is represented by both sex and commerce, or rather, the corruptions of trade can be measured by the extent to which the economic and the erotic are made conspicuous. For Brown, this indiscretion took the form of lewd innuendo; others, such as the *Connoisseur*, saw it in women's clothing, or the lack of it.[17] As a result the process of change, the move to a commercially based society, was one which women were thought particularly to represent.[18] It is this crucial relationship between the commodity and the presentation of desire (and feminine desirability) which provides the most effective context for a discussion of Reynolds's portrait of Elizabeth Gunning.

THE FASHIONABLE IMAGE AND THE COMMERCIAL SPACE

The place to begin the inquiry is in the practice and location of the painting's first public display. As has already been noted, *The Duchess of Hamilton and Argyll* may owe some of its design to the necessity of making a highly visible impression on visitors to the exhibition held by the Society for the Encouragement of Arts, Manufactures and Commerce, which opened its doors on 21 April 1760.[19] Iain Pears has argued that these exhibitions served a variety of purposes, not least of which was the demonstration of saleable talent.[20] Artists who participated in such events, whether as organisers, exhibitors or both, were keen not only to cultivate a taste for the polite arts (over which they would then preside), but also to encourage the purchase of works of art. The two aims could, it was argued, support each other, as an increasingly cultivated aristocracy would, it was hoped, seek to buy more domestically produced art, the increased consumption and ownership of which would in turn raise a taste for, and awareness of, British painting. Despite the assurances made by its proponents, the argument remained open to critique on the basis of its own manifest contradictions. These concerned trade, and the artist's relation to what was always, and clearly, their main objective, which was to sell their wares. Too obvious a desire for financial success ran against the vigorous claims made by the profession's leading figures for it to be considered a liberal art. For, unless painting could be shown to be above the requirements of trade, its claim to a status above that of decorative-painting, metal-chasing, or indeed any other trade seeking to supply luxury goods to the aristocracy, would be vulnerable. Reynolds's work is situated in precisely this context; it was a situation of which he was painfully aware. He would have been conscious that the kind of public to which Shaftesbury had directed his polemic, a public of like-minded landowners, had become a largely unworkable ideal. As a result he has a tendency, particularly in his written work, to try and remodel a version of the classical public, one parallel with the republic of taste. This agenda is at the heart of the *Discourses*, which effect an unceasing, if ambiguous, negotiation with the idea of commerce. The possibility that his paintings, or his practice of exhibiting them, might have been manifestly commercial has, however, until recently, received little attention amongst art historians.[21]

The brief survey of portrait-painter's practices, which André

Rouquet included in his *The Present State of the Arts*, provides a starting point which is both convenient and instructive. Rouquet, like Reynolds, is caught at a particularly awkward intersection of discourses and opinions. As a professional artist, he wants to see an increase in the taste for the polite arts; however, the most prominent moral discourse in which this might be accomplished, that provided by civic humanism, complicates his account. It can justify his position, and that of the arts themselves, but only within certain circumstances. The spread of taste and learning must be a product of disinterested virtue, not commerce. This is not the situation in the England of the 1750s where, on the contrary, money, and not virtue, is the prime mover in the art market.[22] Aware of this problem, and largely critical of the 'present state of the arts', Rouquet's account circles around conceptions of gender and the marketplace. These he sees as irrecoverably linked, so that he begins his commentary 'Of Portraiture in Oils' by reflecting that: 'portraiture is the kind of painting the most encouraged, and consequently the most followed in England; it is the polite custom, even for men, to present one another with their pictures'.[23] The clause 'even for men' marks the limits of acceptability in gendered terms. Clearly the participation of men is something Rouquet takes to be surprising. It represents a vanity and a desire for fashionable self-display not fully consistent with a properly realised civic manhood. Furthermore having one's portrait painted is – and Rouquet is not unusual in this belief – a significant national characteristic peculiar to the English, 'for this nation, especially the ladies, make it one of their chief amusements'.[24] This predilection for portraiture underpins what Rouquet terms the 'very extraordinary manner' in which a portrait-painter obtains his fortune. It is a state of affairs which ensures that the artists' income is secured not by their merit but by a combination of the support of 'some woman of quality' and an ability to seize the current 'vogue'.[25] It is therefore *fashion* – a context which is itself distinctly feminine – and not genius that is the prime mover in the market for portraiture; and while some may only reluctantly succumb to the desire to be painted, 'the women especially must have their pictures *exposed* for some time in the house of that painter who is most in fashion'.[26] Rouquet's narrative succeeds in giving the impression of a market and a painterly practice which he sees as not only highly commercialised but also feminine, as it is women who are both the objects for the art and the means of its transmission.

His closing remarks make this point firmly, if rather curiously. After commenting on the winning delicacy and modesty of English ladies, he embarks on a critique of 'an art, which as yet is only in its infancy in England'. The art he has in mind is that of make-up, or more derisively 'red daub', a practice which he regards as an unprincipled deviation from nature:

Lovely sex, is it to increase your charms, already too inticing, that you approve of an art which nature condemns? Is it to please our eyes still more, that you hang out the formidable vermilion? Surely you cannot please an organ by tormenting it: but I see it is impossible for you to shake off the tyranny of custom.[27]

To follow a discussion of portrait practice with a discussion of make-up would suggest that in Rouquet's mind at least they were closely connected. Both are represented as feminine arts subject to fashion and prejudice, though it is unclear whether Rouquet regards portrait painting as deceptive in the same way as make-up. I would argue, however, that the connection is offered by their juxtaposition in the text, so that portrait painting becomes, like make-up, 'too inticing': a form of self-display which seeks both to seduce and to deceive the viewer.

Given Rouquet's connection of the social and sexual pleasures of being 'painted' with the 'feminine' aspects of British culture, it is worth spelling out exactly the forms of beauty and portraiture that he saw these circumstances as favouring. After noting that each nation, from either habit or prejudice, has its own idea of beauty, he asserts that in England:

the picture of a beautiful women is this: she must have a fine white skin, a light complexion, a face rather oval than round, a nose somewhat longish, but of a fine turn, and like the antiques, her eyes large, and not so sparkling as melting; her mouth graceful, without a smile, but rather of a pouting turn, which gives it at once both grace and dignity; her hair clean and without powder, so as to shew, by its colour, the various effects for which nature designed it; her shape tall and erect, her neck long and easy, her shoulders square and flat, plump rising breasts, her hands generally rather too lean, and of such a make as I think would not be looked upon as handsome in any other country but England.[28]

With some minor revisions this description of fashionable market-orientated beauty would provide a convincing account of the *Duchess of Hamilton and Argyll*. Once the comparison between Rouquet's appraisal and Reynolds's practice is made it appears that Reynolds is producing an image that caters to the 'feminine' desires of the market place as much as it does to the niceties of his 'theoretical system'. It is, furthermore, a form of feminine representation which Rouquet regards as morally suspect.

It makes some sense therefore to examine the other paintings which Reynolds sent to the Society's exhibition, and to examine what, if anything, Reynolds did to palliate the problem of Elizabeth Gunning's desirability, and his own commercial inclinations. The catalogue for the exhibition records four entries under Reynolds's name: '*A Lady, Whole Length*', '*Ditto, Three-quarters*', '*A Gentleman, Ditto*' and '*Ditto, in Armour*'. Modern scholarship has identified the images as, respectively, portraits of Elizabeth Gunning, Lady Elizabeth Keppel, General Kingsley and Lord Charles Vernon.[29] There are complex questions which are raised by the exhibiting, together, of these four canvasses, and which can only be answered tentatively. We can begin, though, by thinking about what the possible significance of this group might have been. On a basic level there is a variety of image and composition on display here: two men, two women; a mixture of full and three-quarter lengths. Stylistically there is also some variety. Elizabeth Gunning is classically attired while Lady Keppel displays a level of genteel fashion, and Lord Vernon's portrait as Walpole observed, owes something to Van Dyck. The result is an impressive display of an artist's range: he can do not only both sexes but also whatever size or major 'style' a potential patron might care to dream up. The intention may well have been similar to Hogarth's depiction of family servants of various ages, an image he used to display the flexibility of his talents. It is not inconceivable that Reynolds intended his submission to be read in precisely this way, functioning as a kind of 'style-sheet'. Certainly the group succeeds in giving a fair display of Reynolds's range of style and composition. However, even for an artist as commercially shrewd as Reynolds, this is an overly narrow conception of how paintings would have acted upon the exhibition visitor.

Assuming that the paintings were hung close enough together to be seen as a single display, we can begin to open some intriguing lines of inquiry. The men portrayed are both army officers, and one at least is represented in the character of a military gentleman, albeit of the previous century. How these two figures may stand in relation to the women Reynolds has painted is an interesting question. It is not unreasonable to suggest that the male portraits locate the images of the women, by providing a frame for the feminine, which combines the public presence of men with their military function as defenders of the nation. Significantly, the women themselves offer rather different models of femininity. The sensual, and I think rather grand, depiction of Elizabeth Gunning, must have contrasted sharply with the more intimate representation of Lady Keppel. Reynolds's biographers Charles Robert Leslie and Tom Taylor describe the latter painting in terms appropriate to its difference from the *Duchess of Hamilton and Argyll*: 'it is one of the painter's loveliest and best preserved female portraits. The dress is white, with a rose in the bosom, and the expression inimitably maidenly and gentle.'[30] Leslie and Taylor's account endorses a fixed division of public and private morals in which the appropriateness of maidenly retirement is contrasted with Elizabeth Gunning's brazen publicity. It is not, as it stands, an inaccurate supposition, as an examination of Reynolds's submissions to exhibitions throughout this period reveals a repetition of the scheme.[31] This occurs most noticeably in 1763 when the *Ladies Elizabeth and Henrietta Montagu* was hung beside a portrait of Nelly O'Brien, a prostitute whom Reynolds liked to call 'my Lady O'Brien'. What this assemblage may have implied about the status of the various sitters or their portraits is, I think, uncertain. There was also, in 1762, the exhibition of *Garrick between Tragedy and Comedy*, a painting which is arguably about the judging of women. The *Garrick* was displayed with a later, more flamboyant image of Lady Keppel, and an intimate portrait of Lady Waldegrave and child. The result is a structure of display which holds in balance, but leaves available for comparison, two forms of femininity, one intimate, the other almost defiantly public. I want to argue that the repeated coincidence of public and private forms of femininity is indicative of an assumption – made by Reynolds, the Society, and later by the Royal Academy – that some kind of reading would have taken place in the spaces between the canvasses. In these terms, the painting functions in such a way as to produce a level of judgement and discrimination within the contrasts represented by the four portraits.[32]

What is not clear, however, is the means by which particular readings were promoted or encouraged. It is possible to begin the process of examining the 'protocols of viewing' that the *Duchess of Hamilton and Argyll* demands by making an excursion into the social and cultural history which surrounds the sitter.[33] I want to contend

that Elizabeth Gunning's presence within the frame of the painting
is far from parenthetical to its overall effect. She is not, as I hope to
illustrate, a figure to whom it is possible to make only a passing
reference, so enmeshed is she by discourses which seek to place her
in relation to many of the abiding preoccupations of the mid-
century. These concerns include not only the facts of her own
beauty, but how that physical presence may be accommodated
within the public and cultured space of the exhibition hall.

THE SOCIETY BEAUTY

The Gunnings (father, mother and at least four children) had come
over from Ireland in 1750, and although their mother was the
daughter of a Viscount they were decidedly poor, so poor in fact that
the two eldest daughters had thoughts of becoming actresses.[34]
What they lacked in finances, however, they more than made up for
in their looks. As Elizabeth Montagu recalled:

The Huntingdon ball was more splendid than I expected. I danced with
lord Sandwich. For beauties we had the two Miss Gunnings, who are
indeed very handsome; *nonpareille*, for the sisters are just a like take them
together, and there is nothing like them, they really are very fine girls.[35]

The Gunnings's incomparable good looks and naïve Irish charms
secured them great celebrity amongst the more excitable members
of the ruling class. But there was, as ever, a catch; depending on
whether they were thought to be emblematic of *Pamela* or *Shamela*,
the Gunnings's pretty faces and rustic manners could stand less as
signs of provincial innocence, and more as emblems of an avaricious
intent.[36] Samuel Richardson himself wasted little time in objecting
to the Gunnings, whom he saw as fishing for husbands. 'When
women turn *seekers* it will not do', he told Miss Westcomb. His
prophecy, that only 'gudgeons may bite' at such dangled wares was,
however, far from the mark.[37]

   The popularity, or the infamy, of the Gunnings was not confined
to the 'Pretty' fellows to whom Miss Westcomb had initially
objected. Horace Walpole, among many others, took considerable
interest in the fortunes of the two sisters, and for a period in the
1750s his letters to Horace Mann and to George Montagu are
replete with 'Gunning stories'. For Walpole, the antics of the sisters
and their admirers seem to have made for a welcome diversion from

the listless nature of politics in the last years of George II's reign. Writing to Mann in June 1751, he confesses that:

You who knew England in other times, will find it difficult to conceive what an indifference reigns with regard to ministers and their squabbles. The two Miss Gunnings, and a late extravagant dinner at White's, are twenty times more the subject of conversation than the two brothers [Newcastle and Pelham] and Lord Granville. These are two Irish girls, of no fortune, who are declared the handsomest women alive. I think there being two so handsome and both such perfect figures is their chief excellence, for singly I have seen much handsomer women than either; however, they can't walk in the park, or go to Vauxhall, but such mobs follow them that they are generally driven away. The dinner was a folly of seven young men, who bespoke it to the utmost expense: one article was a tart made of duke cherries from a hot-house; and another, that they tasted but one glass out of each bottle of champagne. The bill of fare is got into print, and with good people has produced the apprehension of another earthquake.[38]

For Walpole the spectacle of the Gunnings and the 'luxurious heroes' marks out the limits and the extent of modern folly. All of them have deviated from the conduct appropriate to their sex. While women do have a proper function which is associated with display, and men have a role which is concerned with clubbable conviviality, both the Gunnings and the dinner guests overstep this capacity. The conjunction of the two forms (masculine and feminine), of public display and licentiousness are, however, held in balance against the present tawdriness of political 'squabbles'. It is a move which allows Walpole both to register his pleasure at such foolishness, as he clearly thinks here – as elsewhere – that such events have a certain comic aspect, and also to express a note of, albeit ironic, dismay.

It is possible to find the same mixing of good humour and the beginnings of a suspicious dislike in Walpole's account of the two Gunnings's subsequent marriages. It is a passage which is worth quoting at length because it provides a useful narrative of the events with which the Gunnings are most closely, and most personally, associated. After commenting (again) on the dearth of real news, he tells Mann:

The event that has made most noise . . . is the extempore wedding of the youngest of the two Gunnings, who have made so vehement a noise. Lord Coventry, a grave young lord, of the remains of the patriot breed, has long dangled after the eldest [Maria], virtuously with regard to her virtue, not very honourably with regard to his own credit. About six weeks ago [the] Duke [of] Hamilton, the very reverse of the Earl, hot debauched, extravagant, and equally damaged in his fortune and person, fell in love with the youngest at the Masquerade, and determined to marry her in the spring. About a fortnight since at an immense assembly . . . Hamilton made violent love at one end of the room, while he, was playing at pharaoh at the other end; that is, he saw neither the bank nor his own cards, which were of three hundred pounds each: he soon lost a thousand . . . Two nights afterwards, being left alone with her while her mother and sister were at Bedford House, he found himself so impatient, that he sent for a parson. The doctor refused to perform the ceremony without licence or ring: the Duke swore he would send for the Archbishop – at last they were married with the ring of the bed-curtain, at half an hour after twelve at night, at Mayfair chapel. The Scotch are enraged; the women mad that so much beauty has had its effect; and what is most silly, my Lord Coventry declares he will marry the other.[39]

All the key elements for a representation of aristocratic folly and luxury are present in this tale, from card-playing through masquerading and on towards a lustful attention to women. Although Walpole can accept the stupidity of the Duke of Hamilton as something to be expected from such a disgraced character, Lord Coventry is a more serious matter. He has debased himself, sullying the purity of his patriot ancestry and injuring his 'credit' with the world; the marriage can therefore be brusquely derided as 'most silly'. The discursive motivation behind Walpole's remarks would, in the 1750s, have been quite clear. From a strictly civic perspective (though I am not suggesting that Walpole can be defined solely in these terms) the kind of sensuality embodied by Hamilton is to be disavowed because it infects, and ruins, the political capacity of civic manhood. It reflects the loss of the ability to act with calm disinterest, and a descent into the lascivious. Consequently the Duke can no longer be expected to perform the public duties appropriate to his class.

 A similar disavowal is also to be found in a poem published in the spring of 1751, the year before these whirlwind romances began. The poem, entitled 'On a Late Incident. By a Lady', describes an unsuccessful attempt by Maria Gunning to persuade the Duke of Dorset, then newly appointed to the office of Lord Lieutenant of Ireland, to give her indigent mother a pension

> HAIL, *Hibernia*! favour'd isle!
> Thee rising joys await,
> Thy better genius bids thee smile,
> While *Dorset* sways thy state.

Dorset, adorn'd with ev'ry grace,
   Whom happy days attend,
Enlivens commerce, arts, and peace,
   Is Liberty's best friend.

He when the Beaut'ous G–g su'd,
   Was proof against the wile,
And begged the fair would not include
   A pension in a smile.

The people of *Hibernia*'s state
   Are much his sov'reigns care,
Nor will he charge them with a weight,
   Tho' G_____g's face be fair.

The nymph convinc'd by reason clear,
   Her sov'reign's skill ador'd
Agreed her country was his care,
   Since *Dorset* he made lord.[40]

Dorset, unlike Coventry and Hamilton, keeps his credit; and retains his patrician identity intact. The ideological contraction of the poem is breathtaking. It is achieved by making the ability to resist women coincident with the right to hold 'sway' as a colonial overlord. The refusal of the pension becomes, therefore, an act of imperial benevolence undertaken by a rightful, and right-thinking, lord. Excluding for a moment the colonial dimension, it is possible to read in these verses a comparable social concern with the excessive influence of women found in Walpole's letters. Neither Walpole, nor the author of these lines, was alone in regarding the Gunnings as obtaining an unseemly pre-eminence, as, despite earlier enthusiasm, Montagu complains of the Gunnings's 'universal empire'. Indeed she writes that, 'I do not know why Gunning the Great should not sound as well as Alexander the Great'.[41]

Another poem published in the *Gentleman's Magazine* in June 1750, underlines much of this hostility, while complicating its imperial implications. The poem, which takes the form of an 'EPISTLE to a Gentleman of Ireland', provides an account of the two sisters's arrival in London.[42] The poem has two principal movements, the first of which is to place the Gunnings in the context of Ireland's colonial subjugation, while the second offers an analogy with the Roman invasion of Greece.

What tho' *Ierne* knows not thriving arts?
She knows the way to touch hard *English* hearts.
Like some lone isle in farthest regions plac'd;
We think no blessing has the desart grac'd:
But beauty, heav'n's best gift, still chears the land;
Subject to no fierce tyrant's mad command.
The gifts of trade or art may please awhile;
But heav'n alone can give the heart a smile.
Health, peace, and love, are gifts indeed divine;
Ierne's sons for no true blessings pine.
When *Greece* was vanquished by the *Roman* arms;
And the stern conquerors felt the captive's charms:
Such strange unwonted softness to excuse,
A finished model of those charms they chuse:
The *Grecian Venus*, sent to haughty *Rome*,
Pleads for the vet'ran slow returning home.
Thus from a thousand virgins, heav'nly fair,
You cull the *Venus* of the sex with care:
Hither *Ierne* bids her G_____g glide;
Bids her chain those, who would chain the world beside—

There is an ambiguity here within the patriotic discourse which seeks to inscribe the place of Elizabeth and Maria as redemptive, or in some way a compensation for the effects of colonisation. The line in which Ierne 'bids her chain those, who would chain the world beside' implies that the Gunnings can enslave the enslavers – making the 'Empire of Beauty' a retribution for national loss, with the luxuriant falling under luxury's spell. It is however, the Irish and the Greeks who seem best able to accept, albeit passively, the delights of beautiful women. But their pleasure is predicated on their previous defeat and subsequent status as colonies. For the defeated nation, beauty is a compensation (they are, after all, already in chains) while for the victors it is the beginning of an inexorable national collapse.

The figure which most draws my attention, however, is that of the '*Grecian* Venus' and her 'strange unwonted softness'. 'Unwonted' can mean (and this is how it is generally taken) something which is rarely seen, an unfamiliar person or event. But it can also mean something which goes beyond the limits, something which is more than expected. The presence of a quality which is more striking than the merely unfamiliar is suggested by the conjunction of 'unwonted' with 'strange'. In whom such a quality is to be excused is I think uncertain; it seems to hover between the Romans and the Venus herself. 'Excuse', though, does not only mean to provide a plea in mitigation or in extenuation, it also means to indulge. To a degree this clarifies the issue; for it is the Romans who, in taking the Venus home, indulge themselves. They accept a softening of their rough, militaristic masculinity, becoming, like the Greeks and the Irish, supine, passively relishing the seduction of women. Seduction is, however, even in these colonial terms, a dangerous business. The appreciation or enjoyment of beauty marks the onset of effeminacy and national decline; as a state of mind it lacks both the self-possession and self-regard required to resist corruption and defeat.

To a degree, this version of events is consistent with remarks made by Walpole and Richardson, and, in particular, with the former's sense that the Gunnings could be disruptive. However, Walpole never totally rejects the pleasure offered by the spectacle of the two 'beauties'. While his remarks on the Gunnings can be brutally snide, he never quite loses his begrudging affection for them, indeed, there are times when he appears keen to have them around.[43] His strategy for dealing with this ambiguity is to deflect the problem of effeminacy onto the more stable terrain of class politics. To be able to do this, Walpole needed to provide some account of how spectators other than himself responded to the 'noise' generated by the Gunnings's presence. The idea of the 'noise' the Gunnings are said to make is an important one; the word is recurrent throughout Walpole's testimony. It sums up the clamour and gossip of London society in its eagerness to see the two beautiful sisters. More importantly 'noise' is associated with the presence of the 'mob', and with unruly behaviour more generally. The Gunnings are connected, in particular, with two forms of mobbish behaviour. First, there is the mob in the park, or at the theatre; unruly, vulgar and thoroughly plebian, it represents the tumult of the populace as it swarms around the two sisters. Walpole was to regret that the English squandered their liberty 'insulting pretty women'.[44] While the Gunnings, and in particular Maria, are normally held to be in some way responsible for these outrages, Walpole directs his criticism at those, who, unlike himself, lack the politesse necessary for a less exuberant, more genteel leer. The second mob manifests itself in the hallowed space of the Court. Giddy with the excitement of the Gunnings's 'extempore weddings', otherwise dignified members of the patrician elite sent themselves scrambling over tables and chairs in desperate attempts to catch sight of the fair sisters. These and other scenes constitutive of the 'noise' to which Walpole alludes suggest a mania for the Gunnings. The enthusiasm was such that a cobbler in Worcester was able to charge a-penny-a-look to a crowd eager to see the shoes he was making for Maria Gunning.[45] It would be worth noting these incidents merely because they provide an interesting interlude in the history of the fetish. However, their significance lies in the fact that they mark the co-existence of aristocratic and popular enthusiasm and the collapsing of the difference between polite and vulgar pleasures, a distinction Walpole was keen to preserve.

The precise extent of Reynolds's familiarity with these and other stories is unclear, and is likely to remain so. However, Reynolds's correspondent, Miss Weston, seems to have kept him informed of the comings and goings of the English capital throughout his stay in Rome during the early 1750s. Certainly, a letter she posted to Reynolds sometime in early 1751 must have contained some information on this subject, as Reynolds thanks her for news of the Gunnings in his letter dated the 30th of April. What he feels about such events he does not say, but notes that the Gunnings's 'fame had reached here some time agone'.[46] The reference is enough to confirm that Reynolds knew something of the events unfolding back home, though precise details remain elusive. What is intriguing however, is the extent to which such notoriety and beauty might be reworked within the frame of Reynolds's canvas. To be able to follow this process requires a careful consideration of how the sitter's beauty operates within the overall economy of spectatorship which the image offers. In the context of the 1750s, looking at women like the Gunnings might be considered a somewhat dubious occupation. It was suggestive of a popular, vulgar excitement, so that staring at Elizabeth Gunning's painted image, particularly at such a public location as the Society's exhibition, would be an activity to be thought about with some care. It also questions what a 'public' might be: the crowd looking at half-made shoes or a more cultured clientele, eager, as Mannings suggests, to see a society portrait. Eighteenth-century portraiture was not, however, so bereft of iconography as to be unable to focus, or redirect, the viewer's gaze away from the licentious and towards a more restrained form of contemplation.

A LADY, WHOLE LENGTH

In common with the '*Grecian* Venus', the body which Reynolds has chosen to represent is one which claims indulgence, and which seeks to indulge. Cleverly staged amidst a dramatic half-light the Duchess's body radiates a delicate though evident sensuousness. Wrapped in a loose, informal and quite flimsy 'bed gown' of the kind which Reynolds used as a proxy for classical dress, her body is at once disclosed and framed.[47] With strong parallels forming the outline of her legs and breasts, the composition is designed to exploit the volume and curvature of her body. Indeed the image reveals as much of her body as is strictly compatible with the requirements of polite good taste. As I have suggested, it was common knowledge when the painting was exhibited in 1760 that the sitter was a public figure, whose lot it was to be repeatedly stared at. What is striking about Reynolds's image is that it seems to provide, quite deliberately, an occasion for the exercise of that pleasure within the confines of the gallery space. Unquestionably, what is being portrayed is not only a sexually mature woman, but also a woman who is taken to be highly desirable, a beauty no less. Or rather, the painting may be seen to be about her desirability, and as a result seems to bathe in the luxury of that display. The painting moreover signals her sexual availability. While other images of Elizabeth Gunning have a sexual dimension, they appear as more controlled, and more distanced than Reynolds's image. Gavin Hamilton's picture, for example, which similarly represents a scene of gathering dusk, offers a more restrained, less luxuriant rendering of her presence; the Van Dyck costume of grey silk combined with a flamboyant, if improbable, red shawl encases her body in the colours of the Hamilton family.[48] The dress, together with a risibly phallic greyhound, serves to deny the sense of winsome prettiness which might otherwise exceed the forms and claims of male dynasty. Her place in the landscape is similarly restrained, as the wooded valley in which she stands appears to place the young Duchess securely within the Hamilton family's iconography and within their acreage, the source of wealth which underpins their claims to nobility.

Reynolds's portrait is strikingly different, especially as the location of the sitter is much less certain. I do not wish to speculate where Elizabeth Gunning is supposed to be in this picture – it is a deliberately generalised scene and rather beside the point. What is clear, though, is the sense in which she seems much less tied to any particular estate than in either the Hamilton piece, or in Francis Cotes's portrait of 1767, which, as Shawe-Taylor points out, identifies her as the bearer of the Argyll dynasty into which she had married

in early 1759.[49] The uncertainty of location and dynastic affiliation
of Reynolds's portrait may have occurred because the painting's
production coincided with a particularly ambiguous phase in the
Duchess's life. Reynolds's sitter-books indicate that an original sitting
was to have taken place on 16 January 1758. The sitting was
cancelled, however, testimony no doubt to the desperate condition of
the Duke of Hamilton, who died anyway on the 18th.[50] With the
Duke's death, Elizabeth Gunning was detached from any particular
station in the class hierarchies of the kingdom. It would have been
an ambivalent moment, for whatever she may, or may not, have felt
for the Duke, with his passing she gained the freedom of a widow
together with the peculiar status of a woman elevated to the
aristocracy at the behest of a now dead nobleman.

The equivocal status of the woman depicted provides for one of
the most curious aspects of the portrait as a whole: an instability
which is predicated on the ways in which Elizabeth Gunning does
not fit into the high class aspirations of society portraiture.[51] She
had, as contemporary viewers might have reminded themselves,
once been poor, and yet she was later famously rich and the wife of
two successive Dukes. The ducal ermine – the coronation robes
appropriate for a peeress – seem to underscore this ambivalence.
The gown does not appear to be an integral part of her dress, and is
merely hanging, and only just, on her left shoulder, in a manner
which is both negligent and conspicuous.[52] The significance of the
robes is unclear; they could be intended to represent the now dead
husband, and, in particular, the continuation of his line. This would
seem to be discounted, however, by the availability of Elizabeth
Gunning to the gaze of the viewer, and to a new suitor. The ermine
could, on the other hand, signify the difference the viewer was
expected to read, and to understand, between the Duchess of
Hamilton and other 'beauties' represented by Reynolds – most
notoriously Kitty Fisher and Nelly O'Brien. The necessity of making
such a visible separation might however be seen to underline the
Duchess's instability in class terms.[53] With this problem in mind, I
want to focus on two other elements of the painting, the sitter's
posture and the details of the relief on which she leans. This is
appropriate because, more than any other aspect of the painting, it is
the action of leaning upon an emblematic *bas-relief* which signifies
the painting's participation in a complex play of meanings, and a
duality of publics.

Figure 4 Sir Godfrey Kneller, *Mary Compton, Countess of Dorset*, 1690–91

Much of the elegance of the body and its manifest sensuousness comes from the pose in which the Duchess is placed by Reynolds. While it is striking, there would have been little that was unfamiliar to the viewer in 1760. A little less than a year before, the Scottish portrait painter Allan Ramsay had presented *Lady Louisa Connolly* in an almost identical posture. In common with the Duchess of Hamilton, Lady Louisa reclines effortlessly upon the kind of plinth common to eighteenth-century gardens and the paintings which claim to represent them. Ramsay's biographer, Alastair Smart, has proposed Ramsay's work as a possible source for Reynolds's depiction of Elizabeth Gunning. Smart claims that the comparison is 'instructive', though he seems, like many others, to use the juxta-position as an occasion for stating a preference: in this case, for the modernity and politeness of Ramsay over the weary classicism of Reynolds.[54] However, as David Mannings has shown, the sources for Reynolds's composition stretch much further afield.[55] The most immediate source for the pose would, of course, have been Kneller's work, and especially the *Hampton Court Beauties*. The portrait of Mary Compton, Countess of Dorset, in particular, employs a recognisably similar pose and similarly seeks to display a beautiful woman to the gaze of the spectator.[56] This latter point is crucial, as although Mannings's account of the influence of Baroque portraiture on Reynolds is largely persuasive, he does not consider the cultural or social implications of such a reference for a female portrait during the mid-eighteenth century.

To a large extent, the significance of Reynolds's allusion to Kneller's work stems from the uncertain status of the images (and indeed their sitters and patrons) from which he borrowed. Despite their prominence within the Royal collection at Hampton Court, the Kneller *Beauties* are often viewed as a rather problematic set of portraits, and have been dismissed as images all too emblematic of the sexualised extravagance of the Stuart Court; both Henry Fuseli and William Hazlitt, for example, disliked and disapproved of the work, Hazlitt deriding them as little more than 'a set of kept mistresses, painted, tawdry'.[57] More recently, J. Douglas Stewart has argued that what he terms the 'moral problem' of the paintings can be circumvented by an exploration of the Neoplatonic schemes which he claims provide a moral structure for the series as a whole.[58] According to Stewart, the accessories and motifs which accompany each portrait serve to direct and to harmonise desire, transforming lust into the noble passion of love. During the 1750s a few writers did indeed suggest that the Gunning sisters had the capacity similarly to transform appetite into admiration; the following lines constitute the opening of *The Charms of Beauty*, perhaps the most famous of the many poems occasioned by the exploits of Elizabeth and Maria Gunning:

> When *Beauty* spreads her Glories to the View,
> Our wond'ring Eyes the radiant Blaze pursue;
> Enraptur'd we behold the pleasing Sight,
> And lose ourselves in *infinite Delight.*
> *Unruly Passions* urge us to possess
> The richest Treasure of a Mortals Bliss.
> But when *strict Virtue* guards the charming Fair,
> With *Prudence* arm'd, and *chastity* severe;
> Aw'd and chastiz'd by such superior Pow'r
> We stand at Distance, and almost adore.[59]

The poem deploys the Gunnings to offer an admonitory tale directed at the ladies of England. It is, according to the poet, the beauty of the Gunnings's virtue which has attracted the admiration of the English lords; if the English ladies are to be equally successful, then they must lay off their vanity and their paint. The poem, however, is somewhat atypical in its presentation of the Irish beauties, who are more frequently represented as inspiring folly and vice.[60]

The iconography included in eighteenth-century portraiture is much more unstable, and cannot be read as straightforwardly as Stewart's methodology suggests. Crucially, the category of a 'Beauty' is more ambiguous than the overly stark opposition between 'Pin-up' and 'Virtue' put forward by Stewart. There are other parts of the painting, and of this allusion to Kneller, which require elucidation, as an anecdote from Walpole reveals:

As you talk of our Beauties, I shall tell you a new story of the Gunnings, who make more noise than any of their predecessors since the days of Helen, though neither of them, nor anything about them, have as yet been *teterrima belli causa.* They went the other day to see Hampton Court; as they were going to the Beauty-room, another company arrived; the housekeeper said, 'this way, ladies: here are the Beauties'. The Gunnings flew into a passion, and asked what she meant; that they came to the palace, not to be shown as a sight themselves.[61]

This gossipy account – not without its misogynistic overtones – associates Elizabeth Gunning with Kneller and the public face of her beauty in ways which are far from complimentary. Although Walpole is not claiming to be the author of the tale, he presents the story as one taken to be more generally known than merely his own immediate experience. It is used accordingly as further evidence of the Gunnings's folly and caprice – and is indeed part of a series of such stories, of which this is merely the latest. The kinds of judgement taking place in 1760, with Elizabeth Gunning presented in the guise of a royal beauty, could have been quite complex. It may have been possible, for instance, to think about the image more in terms of the Gunnings's conspicuous vanity (and lasciviousness), than in relation to a painterly compliment.

The association between Elizabeth Gunning's portrait and Kneller's *Beauties* implied by Walpole's story is compatible with a civic-humanist account of painting only to the extent to which Reynolds's images may be thought to comment on the *vanitas* displayed by the sitter. Civic humanism is, after all, concerned almost exclusively with the public conduct of men, with their virtues and offices. Reynolds's painting, however, does offer to return the viewer's gaze to the sphere of civic responsibility through the design carved on the *bas-relief* located in the lower left of the canvas. The bas-relief in Reynolds's work, unlike Ramsay's, contains the kind of narrative with which, as David Solkin has argued, Reynolds hoped to raise the style and status of portraiture.[62] The image – which is very indistinct – shows Paris, a seated figure, leaning forward offering an apple to the victorious Venus. Interestingly, Venus herself is not shown, save for the suggestion of her arms on the far left of the canvas, and the two defeated goddesses can only be seen dimly in the shadows behind Paris. This would appear to suspend, or curtail, the narrative process which the relief has inaugurated. This is, however, not the case, as, on the contrary, the narrative can be extended to encompass the whole painting. To complete the image the viewer must insert Elizabeth Gunning as the missing Venus. The process of this narrative completion is further underlined by the presence to the right of the painting of two doves, traditional symbols of the Goddess.

The suggestion that the image on the relief may provide a way into the complexities of the painting as a whole is enhanced by the status of the narrative to which it alludes. The story of Paris's judgement is, along with the Judgement of Hercules, one of the primary texts of civic masculinity. It is certainly central to the ideology of eighteenth-century society, as it suggests the male right to choose, but also the necessity of the right choice. For Joseph Spence, commenting on the story in relation to the Judgement of Hercules, it is the consequences of an inability to discriminate which provide for the greatest drama:

The Choice, or (as it is more commonly called) the Judgement of Paris, seems to me to be the Asiastic way of telling the same story; and it is formed on a larger plan than any of the former. The goddess of Wisdom, the goddess of Pleasure and the goddess of Power, appear to Paris in his youth. They each make him their offers. He prefers pleasure, to whatever the others would give him: and the consequence of this bad choice of his was, the loss of his own life, the suffering of all his friends, and of his country; and finally the overturning of the Asiastic monarchy.[63]

Spence's response, coming from within the discourse of civic humanism, is a familiar one.[64] For Spence, Paris has unquestionably made the wrong decision with predictable and dire consequences. Unlike Hercules, Paris has departed from the civic responsibilities which his status, as a prince, ought to have guaranteed. Moreover, Paris is punished, death and destruction following logically from his lasciviousness.

Spence's response does not, however, exhaust the discursive potential of the figure of Venus, or Paris's judgement. Two plays, written in 1731 and 1768, share the title of *The Judgement of Paris*.[65] Both productions, which graced the stage of the Theatre Royal, suggest a rather different attitude towards Paris's choice and towards Venus herself. The plays are simple tales – certainly much more straightforward than the classical sources to which Spence refers – and tend to see Paris as acting in the main rather sensibly. While the 1731 text, which is more complicated than the 1768 version, does illustrate the rival claims of the goddesses, it is Venus to whom the most effective speech is given. Significantly, while Paris acknowledges that he has forfeited his capacity for self-command, it is not something about which he feels much remorse. And indeed, why should he, as the rest of the characters soon flood onto the stage to congratulate him on the wisdom of his choice. In both plays there is some comment on the forms of destruction and luxury Paris's conduct might entail. But on the whole this seems a hollow rehearsal of a rather tired story; it was preferable, at least on the stage, to proclaim the virtues, assuming they are such, of love.

The attitude to the goddess could then be playful. Desire, while its dangers may be acknowledged, can even be celebrated. To be sure, the differences between the plays and Spence's treatise might be understood as a function of genre. To view the disjunction solely in these terms, however, would be to fail to recognise the ambiguity both of Reynolds's image and of the exhibition as a whole. The question is not only of genre, or indeed of time (James Beattie's poem, *The Judgement of Paris*, published in 1768, is more in agreement with Spence than the play of that year), rather it is a difference of space.[66] The theatre is a site for excited, fashionable pleasure, and, as such, permits a greater indulgence of desire than would be imaginable in Polymetis' patrician seclusion. The exhibition hall lies between the two places, aspiring to the grandeur of the villa, but appealing to the tastes of the crowd. So that, as it hangs on the walls of the exhibition, the *Duchess of Hamilton and Argyll* is forced to mediate between the gentlemanly scholarship embodied within Polymetis' Villa, and the dalliance represented by the Drury Lane productions. Furthermore, the pleasures represented by the Paris of the stage plays coincide with Montagu's invocation of the Gunnings as part of the spectacular repertoire of a society assembly which licenses or takes its animation from the energy of desire, almost acknowledging the slippage between the social and sexual forms of commerce. But it would also coincide with the forms of conventional social practice. Lady Sarah Bunbury, later to be painted by Reynolds herself, writes enthusiastically of the agreeable softening effected by Elizabeth Gunning on her brother:

Charles is in town, & is violently in love with the Duchess of Hamilton; think of his riding out to see her. You know how he hates it; he is all humbleness and respect and never leaves her. I am vastly glad to see him improve so much, he is now quite manly, & much liked, in the world; he is a sweet boy, & I hope will continue as aimiable as he is.[67]

On this account, the admiration of fine women marks the emergence of a fully-matured, male, sexual persona, alongside the possession of a valuable social grace. Montagu makes a similar point when she writes of Sir Thomas Robinson graciously escorting the Gunnings, 'after being master of ceremonies to the French ambassador, and our secretary of state, [he] proposes to be gallant to these fair dames'.[68] Robinson therefore emerges as an exemplary figure, able to balance loyal service and polite entertainment.

The story of the Judgement of Paris may then have been unstable, or at least under revision, in ways of which Reynolds and his audience would have been aware. There were, by 1760, at least two ways of reading the scene on the ancient hillside, and it is here more than anywhere else that the Duchess appears to be located. One version continues the civic-humanist stress on disavowal and another captures a more recent development in the social practices of polite culture. In this sense, the painting constitutes a particularly sophisticated play of meanings, made all the more complex because of the way in which the painting seems to frustrate what remains of a civic agenda. By placing the Judgement of Paris within the space of the canvas, Reynolds appears to be insisting on a considered appraisal, not only of his art, but also of his sitter. This would seem to imply that the viewer ought to recreate the famous judgement: he can, if he so desires, repeat Paris's judgement, or turn away with Herculean disdain (the possibility of a woman's judgement could not be expressed in these terms). However, the choice has, in effect, already been made, for the viewer only encounters the scene at the moment at which the prize is about to be awarded. The only purposeful action available would, therefore, be to stop looking, a rather unlikely, and distinctly foolish, act at an art exhibition. This would seem finally to mark the difference the painting has from a strictly civic morality, especially as, in Spence's terms, 'there can be no virtue without choice'.[69] If Juno and Minerva were more effectively represented, then the viewer could elect to consider their virtues, and to repudiate Venus – this is broadly the import of Beattie's poem. However, with Juno and Minerva scarcely present, there is no higher virtue to which the spectator can appeal. The only recourse would, therefore, be to a more private narrative, one which is more firmly located in the presuppositions of polite social practice than in the art theory represented by Reynolds's critical writings.

SENSIBILITY AND THE VALUE OF THE EXHIBITION

One way for viewers to retain and even restate their capacity for judgement would have been for them to compare the *Duchess of Hamilton and Argyll* with *Lady Elizabeth Keppel*. The two women could, as we have seen, be easily contrasted and their respective characters appraised. Such discrimination would reintroduce choice into the act of looking, while the martial presence of Vernon and Kingsley provided an obvious public frame for any subsequent discussion.

That the action of looking, and of judging, would have been undertaken solely in these terms seems unsatisfactory. Although the process corresponds with Walpole's propensity for evaluating the character and appearance of aristocratic women, and, more importantly with the critical practices outlined in the last chapter, such judgement would do little to dispel the desire which the painting has encouraged from its audience.[70] What could have occurred instead is a redirecting of the viewer's desire into the more permissible channel of sympathy.

So far my account of the *Duchess of Hamilton and Argyll* has focused almost entirely on the painting as representing a problem for the male spectator. However, as recent theoretical work has demonstrated, the much vaunted 'male gaze' rarely acts upon the simple binary of voyeurism or disavowal alone.[71] Furthermore, paintings, like any other form of cultural production, do not exist in one context alone. As a recent essay by Stephen Daniels has shown, a more productive approach lies in the appreciation of a series of contexts all of which produce different, potentially competing, readings.[72] Something very like this has already emerged in the differences between polite and civic reactions to publicly active women. Consideration of the viewer's sensibility, particularly as a mode of compassionate responsiveness to the painting, will provide another means of examining the image produced by Reynolds, one which is concerned, at least in part, with the impact public displays of beauty and sexuality have on the sitter herself. Moreover, a display of sympathetic affection, while it would not wholly deny the expression of sexuality, could have provided a means of condoning both feminine desirability, and male vulnerability to that spectacle.

The grounds upon which the painting may be thought of as evoking a more sentimental response would have been quite clear in 1760. At its centre is an ambivalent working of grieving and loss, an economy of pathos which includes even death. The dramatisation of death, and the deathly, ought not, however, to encourage a hasty identification of sexuality with death. For while such a coincidence is suggested by elements of the painting, consideration needs to be given to the specific processes of loss which the image generates. The coincidence between the Duke of Hamilton's recent death and the production of the painting places the spectre of death centre stage; certainly important aspects of the Duchess's appearance suggest mourning attire, most notably, the loose, unpowdered hair, and the

Figure 5 Sir Joshua Reynolds, *Anne Dashwood* (later Countess of Galloway), 1764

absence (apparently) of stays indicate a funereal image inflecting contemporary fashion. This combines with her pose, which while it has a number of seventeenth- and eighteenth-century sources, also derives from a carving on a second-century sarcophagus.[73] Significantly the tradition of painting Paris in a seated position also derives (via Raphael) from a Roman sarcophagus of the same period. This conjunction of sources, typical of Reynolds's 'witty' allusions, recommends that the plinth is read more as a monument, than an ornament. The suggestion can be supported by considering the funereal or memorial aspect of other Reynolds canvasses, notably his 1764 portrait of Anne Dashwood. In the later painting the young sitter again appears to recline on a monument as if contemplating coming death.[74]

While these elements suggest that Elizabeth Gunning appears in the guise of a grieving widow, a number of other interpretive possibilities are equally apparent. First, throughout the production of Reynolds's portrait, Maria Gunning was dying, and, furthermore, Elizabeth was also thought to be in decline. Walpole, as ever, is on hand to tell the story:

> The Charming Countess is dead at last; and as if the whole story of both sisters was to be extraordinary, the Duchess of Hamilton is in a consumption too, and going abroad directly. Perhaps you may see the remains of these prodigies, you will see but little remains; her features . . . [have] long been changed, though not yet I think above six-and-twenty.[75]

This was in the October of 1760, though her illness had begun its course long before, and, by November, Walpole was candid enough with Horace Mann to tell him that the Duchess of Hamilton would 'not answer your expectation'.[76] The Earl of Chesterfield wrote in a similar vein reflecting, as early as 1752, that the beauties of the Gunnings would be short-lived.[77] The brevity and impending extinction of beauty is a constant refrain in the eighteenth century, and it is not surprising to find the Gunnings used as the occasion for its rehearsal.[78] This connection is supported by Ronald Paulson, who has claimed that an appreciation of the beautiful inevitably constitutes an aesthetic of mourning. It presupposes, he argues, a sensibility based upon expected loss.[79] In this context portraiture occupies a uniquely privileged place. The genre is predicated upon the recovery and re-presentation of what is already absent, or about to be lost. Portraits, indeed, make present those who could not otherwise return to a gallery, or a salon: the dead. This was well understood in the eighteenth century; one commentator writing later in the century noted that it was portraiture's specific responsibility to 'preserve the form which lies mouldering in the tomb'.[80]

In these terms the *Duchess of Hamilton and Argyll* remains a tribute to beauty, but becomes one which proposes the vulnerability of beauty to both age and disease. With this in mind there is an obligation to re-read the disposition of the sitter, and in particular the portrait's primary icon, the bas-relief. Strikingly, the sitter's pose, with its half-reclining posture, is reminiscent of contemporary funeral sculpture, and in particular the monuments in Westminster Abbey.[81] Certainly, there is something sculptural about the way in which the Duchess is depicted, and it was perhaps to this which Waterhouse referred when he described the painting as looking, 'as nearly dead as a Reynolds of a very handsome sitter can be'.[82] The statuesque nature of the pose provides a curious framing presence in Reynolds's otherwise painterly scheme. The heavily incised parallels which construct her body extend the sculptural form outwards from the plinth and onto her whole body. The effect of this is to inter the living within the iconography of death. I have already traced a similar progression from the plinth onto the Duchess's body in the 'Judgement of Paris' narrative. In total, what is transposed is not only the civic iconography necessary for understanding the painting, and its signified of desire and repression, but also a narrative concerning loss and mourning.

Revealingly, Elizabeth Gunning continues to stare grimly at the plinth-sarcophagus upon which she leans; her gaze always returns the viewer to the relief. By gazing at the sarcophagus in this way Elizabeth Gunning might appear to be vulnerable, even penitent. Arranged next to a tomb and posed for its contemplation, the society beauty appears to be on the verge of confronting her own mortality. The very beauty which solicits the gaze, therefore, emerges as fragile, impermanent; it seems to exist only in relation to impending death. It is possible to suggest that this aspect of the painting is not meant to be read as a statement simply about death or aging – though these may be the terms in which the discourse is conducted. Rather, the painting seems to be saying something about the effect beauty-as-publicity (and hence sexuality) has on the Duchess. When her sister died bewailing her lost looks, Walpole reflected that it was 'hard upon a standard beauty' to be so afflicted.[83] Clearly Walpole meant to be sardonic, to point an easy moral at the expense of Maria Gunning's vanity, and to claim that a 'standard beauty' lacks the capacity for any further character or even identity; without her looks she is nothing. However, he seems, as elsewhere, to reflect upon the fact that to be publicly beautiful is to lose something of oneself. While it is important to recognise the existence of Walpole's more misogynistic tendencies, he does appear to be saying that there is something pathetic (in the elevated sense) in the Gunnings's situation. Their ability to seduce leaves them prey to desires not strictly their own: a seduction which, as Susan Staves has argued, was attended in the eighteenth century by the litigious grief of fathers, and the baleful death of young women.[84]

There is something of that sensation of pathos in this picture. This changes the viewer's attitude to the sitter considerably, altering her status and the nature of the viewer's desire. She is no longer merely the object of their anxious pleasure, instead she occupies a position which demands compassion, and a reappraisal of what it is to be a male viewer. Looking away with Herculean forebearance is no longer the issue; what is a concern, however, is the fact that the male spectator may occupy – as a man – two conflicting positions in relation to Elizabeth Gunning. He can seek to seduce her himself (or at least fantasise that triumph) or alternatively he can act as a surrogate father, grieving for her impending seduction and eventual decline. The difficulty – and the impropriety – of Reynolds's image is captured in part within this hesitant double bind. It is however only one of many occasioned by this portrait. There is, for example, a difficulty about distinguishing for whom it is that the viewer is to mourn: the Duke, the Duchess or, indeed, for himself. Most tellingly, there is a profound mixing of functions occurring in Reynolds's portrayal of the grieving Duchess of Hamilton. For while Elizabeth Gunning is represented in relation to the 'private story' of a recent death, this privacy is transformed by the public display of that condition.

The ambiguity of the portrait and its intended audience is indicative of the ambiguity of art production in the 1750s and 1760s. As David Solkin has argued, during this period artists faced a substantial stumbling block when trying to formulate their address to the public.[85] Retaining a convincing address to the public sphere was increasingly difficult prior to the establishment of the Royal Academy in 1768, when Reynolds was able to put civic theory on a 'new footing'.[86] The signs and practices of commerce were too visible for an art representing only classical virtues to have any efficacy. The result was something more hybrid, an art form with two or more competing referents. As a result, the distinction between the references I have been describing can best be seen in the co-existence of competing forms of value within the painting; the civic, the polite and the pathetic. Under the first denomination comes the sign of the 'Judgement of Paris' as a call to civic disavowal, or, at least, a demand to think about the luxury represented by art, and by beautiful women, in those terms. The fact that is has to be included so visibly may signify its vulnerability and not its retrieval as an appropriate discourse for appreciating art. In the early part of the eighteenth century it was customary to produce epigrammatic narratives which regulated the act of looking at Venus.[87] To provide one in 1760 which stresses, instead, the dangers of looking indicates just how much times had changed, as it would seem to imply that the spectator needs reminding of his duty. The civic value of the *Duchess of Hamilton and Argyll* is therefore located in the fact that the spectator can observe, without participation, in the display of beauty, and in the call to its critique.

The creation of the public exhibition, and the formation of a broader audience, abolished the privileged position upon which civic scholarship, at least in its aristocratic form, had relied. This shifted the frame of reference away from art theory, and towards the discourse of social life. Reynolds's portrait cannot be understood without some appreciation of the sitter's life and social position. The 'magazine of common property' to which the painting refers is not therefore, as Malcolm Warner (quoting Reynolds) suggests, the realms of classical allusion, but rather it is common knowledge, gossip; in Walpole's phrase, the 'new story of the Gunnings'.[88] This reworks the classical reference in the painting, just as Walpole's story of events at Hampton Court reworked the reference to Kneller. It makes the problem of the painting less an economy of sexual distance – a choice between responsibility and luxuriance – and more the decision to be contemptuous, or to be sympathetic. It is this dimension of the painting to which the more obviously polite or sentimental readings of the image may be attached. This was the new value system established by the exhibition; the evaluation of Elizabeth Gunning against Lady Keppel, and the weighing of beauty against the recurrence of death.

This kind of social evaluation is not a response which sits easily with the body of art theory propounded by Reynolds later in the century. It is, however, fairly consistent with Solkin's reading of the work of Benjamin West, whose success, even as a History painter, relied to no small degree on the depiction of sensuous and endangered feminine beauty.[89] West's career discloses the irony underlying the exhibitions held by the Society for the Encouragement of the Arts, Manufactures and Commerce, and by the Royal Academy throughout the eighteenth century. For, in order to succeed, they needed to solicit an audience beyond the close confines of the patrician and masculine elites. The polite culture to which they necessarily turned, drawn from the same society which attended Vauxhall and routs at Ranelegh, would be less than impressed by austere injunctions to stoicism. To this end, painterly styles were changed, and historical grandeur brought in line with popular taste. In many respects this is the crucial change. For it is the innovation of the public exhibition, seen as a reorganisation of the business of being an artist, to which Reynolds's work ultimately responds. In this connection it is the spectacle of publicly displayed woman which most catches the eye. It is Elizabeth Gunning's body which provides the focus for the range of references which the painting introduces and then seeks, perhaps not successfully, to reconcile. By evoking and modifying the spectator's reaction to its principal object, the painting appears to be trying to ensure not only its own status, but also its desirability. The ambiguous place occupied by a beautiful woman in eighteenth-century society produced, in this context, an image which referred both to social and sexual mores, as well as to the status of commercial art. In particular the introduction of a sympathetic register indicates an attempted reconciliation of the higher branches of art to what Solkin aptly describes as the 'softer pleasures of the market place'.[90] And it is this 'strange unwonted softness', the softness of commercial art, which Reynolds most wants excused.

CHAPTER FOUR

'Her Whole Power of Charming': femininity, ugliness and the reformation of the male gaze

In the preceding chapter I argued that when Reynolds exhibited his portraits of high-born or beautiful women the paintings were positioned not merely with reference to conventional display techniques, but in relation to a variety of discourses which commented on, or attempted to proscribe the social place of woman within eighteenth-century culture. Such discourses, at least in the grand exhibitions put on by the Society for the Encouragement of Art, Manufactures and Commerce, tended to provide these formulations in terms of a largely aristocratic version of social mores. However, away from the patrician concerns of public men, that address was revised into a discourse which sought to explore and give coherence to the social place of women. This transformation of discourse was enacted in a different social milieu, the location of which was not the grand villas and courtly estates of the aristocrats or anything like, but was instead the parlours and drawing rooms of the middle classes. The account of manners which middle-class writers produced, to be explored in this chapter in its novelistic form, was unconcerned with the notion of men unfit for public office (the middle class were thought unacceptable for this role in any case) but retained the civic sense that women could corrupt as well as polish. The primary focus of such writing, however, was on the conduct of women as agents of sociable interaction. This chapter will explore the degree to which the physical appearance of women was thought to enhance or render problematic that new social role.

According to Terry Eagleton, the middle decades of the eighteenth century witnessed what 'may be called the bourgeois feminization of discourse', whereby feminine values of delicacy, chastity, prudence and charity played 'a more vitally constitutive part in the male public sphere'. Eagleton argues that, 'in a contradictory movement, "feminine" values relegated by the division of labour to the private realm [returned] to transvaluate the ruling ideologies themselves'.[1] Eagleton's formulation, one of the more influential in eighteenth-century studies, is helpful not only in relation to Richardson, the object of Eagleton's inquiry, but to a whole range of texts which celebrated the moral capacity of women. In this context it is significant, that the theoretical discourse on beauty, as my reading of Daniel Webb, James Usher and others has shown, had been feminised; its object and means of address taken to a new and feminine position. However, Eagleton is unduly confident about the degree to which the values of the private sphere were 'transvaluated' into the public domain. His account suggests that there was a comfortable movement between two relatively stable arenas. This was not necessarily the case. Although such assumptions grew in credibility, it was by no means always accepted that 'feminine' values had any place in the 'public sphere'.

As the foregoing discussion has indicated, there were a number of conflicting attitudes about the role of women within eighteenth-century culture and society. To every writer, such as David Hume, who was prepared to suggest that women aided sociability, there was an opposing view which argued that the presence of women tempted men into effeminate assemblies devoid of virtue. The two ideas were not necessarily exclusive. Preaching in 1776 to an audience of young men, James Fordyce claimed that they could improve their morals as well as their manners by entering more readily into the society of women. Women, because they combine 'easy comprehension, natural taste [with] sprightly imagination', are able to offer young men 'some of the sweetest pleasures which the soul can taste'.[2] Furthermore, Fordyce was enthusiastic about the polishing effect which social intercourse with women might have on the emerging sociability of adolescent males. It was, he suggested, precisely the desire of pleasing women which rendered men sociable. Given this connection, it was important that women were not too closely confined or wholly separated from contact with men; predictably, Fordyce added the qualification that women who entered too readily into the 'gaze of the glittering throng' were incapable of virtue.[3] For Fordyce, therefore, while women could embody the private virtues which he believed had a role in reforming young men, it was equally clear that women could not continue to possess these virtues if they themselves moved from the private to the public arena.[4]

This is a point which can be further advanced by a recollection that the advocacy of women's greater emotional sensibility existed in a profoundly ambivalent relationship to the practical politics of marriage during the eighteenth century. As Erica Harth has argued, the 'ideological climate of love and marriage' was particularly fraught by the mid-century; a fact memorialised by the Hardwicke Marriage Act of 1753. By the 1750s, debates about marriage were focused upon the demand for daughterly obedience and the likelihood of feminine desire (concepts given in their eighteenth-century formulation as propriety and passion). According to Harth, such discourses exhibit an interest in surveillance and authority which is in stark contrast to the 'rise of romantic love', or indeed the 'companionable marriage'.[5] Harth's claims are clearly important; however, at this juncture it is merely necessary to note that the tension between the high estimation of women in sentimental narratives and the perceived need for paternal, even political, scrutiny, provides a context in which discourses about women, their beauty and their impact upon men would have a particular currency.

In many respects the repeated coincidence of discourses that placed a high value on women's moral sensibility with texts, even laws, which embodied a far harsher regime of control and scrutiny, represents one of the major fault lines which run through eighteenth-century culture. The last two chapters have explored how a description of a woman's physical appearance became a major part of this ongoing argument, functioning as a sign through which women could be judged. Amongst the most sophisticated, and certainly more interesting, versions of this debate are those to be found in the novels by women published during the mid-century. Responding to what is otherwise a largely male tradition, women writers such as Charlotte Lennox and Sarah Scott (the novelists discussed in this chapter) give the debate a distinctive cast. As Elizabeth A. Bohls has recently suggested, the novel, along with the travel-narrative, provided women writers with a rare opportunity to engage with the 'language of aesthetics'. Bohls argues that the flexibility of the novel form enabled women to respond to aesthetic discourse in ways which were both innovative, and at times, highly critical of conventional opinions.[6] Following the lead provided by Bohls, I want to argue that Lennox and Scott do indeed take up, adapt and to a degree transform the assumptions of male-authored discourses about taste and beauty. Scott, in particular, seeks to move the discussion of a woman's physical appearance away from complacent assumptions about beauty and towards a more individuating discourse on propriety and morality.

Sadly, surveys of eighteenth-century literature have tended to see the women writers of the mid-century as either unadventurous or depressingly conservative. Janet Todd, for example, has claimed that women novelists of the mid-century were overcome by the need to appear morally respectable, and that 'a possible way of signalling moral purpose was to enact the replacement of the power-seeking woman with a new feminine one, to transform the coquettish into a sentimental sign . . . Charlotte Lennox did just this'.[7] It will be part of the intention of this chapter to argue that the literature of the 1750s and 1760s produced a more complex gender politics than Todd's survey allows. Through an attentive reading of their texts, I shall argue that the fictions of Lennox and Scott re-work aspects of the discourse on female beauty in ways which are not easily or accurately described as either radical or conservative. Importantly, both women wrote novels in which descriptions of physical appearance provided a means of representing chaste and virtuous women while also enabling their young heroines to be attractive to a knowing or reformed male spectator. In this context, beauty will have a distinctly uncertain connotation. As we have already seen, eighteenth-century accounts of feminine appearance were profoundly ambivalent and often contradictory. This uncertainty is no more apparent that in Lennox's best known novel *The Female Quixote*, a text now receiving the scholarly treatment it deserves. My reading of the novel suggests that Lennox's text explores and, later, problematises the association of morality with beauty. However, the peculiar nature of Arabella's 'adventures' ensures that the relationship between authority and beauty, sensibility and prestige remains ambiguous throughout the text. It is the ambiguities raised by Lennox's treatment of discourses on beauty which are explored in the next section of this chapter.[8]

TOWN BEAUTIES AND POLITE LADIES: FEMALE QUIXOTICISM AND THE POWER OF BEAUTY

Midway through *The Female Quixote*, an exchange takes place that illuminates the status of beauty for a culture whose conception of itself as social or public is in transition. The conversation, between the quixotic Arabella and her two lovers, Mr Glanville and Sir

George Bellmour, is of interest because of the way in which it foregrounds the use of the word 'Beauty' as the term that provides the most obvious vocabulary for talking about a woman's social presence.[9] The implication of the term is colloquial and familiar; Sir George uses it casually, yet precisely, as he attempts to chide Arabella for her severity: ' . . . you Beauties make very nice Distinctions in these Cases; and think, if you do not directly command your Lovers to die, you are no-ways accountable for their Death'. The particular point of contention ostensibly concerns the nature and the extent of the respect due to beauty; and, by logical extension, to women. Arabella, in the height of her romantic folly, claims for beauty the highest possible status, asserting that, along with love, it is at once the most delightful and the most sublime object of inquiry. Speaking of the various histories she has read she asserts that 'You will there find, that the greatest Conquerors, and Heroes of invincible Valour, reason with the most exact and scrupulous Nicety upon Love and Beauty.'[10] The discussion of beauty in which these warriors engage is taken by Arabella to represent an appropriate public discourse on the physical and social appearance of women. The propriety of their pronouncements lies, however, in the assumption that they will never be uttered in front of, let alone to, a woman. With this opinion determining her thoughts, Arabella asserts that, if a woman is importuned by the solicitations of a lover, she can, and should, banish him. According to Arabella, by sending her lover from her presence a woman not only secures her virtue, but also proclaims her sense of the outrage committed against her person by an impolitic declaration.[11]

Listening to her harangue, Arabella's virtuous and ardent lover, Glanville, is disconcerted by both the obstinacy with which she clings to these high-minded ideals and the embarrassing consequences into which such nonsense must surely lead. While Glanville is undoubtedly upset by her ardent pronouncements, he attempts to gain some consolation from his idol's austerity:

Though, replied Mr. *Glanville*, you are very severe in the Treatment you think it necessary our Sex should receive from yours; yet I wish some of our own Town Beauties were, if not altogether of your Opinion, yet sufficiently so, as to make it not a Slavery for a Man to be in their Company; for unless one talks of Love to these fair Coquets the whole time one is with them, they are quite displeased, and look upon a Man who can think any thing, but themselves, worthy of his Thoughts or Observation, with an utmost Contempt.[12]

In these terms, banishment becomes a kind of freedom – though Glanville hardly thought so when he was banished by Arabella earlier in the novel.[13] The apparent illogic of Glanville's response arises because he and Arabella are describing different places, and, it might be added, different times. Largely blasé about, if not actually unconcerned with, Arabella's romantic ideals, Glanville's thoughts are more recognisably modern. Continuing his argument against the servitude of contemporary manners, he remarks:

How often have you and I, Sir *George*, . . . pitied the Condition of the few Men of Sense, who are sometimes among the Croud of Beaux, who attend the Two celebrated Beauties to all Places of polite Diversion in Town? For those Ladies think it a mortal Injury done to their Charms, if the Men about them have Eyes or Ears for any object but their Faces, or any Sound but that of their voices.[14]

That early editions referred to these two women as 'the Two Sister Beauties' makes it clear that Glanville is objecting to the Gunning sisters. The Gunnings were, as we have seen, the recognised signs of modish luxuriance and fashionable dissipation. Unlike Arabella's austere heroines, the two sisters were seen to enjoy the society of men. It was this behaviour which outraged Walpole who, like Glanville, thought that men debased themselves by such frivolous diversions.

Glanville's reference to the Gunning sisters further suggests that, for him, the problems associated with feminine beauty are very different from the debates which delight Arabella. Unlike Arabella, Glanville is not concerned with the intrusion of women upon a public stage where that activity is thought of in terms of an historic or political intervention. His is the world of polite codes and sublimated sexualities, the kind of public which is formed by admission into theatres, galleries and to the 'public' assemblies for pleasure. Glanville envisions a public that is based on commercialised leisure and enjoyed by individualised family groups; the kind of society, in short, into which Evelina and the Mirvans hurry themselves on their arrival in London in Fanny Burney's novel.[15] This is a world of reciprocal gazes in which each participant desires eminence in the field of social and sexual display and, as such, a realm wholly removed from the ambitious publicity sought by *The*

Female Quixote's deluded heroine. For, while Arabella dreams of a world in which everybody looks at her, Glanville thinks only of a place in which everyone looks at everyone else. Glanville's vision of society is therefore both modern and conventional, and is based, for the most part, on accepted codes of polite conduct. Most noticeably, Glanville believes that the social sphere is the place in which gallant flirtation is not only the accepted norm, but the sole interest of women's lives:

Custom, Lady *Bella*, said *Glanville*, smiling, is wholly on my Side; for the Ladies are so far from being displeased at the Addresses of their Lovers, that their chiefest Care is to gain them, and their greatest Triumph to hear them talk of their Passion; So, Madam, I hope you'll allow that Argument has no Force.[16]

Conversely, Arabella believes, that women can and ought to have serious public roles; this belief is the foundation of her quixoticism. Women should, according to Arabella, act to support dignified public characters: as warriors, princesses, queens, and as distant, but adored, beauties. This is an ideal with which Glanville's idle flirtations can have little in common. Furthermore, there is something inherently aristocratic in the insistence of Arabella's beauty, and the kinds of display envisaged for it (one of Arabella's delusions is that the world is only populated by the nobility and their entourage). Arabella expects to be admired within a splendid public realm for which she is the focus. She does not want, still less expect, anyone else to impinge upon her exalted and adored status as a queenly-beauty. Arabella's predicament lies, of course, in her romantic world view, a curiously disarticulated discourse which reverses the conventional alignment of public and private. Her fantasy of virtuous, historic and, undoubtedly, public action, in its political and social sense, exists solely in an isolated private discourse; the language of the closet.[17] Arabella produces what amounts to nothing less than a private fantasy of the public. Hers is a quixotic vision wherein she is indeed the mistress of all she surveys, yet she sees almost nothing.

Notwithstanding the principled solicitations of the Countess who mediates between the worlds of Arabella and Glanville, Arabella continues to maintain, until the very last moment, that it is absolutely necessary that she should make a great 'Noise and Bustle', a commotion in the world that is concerned not with gaining lovers and estates – the probable extent of the Gunnings's ambition – but with gaining dominion in the 'Empire of Love'.[18] Catherine A. Craft, reflecting on Arabella's repeated assertion of women's historical involvement, comments that her 'retellings of historical events put women at the centre and offer them more important roles than they actually had . . . they are active, they have adventures'.[19] Arabella's aim throughout the novel is to replicate that heroism, and to possess or to inhabit the discourse which most befits her exalted status; that of Romance. Despite its obvious dangers, romance fiction provides Arabella with an effective discourse in which to articulate her 'Entrance into the World', as well as her subsequent conduct. Unlike the hesitant, blushing Evelina, who is forced to appeal for a conduct book which will tell her how to behave, Arabella is both confident of her own conduct and dismissive of the real follies of others.[20] Arabella's reading, though misguided, turns out, ironically, to have been a much better education for the social world than the moral strictures handed down to Evelina by Mr Villars. This fact is the source of the ambiguity of the novel, for while Arabella is clearly deluded, she is neither vicious nor shallow, and her errors are those of naïveté and ignorance, never affectation or vice. This is an appraisal not readily given to her acquaintances in either Bath or London; witness the immoral Miss Groves and the witless Mr Tinsel. It is also a fact she will later use to defend her favourite reading, claiming that romances, 'give us an Idea of a better Race of Beings than now inhabit the World'.[21]

The separation between modern depravity and Arabella's quixotic virtue is also present in Glanville's critique of the fickle 'Town Beauties', and is most readily and most repeatedly offered in the disparity between Arabella and Miss Glanville. Miss Glanville is the embodiment of polite modernity; easy in her addresses and coquettish in her intentions.[22] Through both their discourse and their practice, the two women are widely differentiated and easily distinguished. Arabella is a haughty beauty, not given to admitting favours and advances, while her cousin seeks the attention of all who would offer it. And yet, each produces a species of modesty perhaps most remarkable for the forms of forwardness it introduces. In this instance, Miss Glanville is horrified by what she takes to be Arabella's insinuation that she employs a notion of 'virtue' in order to practise a more licentious lifestyle:

Severely virtuous, Lady *Bella*! said Miss *Glanville*, reddening with Anger: Pray what do you mean by that? Have you any Reason to imagine, I would grant a favour to a Lover?

Why, if I did, Cousin, said *Arabella*, would it derogate so much from your Glory, think you, to bestow a Favour upon a Lover worthy of your Esteem, and from whom you had received a thousand Marks of a most pure and faithful Passion, and also a great Number of very singular Services?

The disagreement – or perhaps the difference – between the two women is entailed in what they take a 'Favour' to be. Miss Glanville, confused and angry at what she thinks Arabella is insinuating, cries out: 'Heaven knows, I never granted a Kiss without a great deal of Confusion', a confession at which Arabella is 'excessively surprised'.[23] While Miss Glanville accepts kisses and makes private assignations, Arabella is prepared to meet men in their bedchambers, believing it her historic and public duty to do so. Arabella bases her claim to publicity on her sense of the pre-eminence of her beauty, a presence which, in her terms, ought to grant her an 'Empire over all [Glanville's] actions'.[24] However, the peculiar nature of Arabella's command ensures that, while her actions are publicly admired, figured within the heroic discourse which pays homage to the virtue of a beauty, they can only be administered in the strictest privacy. For Arabella will only visit her lovers in their bed-chambers. Miss Glanville's social practice might also be private, but it is the intimacy of an assignation.[25]

Although Arabella's absurdity stems from an inaccurate, or wrong, idea of the public space or behaviour, there is a persistently high valuation of what is being mocked. It is not only, as Laurie Langbauer suggests, that Lennox is more involved with, and appreciative of, romance fiction than she is prepared to concede, but that the image of female visibility and action which the novel represents remains attractive.[26] Arabella's beauty is the key to this initiative. Throughout *The Female Quixote*, beauty is retained as an important, though ambivalent, reference that connects the action of the narrative with discourses which described moral or public actions undertaken by women during the eighteenth century. The moral dimension imagined for the discourse on taste by writers such as Spence and Usher has indicated that, for many mid-century commentators. there was a close connection between the appreciation of beauty and the proprieties of modern femininity. In so saying critics were building upon and extending the already highly gendered language of judgement found in contemporary aesthetic tracts; most notably, those by Burke and Hogarth. What was striking about these expositions of the beautiful was that women were assumed to be both 'lovely' and capable of virtue on the basis of their physical appearance. In a curious way, Arabella's quixoticism accepts this connection only to distort it; as such, her assumption that she is a Beauty is both high-minded and absurd. Arabella believes that her status as a Beauty fits her automatically for the public sphere and, consequently, secures her virtue. In her own mind, the force of her beauty is sufficient to grant her both authority and licence. Lennox's own position is rather more difficult to decipher as the excitement and intrigue of much of the novel must be set against its apparently conservative resolution, wherein all Arabella's adventures are finally ended.[27]

In order to explore this ambiguity further, I want to change the ground slightly and examine the issue in relation to what can be described as the moral, or sexual, politics of physical appearance in the mid-century novel. Analysis of Arabella's conduct, in particular her assumptions about her own beauty, has revealed the dangers inherent in the association of a beautiful countenance with moral authority. As many writers were to realise, to propose such an equation not only granted a tremendous authority to the viewed object, but relied on an inherent legibility in the beautiful body which was often hard to find. Too frequently, the beautiful woman was discovered to be unreadable; the signs making up her face and body found to be too uncertain or too mutable to permit a detailed examination of her character. Tassie Gwilliam's reading of Samuel Richardson's *Pamela* has shown that the complexities and ambiguities raised by bodily illegibility were many and various. Gwilliam's close analysis of the text exposes the degree to which Richardson's writing and subsequent editing sought to stabilise what was an unhelpfully vague, visual language.[28] Other novelists, including Lennox, sought to resolve this problem by producing narratives which proposed an opposition between the dissipated beauty and her more ugly sisters, with a corresponding investment in the plain or ugly face as the sign of true worth and virtue. For the face of an ugly woman represented a physiognomy which, while it could not seize the attention of the male gaze, neither could it awaken a woman's sexuality nor deceive the discerning eye of the moralist. Indeed, in many novels of the period, particular stress was placed upon the appearance of women who did not obviously conform to the standards set by the great beauties of the age.

Henry Fielding is, perhaps, amongst the more prominent novelists who sought to give moral dignity to the ugly or deformed face. In his novel *Amelia* of 1751, for example, Fielding was keen to draw attention to the damaged nose of his heroine as an indicator of her social and moral transparency. To underline this association, Fielding's wayward hero Booth, describes his beloved Amelia in enthusiastic tones, claiming that her damaged nose gave him an indication of her greater worth.[29] In examining descriptions of this kind it has often been appropriate to consider the representation of feminine deformity in the light of a comparison with images of the empowered beauty of aristocratic ladies. Such an approach has succeeded in exploring the underlying class agenda which structures texts such as Fielding's novel.[30] However, a focus on the unbeautiful face and its relation to the meaning of virtue and to the nature of feminine sexuality may also yield worthwhile insights. For it is in the presentation and discussion of the apparently ugly woman, that a distinctly middle-class account of virtue becomes most readily evident. This is because, as in the case of Amelia, the woman in question is not really ugly, rather she is imagined to be attractive in ways which do not rely on dazzling spectacle. Indeed, the kind of male gaze which seeks the immediate excitement of extreme beauty tends to be disavowed by novelists such as Fielding, Lennox and Scott. While it would be possible merely to note this repeated image as a reworking, in rather different terms, of Burke's distinction between lust and love, it is more profitable to read these texts with the intention of exploring how the less conspicuous forms of display found in mid-century novels work to reflect middle-class concerns about the nature of self-display and its relation to character and individual integrity. Read in the light of these connections, it is possible to see that within mid-century discussions of ugliness and beauty there is a subtle, yet profound, attempt to change the terms of the debate about taste and to move the debate yet further towards the concerns of middle-class writers. The remainder of this chapter will be taken up with the exploration of these issues. I begin, though, with a reading of Lennox's novel *Sophia*, a text which seeks quite deliberately to represent its heroine as less than beautiful, yet she remains curiously attractive.

SECRET CHARMS AND PRIVATE ATTRACTIONS: THE VIRTUES OF
LENNOX'S SOPHIA

Sophia, first published in 1762, is a revised version of 'The History of
Harriot and Sophia', which Lennox had initially published in the
Lady's Museum in 1760. The story concerns the fortunes of Sophia
Darnley, second daughter to an impoverished gentleman.[31] Sophia's
social position is vital because the issue of female display becomes
more pressing when the woman in question, as in this case, lacks the
forms of social distinction found in *The Female Quixote*, where
Arabella is a Marquis's daughter, and Miss Glanville the child of a
Baronet. At the beginning of *Sophia*, it is the Darnley family's good
fortune, though it rarely appears as such, to be visited by Sir Charles
Stanley, a wealthy and fashionable young man. Sir Charles, in
common with others of his age and status, 'lives in a constant
dissimulation with one part of his species . . . subduing chastity and
ensnaring innocence'. It is wholly consistent with his character,
therefore, that he should find Sophia's beautiful older sister, Harriot,
the ideal target for his scurrilous intentions. Harriot's situation is
precarious, for while 'beauty soon procured her a great number of
lovers; her poverty made their approaches easy'.[32]

However, Harriot's predicament is not one which Sophia shares,
and not only because she is the younger daughter. For physical
appearance separates the two women more firmly than age or
expectation: as Harriot is beautiful, so Sophia 'wanted in equal
degree those personal attractions, which . . . constituted the whole
of female perfection'. Quite whether this is entirely true becomes an
increasingly pressing issue as the passage proceeds:

> Mere common judges, however, allowed her person to be agreeable; people
> of discernment and taste pronounced her something more. There was
> diffused through the whole person of Sophia a certain secret charm, a
> natural grace which cannot be defined; she was not indeed as beautiful as
> her sister, but she was more attractive . . . Harriot's charms produced at
> the first sight all the effect they were capable of; a second look of Sophia
> was more dangerous than the first, for grace is seldomer found in the face
> than the manners; and, as our manners are formed every moment, a new
> surprise is perpetually creating. A woman can be beautiful but one way, she
> can be graceful a thousand.[33]

What structures the plot in *Sophia* is the increasing ensnarement of
Sir Charles in these 'more dangerous' charms. There is, of course,

many an obstacle between the emergence of desire and the successful realisation of his passion, not least of which is the consideration of class difference and power, of which Sophia is to remain painfully aware.[34] One of the most appealing attributes of the novel is the extent to which it dramatises the class-inflected nature of courtship. It is not only being beautiful, as the sign of the sexual, which makes women vulnerable to the solicitations of men like Sir Charles Stanley, but disparity of fortune.[35]

The narrative or moral problem explored in *Sophia* arises from the difficulty of finding an effective means of representing the heroine so that her attractions can be considered virtuous. The narrative seeks to explore how Sophia might function as a virtuous, yet sexual, subject. How she should appear, or how she ought to behave, is, therefore, crucial; but so, too, is the question of how she should be looked upon by the male characters. The opening pages make it clear that Sophia exists for a particular kind of gaze, and a distinct form of pleasure, which is removed from the 'admiration' courted and received by Harriot. That Sophia's presence may be more insinuating, and hence more dangerous to men, is soon evinced when Sir Charles comes to court Harriot, but finds himself struck with the appearance of Sophia. His visual thrill leaves him awed by her reserve, a 'dignity which derived from innate virtue'. Disconcerted by the earnestness of his gaze, Sophia seeks to divert him by opening a conversation:

Then it was, that without designing it, she displayed her whole power of charming: that flow of wit which was natural to her, the elegant propriety of her language, the delicacy of her sentiments, the animated look which gave them new force, and sent them directly to the heart, and the moving grace of the most harmonious voice in the world, were attractions which, though generally lost on fools, seldom fail of the effect on the heart of a man of sense.[36]

Sophia's talking, which combines her melodious voice and fine manners, delights and entrances Sir Charles. With the tableau of these charms unfolded, 'Sir Charles was wrapt in wonder and delight'. Sophia is greatly embarrassed by the insistence of his gaze, and flees the room on 'pretence of business'.The incident represents an image of seduction through sociability, and further discloses the ambiguities of the term 'conversation' which, in its common eighteenth-century usage, might entail sexual as much as verbal intercourse.

The difference between Sophia and Harriot at this point in the novel makes plain the disjunction between vice and virtue. Patricia Meyer Spacks has observed that 'Many women novelists chose to dramatise the absolute separation of virtue and vice by evoking a pair of sisters, one, good in every respect; the other utterly reprehensible.'[37] This is a narrative technique which Lennox's chapter headings deliberately underline, for example: *Sophia continues to act Romantically, and Harriot like a Woman who knows the World.*[38] Unlike her sister, Sophia is modest and genteel, yet with a refined sense of virtue. Hers is a more delicate constitution and her sense of propriety more rigid. She cannot, and will not, countenance a display of sexual feeling, even to herself, and this is a point which the narrator's moralising enforces: 'A young maid has passed over the first bounds of reservedness, who allows herself to think she in love.'[39] The position represents a recurrent dilemma surrounding female conduct. As Harth notes: 'for women, at least, there was something immoral about marrying for love. The conduct books advised them to learn to love their husbands once married.'[40] The situation was, however, more ambivalent than Harth suggests, for it is not love *per se* that is disavowed, but rather certain forms of desire. Arabella's character in the *Female Quixote* articulated something not entirely dissimilar to Sophia's half-expressed, half-repressed desire: 'Our charming Heroine, ignorant till now of the true State of her Heart, was surpriz'd to find it assaulted at once by all the Passions which attend disappointed Love.'[41] Arabella, though, is preoccupied by the nicety of romantic protocol, and attempts to frame her desire within the ponderous pronouncement that, 'she did not hate him', while Sophia's inability to figure her own longing is the most striking feature of her presentation.[42]

Sophia's conduct could not be more dissimilar to Arabella's, and is structured in a crucial relation to the character of Dolly Lawson, as well as to Harriot's behaviour. Dolly, the simple but virtuous daughter of a rural curate, provides an additional or third term necessary to the ideological labour of the narrative. For much of their time together, Sophia and Dolly engage in conversations on the nature of Dolly's passion for William, a neighbour. Her companion's conversation reminds Sophia of Sir Charles, whom she has grown to love despite his wayward character:

Sophia, from the state of her own mind, was but too much disposed to sympathise with the love sick Dolly: these softening conversations were ill calculated to banish from her remembrance the first object of her innocent affections; and who, with all his faults she still loved.[43]

Although, as Spacks argues, Sophia reprimands Dolly for the ardour with which she speaks of William, the text of her 'Simple Story' provides the ground upon which Sophia can exercise her more appropriate discourse, one which takes the form of a sympathetic call to reason.[44] Dolly's story provides an example of how desire may be regulated rather than banished; and the claims of restraint and passion held in balance.[45] Harriot's language and manner is too extreme for this to occur. Although Harriot is important in providing Sophia with a vocabulary for defining, if not experiencing, the sexual, her role is to make plain what Sophia is not, and not what she is or wants.[46] By contrast, and despite differences of social class, Dolly and Sophia are represented by Lennox as occupying a privileged space through which feminine sensibility is reconciled with virtue. Indeed their romantic conversations create a space, because they are both moral and romantic, in which women can represent their desires, at least to one another.[47]

There is an important added dimension to Dolly's story, however: her desire for William, simple though it is, exists in a context of prohibition and denial. For reasons connected with the unwarranted aspirations of William's wealthy aunt, Mrs Gibbon, the pair are forbidden each other's company. Sophia, having already advised constraint, argues for obedience: ' "I would have you keep your passion subject to your reason, so as to make it not too difficult for you to obey".'[48] Fortunately, Dolly's reason is not obliged to undergo too severe a test, because Sophia is able to persuade Mrs Gibbon that there is a wealth beyond riches.[49] By persuading Mrs Gibbon of the virtue of love, Sophia effectively reconciles desire with chastity, while her appeals to Dolly for self-control, frame female sexuality in a way consistent with virtue. Given this conclusion to Dolly's story, Spack's assertion that the moral purpose of the text is heavily reliant on the narrative of Harriot's transgression and eventual fall appears narrow and overly deterministic as Dolly images a rather different trajectory for female desire.[50] Sophia's own path to happiness is more convoluted, because her wish to retain her chastity and her sense of her class vulnerability, makes her unwilling to accept Sir Charles's addresses. Even when he has reformed, she needs chiding, even commanding to abandon a virtue which is increasingly seen as obstinately heroic. Sophia's commitment to her modest retirement and chaste way of living is not easily overcome. In the final parts of the novel she needs to be persuaded repeatedly by her friend, Mr Herbert, that it is acceptable for her to love Sir Charles. That Sophia's friends are forced to these expedients discloses a tension between strictly maintained virtue and the requirements of courtship, one that is resolved through Lennox's depiction of her heroine's unbeautiful attractiveness and its effect upon characters in the novel.[51]

In order to persuade Sophia that her virtue is not threatened by admitting Sir Charles, Mr Herbert must convince Sophia that he is no longer the rake who seduced her sister. Through her heroine's hesitation, Lennox indicated that Sophia could only love and still be virtuous if Sir Charles has abandoned his libidinous pursuit of female beauty and has begun to appreciate modesty and chastity. Appropriately, much of the novel is taken up with Sir Charles's reformation; indeed, if Sophia learns that she can love without impropriety, then Sir Charles is forced to acknowledge that love is impossible without polite attentions and proper manners. In short, he is required to exhibit a more discerning gaze and not to rush lustfully towards merely beautiful or fashionable women. This he accomplishes; at the end of the novel, Mr Herbert praises Sir Charles for the virtue of his passion for Sophia. To Mr Herbert's questions, Sir Charles replies that:

'You attribute to me a virtue, which in this case, I cannot be said to possess; and had my passion for Sophia been founded only on the charms of her person, I might probably ere now have become a mere fashionable husband; but her virtue and wit supply her with graces ever varied, and ever new. The steadiness of my affection for her', pursued he smiling, 'is but a constant inconstancy which attaches me successively to one or other of those shining qualities of which her charming mind is an inexhaustible source'.[52]

Sir Charles's response signals the scale of his reformation. He is no longer a rakish young man; whereas he once sought the splendours of great beauty, he is now contented with the nice distinctions and pretty plays of Sophia's mobile features. The animation of such facial expressions, as the opening description had made clear, is owing to the pleasing function of good manners, themselves ever changing. Sir Charles seems to have fallen for manners over and above the matter of great beauty. His delight now is in the contemplation of a truly domestic virtue, as when he sees Sophia through a cottage window.[53] The expression of pleasing, undeniably polite manners that at once engage the viewer and yet do so with irreproachable chastity represents the forms of a middle-class morality. So much so, that it must appear that Sophia has acquired the art of being pretty.[54]

Crucially, Sophia has acquired her charming appearance through her strict maintenance of a private identity. In particular, throughout *Sophia* the heroine's unconventional beauty appears more uniquely her own. Unlike Harriot's much admired face, Sophia's charms appear to be specifically located in her particular presence, rather than in the judgement of the dissipated multitude. Sophia's presence, determined by her domestic living and particular virtues, is not caught in that play of glances which seems to exhaust the identity of her sister. Harriot, like Miss Glanville and all other 'town beauties', is obliged to restage herself on each and every public appearance. To change one's face and attire so frequently causes her to relinquish any claim to particular identity, or appearance. It is significant, in this context, that dissipation is taken to be the primary characteristic of a Beauty; a view supported by Walpole's sense of the fate meted out to a 'standard beauty'. This discourse is comparable with Pope's in *An Epistle to a Lady*; Beauties, if not all women, have no characters at all.[55] In its novelistic form, this discourse laid particular stress on the propagation of a unique, and uniquely private identity. However, the ambiguous nature of the opposition between public beauty and private plainness remains. For, there is, as Spacks observes, an 'ambivalence about physical appearance – beauty both does and does not matter, since "graces" matter more', and this reverberates throughout the text of *Sophia*.[56] Significantly, both grace and beauty exist visually, and are appreciated as such by Sir Charles, whose gaze troubles the opposition between the retiring aspect of grace and the forward beauties of Harriot and Miss Glanville.[57] Such a suggestion threatens the pious individuation staged by Sophia's self-characterisation. The admiring glance, whether it seeks virtue or beauty, realigns the person so viewed as an object of public scrutiny – this is what, after all, occurs in Spence's *Crito*. This realignment of social place is particularly unpleasant for Sophia who invests so much of her virtuous self-identification in preventing any public appearance, and yet needs also to be seen in order to be loved. The problem is partially resolved by Lennox by making the heroine's conventional, if ardent, virtue the distinctive attribute of her reserved and domestic character. The issue is more effectively treated, however, by demanding that the act of looking, which can transform the position of a woman, is itself transformed. Sir Charles's admiration of Sophia permits her love precisely because it is a private act which both appreciates and validates her privacy. Connections between virtue and personal appearance, privacy and integrity are also prominent in the work of Sarah Scott. I want now to read her work in order to explore the full significance of the private or unbeautiful heroine in eighteenth-century fiction.

LOVE AND THE UGLY WOMAN: SARAH SCOTT'S 'AGREEABLE UGLINESS'

One of the most striking aspects of Scott's novels is the repeated and at times peculiar emphasis placed upon the status of the ugly woman. In many of her works, faces that are scarred or plain; bodies which are twisted or deformed feature prominently. Certainly physical deformity plays an important part, not only in the life of the heroine of _Agreeable Ugliness_, on which I shall focus in this section, but also in _Millenium Hall_ in which a number of the women have bodies which are variously damaged or deformed. Key moments in other novels, such as _Sir George Ellison_, also place an emphasis on the imagined distinction between the ugly and the beautiful woman. It is, however, in _Agreeable Ugliness_, first published in 1754, and to which Scott added the telling subtitle, _or, the Triumph of the Graces_, that Scott makes her commitment to ugliness most apparent.[58] What a reading of these texts suggests is that, for Scott, ugliness had an almost moral quality as the sign of virtuous femininity. Throughout the novel, which is a loose translation of Pierre-Antoine de la Place's _La Laideur Aimable et les Dangers de la Beauté_, Scott focused precisely on the issue of a woman's physical appearance in relation to her social, as well as, sexual identity.[59] The narrative, told in the first person, details the life of a gentlewoman living in France at the end of the seventeenth century. In many respects, the life of the narrator (who is never named) fulfils the reader's expectations of a sentimental novel of this period. She has her lovers whom her father's prohibitions deny her, she has escapades (unwillingly) at masquerade balls; and, finally, belatedly, she is offered reward in the form of a loving and virtuous marriage to her first admirer. What is distinctive about *Agreeable Ugliness*, however, is that the narrator defines herself, quite clearly and deliberately, as 'ugly'. Furthermore, she makes her lack of visual significance the foundation of her relationship with her father. Scott's own agenda adds weight to the formidable, filial identification made by her narrator. Scott makes ugliness, real or merely imagined, the object in an examination of the nature of female propriety, an inquiry which manipulates ugliness as the exemplary sign of gender difference.

Scott's emphatic faith in the virtue of not being beautiful is made consistently throughout the novel, and key scenes are used to give it dramatic realisation. Initially, the narrator uses her ugliness to support her claims of honesty, stating that, 'when a woman confesses her own ugliness, we may believe her sincere'. The conjunction of being truthful with being ugly is striking, particularly when the duplicity of her mother and sister is considered. Yet the narrator concedes that it is beauty, not honesty, which is most likely to arouse 'public curiosity'. 'A Handsome Woman is', she writes, 'by her Beauty, placed in a position more distinguished, and in a more conspicuous Light in the world than a Dutchess.' In comparison, to be ugly is to be 'reduced to a kind of Non-existence'.[60] It is statements such as the last which have no doubt prompted some critics, such as Elizabeth Bergen Brophy, to conclude that *Agreeable Ugliness* is a straightforward attack on the judgement of women's physical form.[61] However, this lack of visual significance is endorsed by Scott's novel. Ugliness, because it has no pretence to authority, produces a temper at once mild and amiable; and these are virtues 'wherein Beauty is often deficient'. The misfortune of ugliness – that it fails to signify – is then balanced by the fact that it appears ideal for mixed sex gatherings.

In a perceptive essay on Scott's novel, Caroline Gonda has begun to explore the connections between virtue and ugliness that I have described here.[62] However, Gonda's focus is on the father–daughter relations represented by Scott, and not upon ugliness itself. What her essay lacks, therefore, is a sense of how the terms ugliness and monstrosity coincide with an increasingly forceful middle-class account of feminine subjectivity and individual integrity. Neither does Gonda attribute any particular meaning to ugliness beyond its opposition to the sexuality condemned by conduct books. By omitting a discussion of this aspect of the text, Gonda misses the problems and ambiguities inherent in Scott's separation of private ugliness from public beauty. Indeed, the two terms become increasingly unstable as the plot unfolds. Initially describing herself as ugly, or 'not formed' for marriage, the narrator chronicles a life in which that identity is under constant threat of renegociation. Her entrance into fashionable society, and most tellingly her depiction by a portrait-painter, disturbs her sense of herself by making her the object (and the subject) of a sexualising as well as socialising gaze. The portrait questions the identity which she, under her father's watchful eye, has crafted for herself as an unobtrusive ugly woman. The repositioning of the narrator as considerably less than ugly is important because of the way it alters her place in society and her self-identity. The narrator, having claimed a plainness which enables a proper converse between the sexes, emerges as a more disruptive presence through her love for a young Count. As the plot evolves, therefore, the narrator becomes engaged in a series of rearguard actions designed to preserve and restate her seclusion and ugliness. She reiterates this point because it marks a sense of herself which is placed under threat by the men in the novel who, because they interact with her socially and visually, reconstitute her position in society. They look at her, either from attraction or admiration, and in so doing begin to give the impression that she is less than entirely ugly, propelling her towards the identity she seeks to resist: that of a beautiful woman. Crucially, this drama is played out through a moral discourse which locates its terms of reference in the opposition between obedience and desire, beauty and deformity. With these concerns in mind, it is possible to read Scott's novel as a highly problematic representation of both women and morality.

THE PHYSIOGNOMY OF OBEDIENCE

Agreeable Ugliness opens with the marriage of the narrator's parents, Monsieur and Madame de Villiers. Monsieur is an earnest, worthy man, who lives in sober and virtuous retirement within the confines of his modest income. Conversely, his chosen mate is a fickle and ambitious woman, but, and this is decisive, she is beautiful; a quality which causes the otherwise prudent de Villiers first to court and then to marry her.[63] In the scenes which follow, her beauty gives her power, as it grants her, rather than her husband, governance in the family. Accordingly, the hierarchy of the family is inverted, and beauty holds sway over and against paternal authority. The undesirability of this situation is most apparent when their first daughter is born. The child, known throughout the novel as the 'Fair *Villiers*', is considered a great beauty, an appearance which immediately claims her mother's love. Finding a malleable companion in her beautiful daughter, Madame de Villiers indulges her every whim, spoiling both herself and her daughter in the process. In time the Fair Villiers becomes, like her mother, vain, shallow and flirtatious.[64] In the period following the birth of the Fair Villiers, her mother's caprices induce a pervasive melancholy in the de Villiers's house. It is at this time that the narrator is conceived:

I suppose it was in some Moment of Vexation, when Mr. *de Villiers*'s Mind was Prey to gloomy Disquiet, that he took it into his Head to beget me. I confess I never had the Air of a Child of Love, for tho' the Repetition is mortifying, I must once more own that a Year after the Birth of my elder Sister, I entered the World in native Ugliness.[65]

That the loveless nature of the de Villiers's marriage produces an apparently disfigured child is not perhaps unique, many eighteenth-century novels – *Joseph Andrews* is a good example – recount how the events of conception determined the features and subsequent lives of their protagonists.[66] While the ante-natal disfigurement is important, what is most striking is that the narrator's face appears to be a property peculiar to her. It is indeed 'native' to her: most obviously it is the face with which she was born. Yet, it is also the sign of the place in which she resides, her father's house. So while her face is distinctly her face, it is connected closely to the cast of her father's mind, and to his home. To emphasise this fact the narrator later describes herself as an 'ugly Resemblance' of her father. The reader is only ever given the narrator's word for this state of affairs. Literary critics are wont to pause over such a problem (and certainly it cannot easily be dismissed), however, it is important to note the enormous stress which is laid throughout the novel on the ideal of ugliness. Even if this commitment were offered only as the narrator's self-persuasion, it would remain instructive in that it seeks to connect virtue, not with beauty, but with a much less assuming appearance. That the narrator further suggests her apparent plainness is the result of a sympathy with her father's gloom, is therefore, striking.

The strength of this moral investment in physiognomy is emphasised when the narrator describes the physical differences between herself and her sister. Throughout the passage the narrator's physical appearance is considerably more elusive than her account of her 'ugly' resemblance to her father suggests; and, from the description she gives of herself, her appearance becomes more equivocal:

My Sister was fair, I was very brown. She was a Picture of my Mother with every Beauty heightened, I an ugly Resemblance of my Father. She had the Superiority in Beauty, I had the Advantage over her in Shape. Her Eyes were of a dark blue, large, and finely formed, but without Fire or Expression, in short they were fine Eyes without Meaning; mine were black, a little too much sunk, tolerably large of very uncommon Vivacity, and seemed to indicate more Sense than perhaps I really had.

The narrator continues in much the same vein throughout the passage, noting that, while 'my Sister's Nose was well-shaped, but rather long; mine was the best feature in my Face'. The effect is to suggest a curious balance, implying that although 'my Sister's skin was as white as possible, it was neither so smooth or as soft as mine'. Concluding the description of herself and her sister, the narrator adds the significant remark that she has 'in drawing my Sister's picture, and my own, without design, given a sketch of the life I lived at de Villiers'.[67] The separation is clear and the terrain familiar; two sisters, one lasciviously beautiful, the other chastely virtuous. The issue though is more complex than this conventional binary allows. The narrator's face is, in a distinctive fashion, doubly inscribed, signed, as it were, in two ways: first by her own presence, her unique and 'native Ugliness', and secondly because that ugliness is in the form of a 'Resemblance' to her father. The place of the narrator is, as such, both verifiably her own and policed by her father's presence.

The ambiguities such an identification may entail are, however, present throughout the comparison the narrator makes between herself and the Fair Villiers. Indeed, the obvious moral separation undertaken in this passage is complicated by the working of resemblance and of similarity: the Fair Villiers is 'the picture of my Mother'; while the narrator is 'an ugly Resemblance of my Father'. In terms of the difference from her sister, the narrator has a countenance and a character distinctly her own; yet the narrative seeks to keep that distinction in abeyance, suggesting that it exists solely as an obedient mimic of Monsieur de Villiers. Furthermore, as a description of an ugly woman, this one is rather flattering, particularly as she is being compared to her supposedly beautiful sister. The manner of the description is responsible for this effect. By isolating the features of her sister's face, she effectively makes them ugly. The passage effectively reverses the convention whereby a beautiful woman is praised by isolating each of her features in turn. The Fair Villiers's face, once broken down to its component parts of eyes, skin, nose and teeth lacks access to any other form of coherence. Her features, though placid and well-proportioned, are not animated by any higher excellence, for the Fair Villiers possesses neither a fine understanding nor her sister's rectitude. Beautiful though she is, the Fair Villiers is an implicitly shallow creature. Her charms are lifeless and unthinking, while the narrator is, by contrast, lively and intelligent.

Scott's manipulation of convention in this passage raises questions about how the character of a virtuous woman can be realised in a visual language. As Diedre Lynch has argued, the problem of defining and representing character, as opposed to mere caricature, was one of the most troubling in eighteenth-century art.[68] In this instance, Scott is seeking to realise character through a representation of facial complexity. In part this move inverts traditional modes of flattery to produce a more varied countenance than that attributed to the narrator's sister, whose attractions collapse when examined singly. As my reading of Lennox's *Sophia* has indicated, the face of a virtuous woman was imagined to require careful decoding. More forcefully, the face had to be of a kind which permitted a prolonged and discriminating gaze. Scott's description of her heroine's face in *Agreeable Ugliness* consciously demands such patient discernment as a means of both defining her identity and of purifying the act of looking. Significantly, the precise and discriminatory descriptions found in the work of Scott can also be discovered in other eighteenth-century texts. A passage from early in Oliver Goldsmith's *The Vicar of Wakefield* illustrates this point clearly:

Olivia, now about eighteen, had that luxuriancy of beauty with which painters generally draw Hebe; open, sprightly, and commanding. Sophia's features were not so striking at first; but often did more certain execution; for they were soft, modest, and alluring. The one vanquished by a single blow, the other by effort successfully repeated.[69]

The phrase 'luxuriancy of beauty' gives the key in this passage, indicating that Olivia's beauty is such that it exceeds the vicar's stilted proprieties. It is this extravagance that Scott's narrator is trying to avoid. By contrast, the polite face (the agreeable face) must represent something rather different if it is to convey character and virtue without becoming overbearing.

The importance of this kind of representation to middle-class accounts of identity and morality can be further evidenced by a consideration of Hogarth's depiction of the detailed lines which compose the face and dress of virtuous, but sensuous women.[70] Indeed, Hogarth's description of a beautiful face is uncannily like that produced by the novels under discussion here. Hogarth writes that: 'the face indeed will bear a constant view, yet always entertain and keep our curiosity awake ... because the vast variety of changing circumstances keeps the eye and the mind in constant play, in following the numberless turns of expression it is capable of'. In the present context, Hogarth's question – 'How soon does a face that wants expression, grow insipid, though it be ever so Pretty?' – has a clear significance.[71] Intriguingly, Hogarth's readable face offers both pleasure and definition, chastity and a more ambiguous pleasingness, in ways which are coincident with key passages in Fielding's *Amelia* and Lennox's *Sophia*. Although Hogarth denied being a 'physiognamist', he is clearly committed to the physiognomic assumption that the face represents character in a legible form. However, Hogarth is also committed to an aesthetic in which variety indicates not merely potential pleasure, but also provides the grounds for work and the exercise of judgement. It is a position in which the intricacy and individuality displayed by Scott's narrator would have had a high value.[72]

With this ideal very much in view, the narrator seeks, when describing herself and her sister, to emphasise her own distinction and separateness without appearing to endorse the showy distinction which characterises her sister. In part, this explains the repeated association with her father; however, the father's presence not only lends authority, but also grants readability. Accordingly, in contrast with her sister, the narrator's face appears easily deciphered by those who might take the trouble. The contrasting education received by the sisters makes for a similarly clear separation between them; while the Fair Villiers is apprenticed in the public arts of female allure, the narrator learns from her father the private values of chastity and modesty. It is an education for which she appears grateful: 'I esteemed it a Consolation even for the harsh Treatment I received from Madame *de Villiers*, who never gave me any other Name than the *Shocking Monster*.' The issue of consolation is an important one and will re-emerge throughout the novel; indeed Monsieur de Villiers identifies the narrator as a consolation for her mother's indifference towards him. De Villiers is, moreover, a shrewd manipulator when it comes to the management of his youngest daughter. Unwilling to let her fall into the same errors as her mother and sister, he insists upon the facts of her plainness and the necessity of her obedience.

He could not indeed conceal from me the Misfortune of having been so ill-treated by Nature, but far from chusing to make it the Subject of Vexation, he talked to me of the Charms I wanted, only to excite in me a desire of acquiring such, as were more valuable and lasting: These were Advantages he was well qualified to give me; and while Madame *de Villiers* had no other Employment than the pursuit of Pleasure, he made it both his Pleasure, and his Duty, to instruct me in all the useful knowledge which he possessed.[73]

By returning to the fact of her absent beauty, her father hopes to instil in her the impossibility of transgression and to suggest that even if she sought to act improperly, she lacks the wherewithal to do so. The place of her ugliness is central to the morality visited upon her by her father's calculated education. It is a remonstration in the fullest sense of the word, keeping her always in the sphere of obedient ugliness. De Villiers's advice endorses a restricted sense of the proper place of women, dictating the necessity of their domesticity, and his resistance to their display.

Significantly, the monstrosity of the narrator is the only thing on which Monsieur and Madame de Villiers can agree; it is the name given to her by her mother, and an act of dismissal explicitly supported by her father's teaching. Secured by habit and a shared nomenclature, the notion of her ugliness is crucial to the way in which the narrator forms her self-image, as a distinctive non-presence. It is an identity that is only partially individuated, becoming almost a non-identity, a mere resemblance. The terms through which her identity is discovered – outside of the doubly marked face – will emerge more fully as my account proceeds. However, it is possible to give a simple example from the opening passages of the novel, when the narrator writes about being 'reduced to a kind of non-existence'. In this passage she is recording a contemporary disregard for women who do not function visually. A sense of this is articulated by Madame de Villiers, who, when she looks upon her languishing daughter, reflects that: 'The Girl is in a

Manner dead already; alas! death will be a Blessing to her, what could that Thing do in the World!'[74] Failing to signify in the World – that is to say, in the social and public world of assemblies and marriages – is, by Madame de Villiers's account, to face extinction, so that bodily death comes to lack any meaning. Living privately on this version of things, is not living at all. Madame de Villiers's view, however, does not go unquestioned. Scott's narrator is not keen to make a 'Noise' in the great world, which on the evidence of her mother's conduct, she knows to be ruinously dissipated. The social world – the realm of beauty and the visual – is rejected in favour of companionable obscurity, the native place of the ugly. This is the moral agenda of the novel: the opposition between ugly seclusion and publicly gazed upon beauty.

Furthermore, while exciting 'public curiosity' may be enviable, it is by no means virtuous. This is something to which the sub-plot concerning Madame de Villiers and her eldest daughter powerfully attests. On her arrival in Paris, mid-way through the novel, Madame de Villiers readily enters into a fashionably dissipated life; Madame it is noted, still enjoys a good romp, despite her advancing age. More pertinently, she has not given up the desire for 'Admiration'. Her presence at Parisian assemblies, together with the Fair Villiers, is sufficient to draw 'the Eyes of all present'. Appalled at such indecorous conduct, the narrator is easily prevailed upon to forego any further public appearance with her mother and sister.[75] The mother's folly is less easily prevented and, heedless of all advice, she continues to cavort across the ballrooms of the capital. Haughtily indifferent to the advice and command of husband and friends, she spurns every one of real value and involves herself in a series of scandals, which culminate in the Fair Villiers being brought before a Justice: arraigned, in effect, before the bar of middle-class morality. That she is accused of being a common and infected prostitute highlights the confusion that their appearance, combined with their conduct, generates.[76] In this context beauty becomes a moral as well as physical property in a narrative concerned with sexual proprieties, as well as with class instability.[77] The narrative indicates that the two women are guilty of not knowing their proper place in society, and that they have assumed that a magnificence of appearance translates into a magnificence of social place. They have further presumed that the command and social pre-eminence granted to them by their appearance makes them exempt – as royalty might be exempt –

from social obligations and polite decency. But they are mistaken because that connection between beauty and social elevation is rejected and devalued by the emerging culture of the commercial middle class which regarded obedience and chastity as more valuable qualities. The novel clearly condemns the dangers of such indulgence, and rejects the notion that beauty is connected to a dignified place in society.

The connections these passages establish between seclusion, paternal authority and ugliness are not uncommon within Scott's work. In the *History of Sir George Ellison*, the sequel to *Millenium Hall*, the youngest Miss Tunstall is congratulated, albeit cruelly, on the loss of her beauty to the ravages of smallpox. The disease, by obliterating the pliancy and vivacity of her character, has, according to Sir George, kept her virtue by excluding her from the public diversions into which pretty women are naturally drawn.[78] Like the narrator of *Agreeable Ugliness*, Miss Tunstall acquires virtue and understanding as a result of her loss; finally, however, she finds a suitor, who is not only rich, but sensible enough to find her ugliness 'agreeable'.[79] In these terms the striking aspect of Scott's work is the degree to which she disrupts the conventional correspondence – advanced by, for example, Spence – between femininity, beauty, and virtue. In both *Agreeable Ugliness* and *Sir George Ellison* beauty is made into the disruptive term transforming young women into coquettish and daring schemers. In terms of an emerging discourse on female sexuality, what seems to be at issue is the degree to which women, and particularly unmarried daughters, should have identities constructed beyond the confines of the paternal home.[80] In the case of *Agreeable Ugliness*, any movement beyond the domestic sphere of the de Villiers's paternal and private authority can therefore only be undertaken with a great deal of anxiety.

A PICTURE WHICH COULD NOT BE DRAWN FOR A MONSTER

Perhaps the moment when this slippage between public and private identity is most apparent is the scene in which a portrait-painter is commissioned to paint the narrator. Occurring half-way through the novel, it is an event constructed around the competing claims of feminine modesty and the need for self-display. The narrator's appraisal of events is indicative of this competition:

I do not know whether the relating of these trifling Circumstances about my Picture, will not lead my Readers to accuse me of some Self-conceit; but they will hereafter be sensible that it was necessary they should be acquainted with Part of them. I therefore enter a Caveat against every Jest that People may be inclined to make upon me, and I continue to tell the Truth, in frankly confessing, that I was very pleased to find that a Picture, which could not be drawn for a *Monster* was acknowledged by my Friends to resemble me.[81]

There is in this short passage a complex working of what it is to be both private and feminine. The stakes are raised because of the way these ideas seem to pose, quite explicitly, a question of truthfulness. The problem arises because the narrator tries to maintain a clear distinction between public and private codes when, in the context presented by the novel, no such separation can be achieved. The 'trifling Circumstances' of the painting's production are, as the phrase suggests, a relatively intimate affair, comprising a private contract and an arrangement to sit at a friend's house. However, the demands of the novel require their publication. In a sense, the narrator is caught in a trap of her own making: the publicising of events is 'necessary', otherwise the reader will lose the sense of what is being related, yet it requires a 'Caveat' and a further declaration of truth in order to make it properly acceptable. And here lies the rub: for by opening the events to a wider audience the narrator is exposed to the charges of imprudence and vanity, and accordingly only a confession will resolve the problem. By declaring her pleasure, the narrator hopes to turn the unrealised distinction of public and private to her advantage. Because she acknowledges her private pleasure at the portrait – making it the subject of a public declaration – she dismisses the suggestion that she harbours such gratification, and the desires from which they spring, in secret. She is, therefore, open and honest, and hence virtuous. Furthermore, the narrator has been careful to place the sensation of her pleasure, and the reader's awareness of it, at one remove from any immediate gratification arising from her own physical appearance. It is only because the resemblance between portrait and sitter is 'acknowledged by my Friends' that the narrator is satisfied. The rhetorical function of these friends is to mediate between that which is overtly public and the narrator's more immediate sphere. By making the recognition of the semblance, and the pleasure it gives, the act of a third party, the process of making it public has been reduced in danger, if not in significance.

The problems of portrayal remain, especially as the security of a 'resemblance' is undermined by the intrusion of individuality and desire. As Marcia Pointon has argued, having one's portrait painted was a serious business, one which necessarily involved the formation of an identity on the canvas, and its subsequent re-presentation. Pointon further suggests that it is through the constructed image of the portrait that women entered the world. Pointon situates portraits of women in a further context, that of marital property and exchange between fathers and husbands.[82] The circumstances depicted by Scott operate within a comparable social and discursive environment, and they raise similar kinds of problems for the woman portrayed. In this context, it might be profitable to keep in mind William Hazlitt's enthusiastic appraisal of the pleasures of portrayal:

The fact is, that having one's picture painted is like the *creation of another self*, and that is an idea, of the repetition or reduplication of which no man has ever tired, to the thousandth reflection.[83]

Hazlitt genders his account throughout; the subject of this passage neither aspires to, nor deserves, universality. He makes it clear that while men can experience representation as pleasure, women must endure the uncertainty of exposure. The production of 'another self' for women is a more anxious moment, marking an entrance in to a complex play of glances which construct the sitter as a sexual subject. Throughout Scott's novel it is possible to see these problems as those which the narrator is attempting to avoid with her caveats and confessions.

Given the tension between the narrator's desire for transparent representation and the conventions of portraiture, it is telling that the painter is only commissioned after he, like the narrator's first husband, Dorigny, has been captivated by the sweetness of the narrator's disposition, and agreed to paint her as she really appears. Within the terms of the novel's ideological parameters, he is set a difficult task, as he must blend the claims of modest ugliness with those of painterly portrayal. It is striking, therefore, that his promise to the narrator is to make her, or, at least, to represent her as, the 'handsomest woman in *Paris*'. He does not stop there, however, as he asserts that 'this Lady, has one of those countenances – of which I would be happy to draw an exact Likeness'. The perhaps unlikely combination of verisimilitude and pleasingness is seized upon with some enthusiasm by Dorigny, who declares a wish to know whether the painter's 'Eyes are as good as mine'.[84] The painting once begun is rapidly completed, and Dorigny 'charmed' with the result. His pleasure, and those of other close friends, is such that they order a number of copies. It is during this private act of purchase and praise that de St Furcy, the narrator's former lover, enters the room. It is a telling moment:

We had just settled this Point when the young Count *de St Furcy* came to visit the Countess; in vain I endeavoured not to see him, [but] the Viscountess and my Husband obliged me to stay. The Count turned pale at the Sight of me, I red at the Sight of him, but after the first Compliments were over, Mr. *Dorigny* would have Monsieur *de St Furcy* consulted about my Picture, which put me quite out of countenance. The Count thought it exactly like.[85]

The encounter is traumatic because it represents a new and unlooked for level of exposure; that her lover is allowed to comment on the new portrait only underlines the anguish. For it is not only the return of the Count, unexpected though it is, that is the cause of the narrator's distress; rather, it is the precise moment at which he has walked in that is vital. It is a moment of her utmost vulnerability and exposure. Hung up as a portrait she exists for another, for de St Furcy: for a man who is not her father, and who has no interest in her resembling him. So displayed, she solicits, even if unwillingly, the gaze which will represent her as a sexual subject. She experiences the moment as one of radical displacement (she is 'out of countenance', not of her own face); most worryingly, she is no longer an 'ugly Resemblance' of her father – but looking like herself, or rather looking 'like' she does to de St Furcy.

What really seems to be at issue is the portrait, which is 'acknowledged by my friends to resemble me' and yet 'cannot be taken for a *Monster*', represents her not as an obedient daughter but as an attractive young woman. As such the image represents her, if not as a beauty, then certainly as a woman who attracts the attention of men. This is new territory for the narrator, for it takes her away from her 'native Ugliness' which characterised her youthful education. Suddenly, she is both desired and displayed, and not through her own devices, or desires, but through a painting. St Furcy's sight of the portrait disconcerts the narrator because it threatens to transform her into the kind of public beauty her father has taught her to avoid. Throughout the novel, the narrator is at pains to maintain her status as a *'Shocking Monster'*. This is her 'native' quality, that which makes her different from her mother and sister physically and morally, and which marks the location of her sincerity: in her person, and at home. The painting questions that intimate connection. Commenting on the image in more detail, she reflects:

Tho' one is not the best Judge of one's own Picture, I could not mistake mine. I saw in it some Beauties which I did not suspect in myself, and whose momentary Appearance in my Countenance there must have been great Art in seizing when I was gay and happy; and in short, when without knowing why or how, it endeavoured to render itself agreeable. This was what the Painter had so well expressed, that agreeing to the Resemblance the picture bore to me, I thought myself obliged to accuse him of having greatly flattered me.[86]

Although the portrait resembles her, the narrator cannot, or will not, recognise it as a representation of herself. Her description of the painting is inlaid with what is either an attempt to evade the implications of the portrait or an inability to comprehend how such a production might represent herself. What the canvas depicts is therefore said to be something unsuspected, whose fleeting appearance is testimony to 'great Art' – in the sense of artifice – rather than to any great perspicuity on the painter's part.

To agree that the portrait represents, or, worse still, resembles, her would be to concede that she is pleasing; and therefore more like her mother than her father. This is the dilemma which she faces. It is an ambiguity which is underscored by the syntax of the passage, as the second 'it' is uncertain in its reference and could refer either to her face or to the portrait. What is most disturbing, however, is the deep sense of alienation the passage instils, the narrator appears wholly divorced from herself referring to her face, painted or physical, merely as an 'it'. It is that 'it' which, in the narrator's testimony, is assumed to have endeavoured to become agreeable and not herself. The narrator cannot deny, however, the force of the resemblance, and this leaves her to charge the portraitist with flattery. What the narrator seems most fully distanced from is the desire to be desired, the wish to be sought after. Or rather she wants to love, or to be loved, but cannot, or will not, find a place in which that wish can be fulfilled. She is denied it on several points, and on numerous occasions. There have always been her father's instructions, which are combined with her own deep sense that his teachings are correct. In his terms, to be desired is not to be esteemed.

Significantly, the new portrait embodies a form of display which entails becoming available, not only to a desiring male gaze, but a gaze at oneself; it is to consider oneself as sexual. The portrait-scene indicates that display acts as a moment of sexual awakening, one that is experienced as a process of being split or divided. Indeed, throughout *Agreeable Ugliness*, passion is represented as a painful disembodiment or multiplication.[87] In these terms, de St Furcy's presence serves as a warning of the dangers of self-display. In the context of Scott's novel it is self-display, not ugliness, that is monstrous. The portrait-scene is critical because it denies the identity which has been so carefully crafted earlier in the novel. However, it is equally clear that there would not be much point to such a character if she were never to be seen. If Scott's vision of virtuous domesticity is to be effective then its non-presence, its invisibility, must be displayed. It is only at the moment of her exhibition that the narrator's prior (and perhaps ongoing) innocence can be realised. This is the catch which Scott, via her narrator's circumlocution, is trying to negotiate. Indeed, what the twists and turns of Scott's narrative illustrate is not the folly and self-deceit of the narrator, but an anxious attempt to define the social position of a virtuous woman which at once accepts the need for her retirement, and yet needs to display that very disguise. It was by forcing her narrator to adopt this apparently contradictory position, that Scott hoped, at least in part to refashion the discourses on beauty and femininity.[88]

NO OIL PAINTING: THE CHARMS OF AGREEABLE UGLINESS

In order to understand the full significance of the portrait scene in *Agreeable Ugliness* it is necessary to consider the disjunction between the 'native ugliness' which the narrator believes (and wishes us to believe) she possesses and the strangely attractive 'agreeable ugliness' which determines the conduct of the novel. The distinction is crucial; for the notion of agreeable ugliness is oxymoronic, and, as such, would appear to suggest that the narrator is not, perhaps, as ugly as she claims. This is not merely a case of fraudulence, but something more particular. Nowhere in the novel is the fact that the narrator is plain, ugly or monstrous distinctly refuted (though we might wonder how the narrative slides so easily between what are properly separate conceptions). Certainly, her father does not deny that she is ugly, indeed, like her mother, he is keen to remind her of the fact. He tells her constantly that she is not beautiful, yet, like many of the other characters in the novel, seeks also to reassure her that she may yet prove agreeable. What is being sought here is a description of a woman which accords her a place in a refined society while not attributing to her an undue importance. The concept of agreeable ugliness offered by Scott's text is a means of holding that precarious balance. In a culture in which an increasing stress was placed upon the conduct of polite sociability, 'native ugliness', with its associations of isolation and seclusion, could have little value. Agreeable ugliness by contrast, could connote a modest, yet pleasing, disposition which offered refinement without luxuriance.

Within what is an otherwise fairly conventional narrative, the attempted reconciliation between physical appearance and moral security attempted by Scott's fiction is a bold initiative. In a gesture which rewrites both the discourse on taste and the assumptions of the conduct books, Scott represents feminine ugliness as a more attractive quality than beauty throughout *Agreeable Ugliness*. Furthermore, like Lennox in *Sophia*, she also makes the capacity to see what is agreeable about ugliness an ability shared by only the virtuous men of the novel. The tension generated by the novel stems therefore from the need to reconcile these imperatives with a sentimental narrative which has a loving marriage as its desired conclusion. This division of intentions ensures that the narrator is required to restate the circumstances of her ugliness, while also describing how she appeals to men; as a result she appears to be locked into an ongoing battle to keep her ugliness as the source of her identity. Unlike Fielding's Amelia, Scott's narrator has not lost beauty, as it was never hers; rather she fears its acquisition. She becomes beautiful at several points during the novel: while in residence at the de Beaumont's castle, through her subsequent singing, and by being painted.[89] Each instance turns on a level of exposure, of being made public. So, it becomes clear that to become visible is to accept, or to display, beauty. Only that which is properly retired, and hence private, can avoid the imputation and scandal associated with beauty. To be agreeably ugly, therefore, is to refuse the adult, and adulterating, leap into public life, and to remain both unlooked for and unseen. However, she must also be seen in order that de St Furcy can first discover and later desire her. As such she is both displayed and hidden by the events of the novel, indeed her agreeable ugliness relies on precisely the attraction of the being seen to be hidden.

The display of the individual who declines exhibition is something of a trope in Scott's writing. In many respects, Sir George Ellison's first visit to the society of ladies in *Millenium Hall* typifies this recurring double movement. Early in Ellison's stay, both he and the foppish Lamont are taken round the park and gardens of the house. In the course of their tour, they pass an enclosure which 'bore some resemblance to one of Lord Lamore's, where he kept lions, tigers, leopards and such foreign animals'.[90] The two men are intrigued; however, the ladies protest that the kinds of cruel exhibition Lamont wishes to enjoy are not practised on their land, rather the reverse. The 'inclosure' is indeed for 'monsters', but for dwarfs and giants of the human variety. The purpose of the enclosure, though, is to shield the 'Monsters' from display, to remove them from the cruel gazes to which they had, hitherto, been exposed. However, Sir George's narration serves to make the lack of exhibition exemplary. His zeal to portray the ladies' virtue ensures that he must expand upon the appropriateness of their conduct; in effect, he displays what is hidden. Moreover, the shrouded 'inclosure' first attracted Lamont's gaze because it appeared to be constructed for display, the people it contains also retain the name 'monsters' designating them as those individuals destined for display.[91]

Sir George's narrative of the monsters' enclosure is not the only instance of concealed exhibition in *Millenium Hall*. The histories of the women who make up the society evidence similar rhetorical habits. Miss Trentham's story, for example, once again suggests that a woman's beauty disrupts her domestic arrangements, in this case by making it impossible to live with her childhood friend Mr Alworth. Her charms made him desire her, and confused her own sense of her place and her virtue. Her sociable intentions are consequently destroyed by the fact of her own appearance.[92] Confused and dissipated Miss Trentham catches smallpox:

When she came to her senses, she at first seemed mortified to think Mr. Alworth had seen her in that disfigured condition; but on reflection told me she rejoiced in it, as she thought it must totally extinguish his passion; and her greatest solicitude was for his happiness . . . When she recovered, she perceived that the small pox had entirely destroyed her beauty. She acknowledged she was not insensible to this mortification; and to avoid the observation of the envious or even of the idly curious she retired, as soon as she was able to travel.[93]

Like the narrator of *Agreeable Ugliness*, Miss Trentham finds ugliness consoling: 'she became perfectly contended with the alteration this cruel distemper had made in her . . . and she regained the quiet happiness of which flutter and dissipation had deprived her'. The purpose here is two-fold: to display to Sir George and, by extension, to the reader, the femininity of Miss Trentham, and to call attention to the fact that Miss Trentham does not display herself. Furthermore, as an ugly woman, Miss Trentham may retire into Millenium Hall, a community of similarly persecuted and virtuous women. Although Millennium Hall is remarkable, not merely for its idyllic setting, but also for the spectacular wealth and the peculiar ugliness of its domestic staff, it also images a scene were women's worth and wealth can operate, even conspicuously so, without address to the necessity of display.[94] And yet, the zeal of the women, and the prospect of their virtuous persons, form an alluring spectacle, precisely because they appear to resist the desire to the seen. The women's virtue exists, therefore, not because they abolish display, rather that they invert it. Virtuous seclusion appears, therefore, only to the extent that it can be meaningfully displayed; a total disguise can have no rhetorical impact.[95]

That such modest and yet manifest virtue should be seen by the otherwise foppish Lamont is crucial to the novel's purpose as a reforming text. As James Cruse suggests, part of Scott's aim when writing *Millenium Hall* was that the text should improve men by encouraging them to adopt more enlightened ideas towards virtuous and educated women.[96] In each of the novels I have been describing, therefore, a distinctly middle-class, cultural politics can be seen to emerge; attitudes which, in common with the discourse of polite taste, concentrate on the physical and social circumstances of middle-class women who aspire to virtue. However, this is also an account of taste and appearance which is consciously feminised, resisting many of the assumptions found in texts, such as those by Burke and Spence. Scott and Lennox use their fictions to negotiate with a complicated array of discourses which associated female beauty with dangerously unlicensed display. What a reading of Scott's fiction reveals is that by mid-century the best way to signal a woman's moral integrity was to describe her as ugly, plain or at least unbeautiful. Indeed, what the moral discourse found in Scott's writing suggests, and *Agreeable Ugliness* is the foremost example of this investment, is that there is a violent disjunction between a woman's polite sociability (secured by ugliness) and the imagined deviance of a public life. The most obvious consequence of this investment is that the public sphere – the world of vision and beauty – is rarely represented as a virtuous space for women. It is the purpose of the next, and final, chapter to re-examine the gendering of publicity and display and to explore how the ideal of feminine modesty came to have a determining influence in the definition of taste and culture at the end of the eighteenth century.

CHAPTER FIVE

'The Accomplishment of Your Long and Ardent Wishes': beauty, taste and the feminisation of culture

It has been the argument of this book that during the course of the eighteenth century the question of taste achieved a new and peculiar prominence within the polite culture of the newly wealthy middle classes. Indeed the period might justifiably be characterised as one in which a profound change occurred in both the mode and manner of critical judgement. The eighteenth century was, after all, the period which saw the publication of William Hogarth's valedictory *Analysis of Beauty* and Edmund Burke's more insinuating *Enquiry*. However, neither the ingenuity of Hogarth nor the more detailed arguments of Burke's work can give anything but the briefest indication of what was a large and diverse area of debate, one in which the participants sought tirelessly to redefine what was good, beautiful or merely proper. The foregoing discussion has explored how British accounts of taste and beauty, beginning with Addison's 'Essay on the Pleasures of the Imagination', endeavoured not only to accommodate the thrill of private pleasure but also to adapt themselves to the needs of a society which was no longer defined by the public pronouncements of male aristocrats, such as the Earl of Shaftesbury. Notwithstanding the persistence of civic-humanist ideals, debates about the significance of beauty gained a currency beyond the narrow confines of aristocratic privilege. As the century progressed, more people wished to be able to explain and to defend their preferences in art and culture and to be able to claim social distinction. The discourse on taste provided the most readily available means through which those aspirations could be voiced. As recent essays by John Brewer, David Solkin and others have shown, the motivation for this frenzy of reading, writing and rushing into print lay in the changing social and cultural make-up of British society. In this context, it is not unreasonable to argue that the upheaval in social relations occasioned by the expanding commercial economy filtered into a corresponding, though disproportionately sensitive, fluidity of cultural relations.[1]

While the claims of Brewer and other historians have been important to the development of the argument advanced in this book, I have also been keen to investigate how the languages which defined debates about taste were redeployed, even redefined, within discourses about conduct and sociability. The last two chapters have explored these connections with specific reference to the representation of women and sought to examine the concept of beauty in terms of debates about taste, public visibility and female virtue. This chapter seeks to return to the relationship between those issues and the more philosophic inquiry into the nature of beauty represented by texts such as Burke's *Enquiry* or Lord Kames's *Elements of Criticism*. Importantly, it is the affinity between the practices of tasteful discrimination and the gender politics of the novels and painting which make the issue of beauty an object of such pressing critical concern. By focusing on how debates about taste represented or made apparent concerns about gender roles and identities, I hope to be able to give some indication of how the debate about beauty raised questions about pleasure, luxury and virtue and how an address to femininity both made apparent and, to a degree, resolved the anxieties of middle-class culture. I can begin this inquiry by returning briefly to the career of Joshua Reynolds. Despite his pre-eminence as the foremost civic art theorist in the late century, Reynolds appears to both accept and deny the possibilities of Britain's newly wealthy culture. Significantly, Reynolds bolstered his otherwise cautious stance by a firm commitment to an account of masculinity with which he sought to resist the effeminising force of fashion and commerce. Later in the chapter, the opinions of his sister, Frances, will be discussed as a means of appraising some of the larger cultural and social changes to which the debate about taste and beauty both contributed and was subjected during the later part of the eighteenth century. It will be argued that it was perhaps Frances, and not Joshua Reynolds, who was ultimately able to reconcile the enjoyment of culture with the habits and inclinations of a 'polite and commercial people'.

OPULENCE AND POWER: MASCULINITY, TASTE AND CULTURE

Despite the excitement and temptations of fashion and commerce which seemed to define the Hanoverian age, it was still possible to found new, public bodies in fulfilment of long-meditated and well-established ambitions. In January 1768, for example, Sir Joshua Reynolds, newly created baronet, was able to announce that:

An Academy, in which the Polite Arts may be regularly cultivated, is at last opened among us by Royal Munificence. This must appear an event in the highest degree interesting, not only to the Artists, but to the whole nation.

It is indeed difficult to give any other reason, why an empire like that of BRITAIN, should so long have wanted an ornament so suited to its greatness, than that slow progression of things, which naturally makes elegance and refinement the last effects of opulence and power.

An Institution like this has often been recommended upon considerations merely mercantile; but an Academy, founded upon such principles, can never effect even its own narrow purposes. If it has an origin no higher, no taste can ever be formed in manufactures; but if the higher Arts of Design flourish, these inferior ends will be answered of course.

We are happy in having a PRINCE, who has conceived the design of such an Institution, according to its true dignity; and who promotes the Arts, as the head of a great, a learned, a polite, and a commercial nation; and I can now congratulate you, Gentlemen on the accomplishment of your long and ardent wishes.[2]

When, with these words, Reynolds began his inaugural address to the Royal Academy, he spoke with a confidence and a flourish which had not been imaginable a decade or so earlier. The road to the fulfilment of the 'long and ardent wishes' had been a rocky and uncertain one, a path too daunting to many a modern Hercules. However, with the negotiations surrounding the foundation of the Royal Academy completed, the preceding December, Reynolds and his fellow academicians could look forward to an era of dignified prosperity. In his assured style, Reynolds argues that the inception of this new public body ensures the high valuation due to the arts in a civilised and polite state. He is furthermore prepared to suggest that 'elegance and refinement' is the effect of 'opulence and power'. Reynolds claims that the Royal Academy is a product not only of 'Royal Munificence', but of the superior, commercial and imperial fortunes of Britain.

Reynolds's address to the new institution is of interest for the way in which it repeats earlier concerns about the dangers of unregulated wealth while expressing a new-found confidence. Throughout his speech Reynolds tries to persuade his listeners that the quasi-civic aspirations to learning and greatness embodied by the Royal

Academy could be reconciled with the practices of a polite and commercial culture. This was a crucial endeavour for Reynolds, and similar attempts to resolve the tension between 'opulence' and the higher arts can be found throughout Reynolds's later addresses. Despite his zeal in exploiting the new opportunities which fortune and prestige granted him in the 1760s and 1770s, Reynolds's public account of Georgian modernity remained rooted in a vocabulary which stigmatised all that was not classically sanctioned as effeminate and corrupt. In subsequent lectures to the Royal Academy, the rhetoric of his inaugural address was put to one side, allowing Reynolds to express the view that mere commercial wealth introduced the kinds of sensuality and luxury which would inevitably corrupt taste. Reynolds's analysis of Correggio in his fourth Discourse, a description which both derided the painter's alleged effeminacy while accepting his success as a painter of polite synthesis, has already provided an instance of how Reynolds's reservations about all but the most chaste – even austere – classical style could find expression in his Academy addresses. Reynolds believed Correggio's error was one into which British art could easily succumb through an over-attention to the caprices of fashion or the false refinement of an effeminate politeness. Responding to this imagined crisis Reynolds argued that the utmost vigilance was required to prevent the arts from being 'debauched' and 'contaminated' as they had been in other European cultures (most notably Holland and Venice), by the corrupting influence of fashion or luxury.[3]

The theme of cultural and artistic pollution and contamination was one to which Reynolds was to return frequently. In a telling passage in his seventh Discourse of 1776, Reynolds warned his audience that unless they maintained a clear commitment to the fixed and general rules of taste, then their conceptions, like the pockets, would be infected with the bad currency which is perpetually in circulation. Expanding his initial observation, Reynolds suggested that, 'we are used to take without weighing or examining; but by this inevitable inattention many adulterated pieces are received, which, when we seriously examine our wealth, we must throw away'. Reynolds, however, was far from wishing that his students should remove themselves entirely from circulation, indeed, he advised them to remain in contact with 'the conversation of learned and ingenious men' and to endeavour to 'enlarge their stock of ideas' whenever the opportunity presented itself. Accordingly, the passage, with its blend of fearful prudence and zealous acquisitiveness underlines Reynolds's sense of the need not only to acquire riches, but also to judge and regulate wealth, to ensure, in his ambitious formulation, that 'elegance and refinement' really are the final results of 'opulence and power'.[4]

In line with his image of the 'adulterated pieces' of coin and opinion which require careful sifting and scrutiny and are yet desired and necessary, Reynolds represented the opportunities of the modern, implicitly commercial, age as both dangerous and welcome. Reynolds's position, though ambiguous when viewed from a strictly civic perspective, was neither unusual nor unsustainable with the context of his overall sense of how the British school could be advanced by the Royal Academy. Reynolds's occasional reflections in the *Discourses* on the position of the portrait-painter are justly famous, particularly as they seem to reflect on the President's own predicament. Given these connections, they are worth quoting again as an illustration of how Reynolds was willing to accommodate necessary practice with theoretical ambition:

He therefore who in his practice of portrait-painting wishes to dignify his subject, which will suppose to be a lady, will not paint her in the modern dress, the familiarity of which alone is sufficient to destroy all dignity. He takes care that his work shall correspond to those ideas and that imagination which he knows we regulate the judgement of others; and therefore dresses his figure something with the general air of the antique for the sake of dignity, and preserves something of the modern for the sake of likeness. By this conduct his works correspond with those prejudices which we have in favour of what we continually see; and the relish of the antique simplicity corresponds with what we may call the more learned and scientific prejudice.[5]

In these terms, Reynolds argued that the dignity of the portrait-painter's work lay in his ability to grasp the 'nobility or elevation of all arts, like the excellency of virtue itself, consists in adopting this enlarged and comprehensive idea'. To do so he must rise above the predilections of the moment and embrace the more 'learned and scientific prejudice' of antique forms. [6]

Reynolds commitment to this ideal was such that he could be provoked to considerable anger by any suggestion that the artist should do other than express the 'eternal', 'general' or 'invariable' truths of nature. In what Solkin rightly describes as an 'uncharacteristically nasty' passage in the eighth Discourse, Reynolds attacks du

Piles for his suggestion that grace or dignity can be conveyed or rather added to a painter by the addition of motifs and accessories. To Reynolds such a course of action meant a deviation from all that is noble or elevated, accordingly such painting 'betrays vulgarity and meanness, and new-acquired consequence'.[7] It is clear from the vehemence of Reynolds's attack on du Piles that he regarded such opinions, like Correggio's paintings, as a dangerous step towards what he considered the brink of hatefulness, affectation, fashion, effeminacy. In these terms, Reynolds offers a more aggressive image of the Man of Polite Imagination than that intended by Addison earlier in the century. The easy poise of conversation and contemplation is abandoned for a more belligerent assertion of both pride and principal. In the eighth Discourse, Reynolds advocates definition of a taste which, while it is refined, is also robust, even manly: moreover, although Reynolds acknowledges that 'our taste has a kind of sensuality about it, as well as love of the sublime' it is a quality which he thought required constant examination, lest it fall into a mere craving for grace and softness.[8] As such, an indomitably masculine as well as civic aesthetic is evident throughout the *Discourses*, indeed Reynolds's theoretical concerns are most often expressed as a resistance to effeminacy. It was a cause which Reynolds knew required both public watchfulness and professional integrity, indeed, his sense of the painter's masculinity resided in the 'long laborious comparison' through which true genius separated the worthy from the insipid.[9]

However, Reynolds did not wish merely to repudiate, though the need for resistance and stoic defence remained, as such, he often appears willing to incorporate and adapt that which otherwise might be thought of as dubious or merely ornamental. His comments on the possibilities of portrait-painting is one such example. Harriet Guest has argued that this ambivalent attitude is most strongly marked in Reynolds's treatment of the gothic style, an artistic mode which he regarded as both effete and luxuriant, yet capable of reworking into something more noble. Guest further suggests that Reynolds sought to establish the masculinity of the artist, and hence his claims to true greatness, by associating the gothic with an image of an unformed, excremental feminine mass. To Reynolds's mind, it was the achievement of genius that it could incorporate such unpromising material. He writes: 'a skilful painter, who is sensible of what he wants, and is in no danger of being infected by the contact of vicious models, will know how to avail himself', he would know more importantly, by what 'nice chymistry' dunghills could become gold.[10] However, as Guest notes, this triumph requires an acknowledgement not only of the attractiveness of the lesser style, but also of the deficiency of the grand style itself, 'it is because Gothic is excremental, feminine and wanton . . . that it can "add" to a chaste masculinity austere in its lack'.[11] On this reading, Reynolds accepts the necessity of bad coinage, of unrefined material, as the source for art. Certainly, by the time Reynolds was writing his later lectures, he was far less concerned with an austere, civic art which exhibited its claims to excellence via a call to public virtue. Indeed for much of the eighth Discourse, Reynolds is keen to assert the necessity of an appropriate blending of uniformity and variety, too much simplicity he suggests is 'penury'. The task for the painter, and Reynolds never slackens his belief that it is an arduous task, is to use the 'abundance' and 'riches' with a 'sparing hand'. Once again, it does not seem inappropriate to read Reynolds's image as a reference, albeit indirect, to the more general situation of the artist; the opportunities wealth offered were not to be scorned even if they demanded scrutiny.[12]

Reynolds's ambiguous address to commercial prosperity is evident in his advocacy of painting as an art which both expresses an age's refinement but which also makes evident its capacity for decline. Reynolds's argument in the *Discourses* is one which represents a peculiarly anxious perception of the connection between refinement and corruption: that which flowers is always on the verge of decay.[13] Reynolds's attitude to the opportunities afforded by 'opulence and power' can be compared with the dour appraisal given to the nation's arts in 1755, when André Rouquet believed them beset by the calculations of a narrowly mercantile culture.[14] Rouquet's estimation of the English public was, as we have already seen, not high:

We cannot say that the public are really the dupes of all the puerilities . . . ; no, they are only dupes to the fashion which they follow, even with reluctance: it is the fashion that carries them to a painter of whom they have no great opinion, to engage him out of vanity to draw their picture, which they have no occasion for, and which they will not like when finished. But the women especially must have their pictures exposed for some time in the house of that painter which is most in fashion.[15]

Commercial, vain, epitomised by the conspicuous consumption of society women, and, as he goes on to argue, riven by party interests, the public described by Rouquet is no place for the 'Polite Arts' to flourish. Conducting his argument in highly gendered terms, Rouquet, as much as, say, Edmund Burke or John Brown, has a capacious distaste for the effeminate, and at times for the feminine. Although he makes the general claim that 'the spirit of commerce and that of the polite arts, seem to be derived from two very different sources', Rouquet tends to associate the failings of British art either with fashionable excesses which he genders as feminine or with women in particular.[16] It is a repugnance that is characteristic of all those who are wary both of the commercial nature of polite culture and of women's involvement in that environment. Although Reynolds himself makes no such specific connections, it would have been well understood by his largely male audience that his references to fashion and to the 'corruption' of the arts contained similar assumptions about the need to maintain the dignified masculinity appropriate to a 'great . . . nation'.

However, the often acerbic opinions of Reynolds and Rouquet need to be contrasted with the vast array of eighteenth-century writers who believed that the involvement of women in the discussion of taste and beauty improved and enlivened what might otherwise have been arid or cumbersome debates. For Burke, indeed, it was the pleasures of association with women, figured as the beautiful, which carried men into society, and even the curmudgeonly *Connoisseur* was obliged to rehearse an appeal to 'the Ladies' in order to secure itself a polite audience.[17] Similarly, the lucubrations of John Gilbert Cooper relied upon a deliberate incorporation of women as agents as well as objects of tasteful discourse. Speaking of his desire for residence with his beloved Amelia, he exclaims:

I am one of the loyalist Subjects the Sex ever had, and, I dare say [they] will not be displeased with this fresh Proclamation of their Dominion. You may add farther, that I think Women are the Fountains from whence flow the blended streams of Taste and Pleasure, and that the Draught of Life is more or less Sweet as they are blended in the Cup.[18]

In this extract Cooper wishes to reside in a place where women are not only appealing in themselves, but actually control and mediate judgements about taste and beauty. Women he writes 'harmonise the souls of men' and not only provide as the basis for judgement in the more general or public forms, but also prevent the forms of corruption Reynolds thought potentially disastrous to a commercial nation. It is women, Cooper suggests, who can best bestow politeness on commerce.[19]

The association of women with the arts, particularly as consumers of tasteful ornamentation and rich furnishings, fulfilled an important role in the refashioning of eighteenth-century society. The basic proposal could find a number of different expressions depending upon the genre in which it was found. The notion that feminine taste (or at least a woman's presence) could alleviate the luxuriant effects of commerce seems to underlie, or at least make sense of, Mr Warner's extravagant action in Frances Sheridan's novel, *Memoirs of Miss Sidney Bidulph*. Returning from the West Indies and possessed of an embarrassingly large fortune for which he has no immediate purpose (Warner has lost his own wife and children prior to the novel), Warner effectively launders his money by purchasing elegant vases and furnishings which he then gives to the impoverished Sidney. In the context of the novel's sentimental plot, Warner's sudden appetite for consumer purchases appears to secure a domestic felicity as well as an 'abundance' of fine china, glassware, carpets and other fine furnishings.[20] However, more interestingly, Sheridan's novel (which was published in the same year as *Elements of Criticism*, 1762) offers, via a different genre, an elaboration of Kames's opinion that wealth could cleanse itself by offering an encouragement to the arts. While Warner and Sidney cannot achieve such public triumphs, they do manage to distribute Warner's wealth and riches in a way compatible not only with good taste, but also with decorum and politeness; in short wealth once passed through Sidney's feminine domain, becomes not luxury, but almost virtue.

Given the connections proposed or implied by Cooper, Sheridan and others between an appreciative and uncorrupted taste and a refined femininity, I want to conclude this study by examining what is an important, but often undisclosed, aspect of the discursive structure which both underpinned and represented judgements about beauty. Once again, the contested place of a woman will receive particular attention as a means of disclosing the ambivalence within eighteenth-century culture regarding the nature of both taste and society. In many respects, the question of femininity was the fault line upon which Reynolds's portrait of Elizabeth Gunning was situated. The problem of defining femininity was also present in the

fictions of Sarah Scott and Charlotte Lennox, and became the object
of close scrutiny in the work of Joseph Spence and James Usher. A
reading of these writers has suggested the means by which middle-
class discourse sought to limit the power of the 'factitious beauty' by
requiring women to exhibit a pleasing modesty. The disquiet about
the social place of women found within these texts is perhaps
indicative of the ambiguity of expected behaviour in mixed, part-
public, part-private spaces found in many eighteenth-century texts.
Such expectations, formulated in conduct books and in various
advice literature, had, as earlier discussions have explored, a considerable impact on the debate about what constituted a refined
taste in the eighteenth century. The strength of this conjunction of
terms and concerns is exemplified by the timid and yet gifted career
of Frances Reynolds. Although Frances Reynolds's piety and strict
adherence to social protocol is almost infamous, her opinions on the
questions of taste and beauty are often illuminating when taken in
the context of the gendering of such debates in the late century.[21]
While not ignoring the religious aspect of her writing, I want to
concentrate on her account of taste in relation to her description of
gender difference, as it is this dimension of her writing in which her
disagreement with her brother and her allegiance to dominant social
codes is most apparent.

THE PRIVATE HONOUR OF THE HEART: FRANCES REYNOLDS AND THE DOMESTICATION OF TASTE

It was suggested, much earlier in this study, that the discussion of
beauty encompassed more than a taste for this carriage or that.
Taste, it was claimed, was a more complex issue than a liking for this
phaeton or that curricle, or so it appeared. This was, to use a phrase
of Sir Joshua's 'inadvertently said'.[22] Indeed the converse is true, or
almost. Throughout the eighteenth century, possession of the accou-
trements of fine living – the right clothes, plate, portrait and what
have you – was part of the ritual of acquisition which permitted
entrance into the debate about beauty. For Reynolds it was particularly so. Embarrassed by a provincial accent and by his rough
features, the President of the Royal Academy was conscious that his
claims to polite taste were forever vulnerable. His status as a
practising portrait-painter can only have made his predicament
more apparent; indeed, the marshalling of classical tastes and the

eager fraternity with Dr Johnson and Oliver Goldsmith underlines the anxiety he sought to hide. For Reynolds, possession of the right kit for being tasteful was crucial, and perhaps a carriage, again in his phrase, was the 'all-in-all'.

His carriage was indeed magnificent, and was justly celebrated for the immodesty with which it proclaimed both newly acquired wealth and the novelty of rank. In Northcote's sarcastic testimony, it was a 'chariot on the panels of which were curiously painted the four seasons of the year in allegorical figures. The wheels were ornamented with carved foliage and gilding; the liveries also of his servants were laced with silver.'[23] But there was a contradiction even within such avowed showmanship. For in order to pay for such luxuriance Reynolds had to paint and paint. Indeed he had to work so much and so often that he rarely had the time or the occasion to use the carriage upon which his labour was expended. Unwilling to countenance such waste Reynolds insisted on the compliance of his sister, the unlucky Frances, in a scheme designed to keep the evidence of his success in motion around the streets of London. Frances was obliged to traverse the highways and places of public resort encased within the carriage, her brother's wealth visible despite his absence. Throughout these excursions the blinds on the coach's windows remained down. Frances was to display the equipage, symbol of fraternal success; there was no suggestion that she should display herself. The image of woman locked into the material expression of her brother's wealth is poignant. It acts as a reminder of the politics and proprieties of display, and of being displayed in the eighteenth century. Northcote notes that the 'coachman frequently got money by admitting the curious to a sight of it', a point balanced by Frances's sense of shame at the coach's ostentation. She thought the carriage was 'too fine' and most damagingly 'too shewy'.[24]

Despite her embarrassment, and the many obligations heaped upon her by her brother, Frances Reynolds was not without resource, and, though she is most often remembered merely as Reynolds's long-standing housekeeper, she was also able to furnish the world of learning with a competent, though brief, work on the beautiful. It is a text which, after some huffing and puffing, Johnson was able to praise with a degree of complaisance: 'there are in those few pages or remarks such a depth of penetration, such nicety of observation, as Locke or Pascal might be proud of'.[25] While perhaps less magnificent than Johnson's remark suggests, Reynolds's *An Enquiry Concerning the Principles of Taste and the Origin of Our Ideas of Beauty* is an interesting intervention in a field crowded with amateur treatises of a highly variable quality. Reynolds's *Enquiry* is an intelligent and, at times, original synthesis of the prevailing opinions of eighteenth-century thought. It is possible to find her introducing William Hogarth's waving-line, the Burkean sublime, her brother's notion of the 'common form' and the moral sense of Francis Hutcheson.[26] However, it is Reynolds's commitment to the discussion of the beautiful as a representation of personal, moral excellence – a discursive technique which I have already analysed in relation to the work of Spence – that she offers her most suggestive conclusions.

The eclecticism of Reynolds's reference and the tenacity with which she pursues her argument is such that a careful reader is easily persuaded that Peter de Bolla was a little hasty when he concluded that the *Enquiry* is to be read as a 'minor work on the moral sublime'.[27] De Bolla underestimates Reynolds's text because he is only concerned with what, in Reynolds's terms, is a presumptuous, masculine obsession with the sublime. True, Reynolds relates the experience of the sublime in the same exciting and excited prose style as Burke, and offers her opinion that the sublime constitutes 'the pinnacle of beatitude, bordering upon horror, deformity, madness! an eminence from which the mind, that dares to look further, is lost'.[28] However, her concerns – sanctioned always by divine ordination – remain more earthbound, and more sane, than this outburst suggests. In fact, Reynolds is far less concerned with the sublime, with its unearthly or absolute beauty – the point of 'undetermined power' – than she is with the sphere which is just below it; 'Grace'. For, as her Dedication to Elizabeth Montagu makes clear, Reynolds focused her attentions on what she defined as 'moral excellence', by which she intended all that was good, beautiful and worthy. What the Dedication to Montagu also indicates is the gendered nature of Reynolds's project. Her application to the famous Bluestocking negotiates the purpose and publication of the *Enquiry* in relation to known female intelligence and admired virtue: 'your character not only secures me from all imputation of flattery, but this public avowal of my admiration of its excellence conveys an honourable testimony of the consistency of my principles'.[29] The praise for Montagu suggests that the relationship between taste and personal virtue is central to the claims of the

Enquiry. Indeed, the connection is made so forcibly in later pages, that it is necessary to read Reynolds with some care, in order to understand fully the degree to which she unites the two terms within a profoundly gendered account of the social.

From the outset, Reynolds is clear that beauty is a moral good, the emanation or expression of virtue. According to Reynolds, the idea, or rather principles of beauty are incontrovertibly moral. She writes: 'I have no more doubt that the principles of beauty are moral, than the principles of happiness are moral.' She writes that 'it is, I imagine, the moral truth, that is the characteristic truth of beauty . . . and hence the universal interesting charm of beauty'. The measured stress on moral certainty, evident throughout the text, underlines the fact that for Reynolds, all perceptions of beauty arise because the perceived objects accord with 'some preconceived idea of beauty'. The connection is sufficiently strong to ensure that, whatever appears 'to each individual, the most excellent in the human system, at once constitutes his idea of *happiness*, of *morality*, and of *beauty*; and all mankind, I imagine, would agree in the same idea'.[30] Furthermore she has absolute confidence that personal beauty is pleasing because it is the emanation of inner character, indeed she quotes Edward Young's opinion that: '*the body charms because the soul is seen*'.[31] In the same vein Reynolds claims that, 'the strongest proof that the moral sense is the governing principle' is the realisation that:

the human form, from infancy to old age, has its peculiar beauty annexed to it from the virtue of affection that nature gives it, and which it exhibits in the countenance. The negative virtue, innocence, is the beauty of the child. The more formed virtues, benevolence, generosity, compassion, &c. are the virtues of youth, and its beauty. The fixed and determined virtues, justice, temperance, fortitude &c. compose the beauty of manhood. The philosophic and religious cast of countenance is the beauty of old age.[32]

In these terms, the representative marks of each character – the signs variously of youth, maturity and old age – would, were they to be misplaced or misapplied invariably displease, for 'without congruity there could be no virtue; without virtue, no beauty, no sentiment'. The importance of congruity, as Reynolds emphasises, is based upon the observation and preservation of key moral and social divisions, first between age and youth, latterly between genders:

the beauty of each sex is seen only through the medium of the virtues belonging to each. The Beauty of the masculine sex is seen only through the medium of the masculine virtues . . . The softness and mildness of the feminine expression would be displeasing in a man. The robust and determined expression of the rigid virtues, justice, fortitude, &c. would be displeasing in a woman. However perfect the Form, if an incongruity that touches the well-being of humanity mingles with the idea, the Forms will not afford the pleasing perception of beauty: though the eye may be capable of seeing its regularity.[33]

Significantly, Reynolds described a similar progression earlier in the text when she writes of the artist's progress from the tastes of his own nation to those of ancient Greece, a culture which she defines as possessing the highest excellence.

I want to stress two points at this stage, first, the fact that Reynolds is arguing that beauty and taste are acquired cultural characteristics that are capable of cultivation, as witnessed by their relation to the maturation of the individual. In each case the evolution, whether personal or national, is associated with the acquisition of a more dignified and general character, a tendency which is made manifest by a greater conformity between the bodily and intellectual forms of beauty.[34] My second point is that Reynolds believes not only in the necessity of identifying the differences of age and gender (she comments elsewhere on the issue of race) but in keeping the terms apart once they have been so designated. Such distinctions are crucial, according to Reynolds, as it is 'to the principles of the masculine and feminine character, that we owe the perception of beauty or taste, in any object whatever, throughout all nature and all art that imitates nature'. Reynolds's sense of the significance of this division is surprisingly capacious. She writes, 'it will be found, that, there exist principles which are analogous to those that constitute beauty in the human species' throughout the created universe.[35] Flowers, for example, please precisely according to this connection:

In the form and colour of flowers, there appears to me a striking analogy to the character of human beauty. They afford an ocular demonstration, in the pleasure with which we contemplate their particular forms, that the pleasure, we receive from the beauty of the human form, originates from mental characters: witness the charms of the infant, innocence of the snow-drop, of the soft elegance of the hyacinth, &c. and, the robust, unmeaning, masculine, piony, hollyhock, &c. &c.[36]

As curious as the idea of a butch 'piony' may seem, it constitutes what Reynolds terms a '*moral good*', one which makes judgement possible. It is also worth stressing how deliberately and how carefully the words 'robust', 'unmeaning' and 'masculine' have been reduced to a rough equivalence.

The extent to which de Bolla's reading is both hasty and partial should now be clear. The question for Reynolds is not about subordinating ethics to the 'topology of the sublime', as de Bolla suggests, but finding a moral language which can express gender difference through an account of taste.[37] Within Reynolds's scheme, the sublime exists beyond the limits of both comprehension and cultivation, as a result, she is more interested in what she defines as the agreeable. The cultivated aspect of the agreeable is stressed when Reynolds claims that in order to be agreeable an object must be 'able to assimilate . . . some amiable interesting affection'. In this respect addition and assemblage play an important part in determining the value of a given body.[38] A more fulsome definition of the terms is given when she writes that:

The agreeable, in person, is composed of beauties and defects, as is the common form, but differently composed. The beauties and defects of the latter are blended into the idea of mediocrity; those of the former are always distinct and perceptible, contrasting each other, they engage the attention, and create a kind of pleasing *re-creation* to the mental faculties; and, in proportion as we can bring them to unite with our governing principles of pleasure, they create affection, which gives the person a more fascinating charm than beauty itself.[39]

The passage easily recalls the description of women's faces found in Scott, Lennox and Hogarth. As this connection would imply, the degree to which the agreeable is gendered as feminine throughout the *Enquiry* is striking. Indeed, Reynolds explains how the superaddition of 'some amiable interesting affection' ensures that 'it is the feminine character that is the sweetest, and most interesting, image of beauty'.[40] As she continues her account, Reynolds not only genders beauty as feminine, but begins to suggest that feminine beauty is the more likely (in the sense of both more frequent and more probable) and more acceptable form of beauty. Masculinity, by contrast, remains associated with the sublime, but only in the sense of its overweening ambition; as such it is unreachable, improbable and, quite possibly, unpleasant.[41]

In her explication of taste – I have been focusing on her account of beauty – Reynolds makes these claims still more emphatically. More importantly, she connects her claims with an account of the rise and progress of the arts. Therefore, although Reynolds begins her discussion by stating that taste appears to be 'an inherent impulsive tendency of the soul towards true good', her argument falls more readily on the social and cultivated aspects of judgement.[42] Initially preferring to remain broadly schematic in her account of taste, Reynolds abruptly engages with the discourse on luxury, in order to attack the corrupting progress of false taste. In common with her brother, her pronouncements upon the spread of refinement indicate a creeping suspicion of commercial wealth:

In the progress of civilization, the polishing principle, which I call taste, is chiefly found in the highest sphere of life, highest for both internal and external advantages, wealth accelerates the last degree of cultivation, by giving efficacy to the principles of true honour; but it also accelerates its corruption, by giving efficacy to the principles of false honour by which the true loses its distinction, becomes less and less apparent, nay, by degrees less and less real. Wealth becoming the object of honour, every principle of true taste must be reversed. Hence the *dire polish* of the obdurate heart, repelling the force of nature. Hence avarice and profusion, dissipation, luxurious banqueting, &c. supercede the love of œconomy, domestic comfort, and the sweet reciprocation of natural affections.[43]

The decline of taste is a particular problem with respect to the position and inclinations of women, who are more prone, in Reynolds's view, to the depredations of fashion. Warming to her task, Reynolds concedes that the corruption of taste is a subject upon which she could 'expatiate largely' and, yet, she retains a clear sense that women are also more likely to offer resistance to the follies of wealth and fashion than their male counterparts, a point underlined by the femininity of the virtues which are disregarded by more opulent cultures.

Partly in response to the pressures of refinement and over-polishing, Reynolds maintains that there are three major components of the tasteful 'virtue, honour, and ornament' which secure taste. Interestingly, although the terms are offered as a triptych, each of these principles of taste corresponds to a particular 'order' or 'sphere', though Reynolds is not always clear as to their precise distinction. The first order of taste is that which is divine, the next that which is social, embracing the external effects of 'true taste' and 'moral virtue'. Lastly, there is the third order, that of 'general ornament' which encompasses the arts, fashions and decorations of the world.[44] The last category, that of ornament, is the one most open to corruption, an opinion in line with Reynolds's general view of fashion and high life. The ornamental sphere is also, logically enough, the sphere which will prove most receptive to regulation and correction.[45] The distinctions between the various 'spheres' of taste are important because, although adherence to the principles embodied by these orders guarantees taste, this is achieved differentially:

> The three grand co-existing principles of taste, virtue, honour, and ornament, run through all its perceptions. Their triple union cannot be broken; but taste is nominally distinguished by one or the other, according as its objects, situations, circumstances, &c. vary. Ornament and honour seem the public character of taste; virtue to be the private and domestic, where, though unperceived by the vulgar, to the eye of taste, she appears in her highest ornament, highest honour.[46]

Characteristically, the difference between the public and the private aspect of taste is defined by a consideration of gender. Reynolds notes that 'as the virtues differ, in some degree, as the character of the sexes differ, of course so must the sentiment of taste differ'. The supposition is the basis upon which Reynolds builds a telling hierarchy of values:

> The cultivation of the social moral affections is the cultivation of taste, and the domestic sphere is the true and almost only one in which it can appear in its highest dignity. It is peculiarly appropriated to feminine taste, and I may say it is *absolutely* the only one in which it can appear in its true lustre. True taste, particularly the feminine, is retired, calm, modest; it is the private honour of the heart, and is, I imagine, incompatible with the love of fame.[47]

The place of woman as both most likely to fall victim to the corruption of wealth and fashion and as the emblem of that which is truly virtuous was a familiar image in the eighteenth century. Reynolds enforces the conception she has advanced by suggesting that 'exterior feminine grace is the most perfect visible object of taste, the highest degree of female excellence, externally and internally united, must of course constitute woman, the most perfect existing object of taste in creation'.

Reynolds's advocacy of the excellence of female taste is detectable throughout the *Enquiry*. What is more interesting, however, is the extent to which Reynolds opposes this prescription, if only implicitly, to the love of fame and riches which constitute the character of the upper-class male. It is a diffidence which may go some way to explain the disagreement between herself and her brother concerning his overly opulent coach.[48] Compared to this showy munificence, the ornaments of the domestic sphere, no matter how precarious, are always to be valued. In these terms, Reynolds proposes an ideal of the private or domestic world as the true arena of taste. It is a realm which she takes to be distinctly and appropriately feminine, its modest and retiring virtues making plain its gendered character. In particular Reynolds's embarrassment at the ostentation of her brother's equipage, and her own investment in the retiring charms of femininity suggests a compelling connection of eighteenth-century ideologies.

LUXURY PRIVATISED: THE ART OF BEING MIDDLE-CLASS

The separation of feminine taste and privacy from masculine hubris recommended by Frances Reynolds makes for a clear distinction between the sexes, one which is not only capacious but the contrary of that advocated in her brother's writings. Certainly, Reynolds imagined an entire epistemology based on the distinction between femininity and masculinity, one in which femininity was a highly valued term.[49] In this context Johnson's response to the *Enquiry* is once again intriguing. I have already noted that, after some considerable hesitation, Johnson was willing to praise Reynolds's book with some effusiveness, however, it is worth drawing attention to the precise reasons Johnson gave for delaying his commendation. In his letter of 8 April 1782 Johnson managed to appear fulsome in his praise, yet withheld final approbation:

Your work is full of very penetrating meditation, and very forcible sentiments. I read it with a full perception of the sublime, with wonder and terrour, but I cannot think of any profit from it; it seems not born to be popular.
    Your system of the mental fabrick is exceedingly obscure, and without more attention than will willingly be bestowed, is unintelligible. The Ideas of Beauty will be more easily understood, and are often charming. I was delighted with the different beauty of different ages.
    I would make it produce something if I could but I have indeed no hope. If a Bookseller would buy it at all, as it must be published without a name, he would give nothing for it worth your acceptance.[50]

Johnson's letter accomplishes a subtle balancing act, in which praise and confinement are meted out in equal measure. The letter represents Reynolds in terms of her perceived deficiencies (her lack, tellingly, of logic and control) and with reference to her departure from the domestic sphere. Throughout the letter, Johnson regrets that she should venture into the public stage while also implying the improbability of her success. Significantly, Johnson suggests that while he is ready to attribute to her a feeling for taste (note his praise of her account of beauty), he is unwilling to believe that taste is a subject upon which she can effectively pronounce. Indeed, close examination of Johnson's correspondence with Reynolds reveals his serious reservations about her capacity for reasoned argument, a limitation which Johnson regarded as gendered. Most noticeably, Johnson's letter seeks to separate a feminine capacity for feeling from a masculine ability to describe that sensation.

The limits Johnson sought to place upon Frances Reynolds were typical of attitudes towards women's intellectual capacities during the eighteenth century, furthermore, they reflect an assumption that women could embody the aesthetic, but not define it. As Ann Bermingham has argued, eighteenth-century women were often expected to display accomplishments and fine feelings, yet were not expected to be able to comment critically on what they achieved. Instead, the spectacle of their refinement and their talents provided an act of exhibition which was intended to display not only unmarried women but also familial wealth in a setting which was both private and convivial. As such, the taint of luxuriance was deftly avoided, and sexuality passed into polite responsiveness.[51] Approaching the issue from a slightly different perspective Marcia Pointon, has argued that, for the middle classes, distinction from their social inferiors, and, just as importantly, from the luxuriant aristocrats they affected to despise, could be achieved by an image of domestic propriety and 'familial coherence' in which women featured prominently. Pointon argues that, in order to overcome the luxuriance of commercial culture, painters and essayists represented domesticated women as the means through which the ownership of property could be transformed into something like a virtue. The conversation piece, in particular, represented women as both passive objects and as the organising principle which prevented the onset of luxuriant appetite.[52] In this context, images of middle-class women became profoundly resonant, if also ambiguous, symbols of the new culture. Women were imagined, by those seeking to defend commercial culture, to be able to refine the mere ownership of a good into the acquisition of exemplary signs connotative of distinction as well as forbearance.

Representations of the polite, virtuous woman were, therefore, central to the enormous ideological endeavour through which eighteenth-century culture sought to rid itself of the fear of luxuriance. Harriet Guest has argued that such discursive alignments can be understood in terms of an evolving articulation of both class positions and gender roles. Guest suggests that what she terms the 'moralisation of commercial society' required, not the simple confinement of women to the domestic sphere, but rather that such an act of retirement should be itself displayed. The image of a disclosed retreat allowed for a 'distinctive display' through which the goodness of chastity, modesty and prudence could most effectively be portrayed.[53] As a result of this realignment – one which is clearly endorsed in novels such as *Sophia* and *Agreeable Ugliness* – the domestic sphere comes to be highly valued. It is in such enclosed, yet visible, spaces that the virtues of middle-class refinement are most evident.[54] This is an ideological position to which Frances Reynolds was firmly committed. As we have seen, it was the security of feminised and domesticated taste which Reynolds felt could best maintain its virtue. In common with Reynolds, many discourses which sought to describe the new patterns of cultured women, or rather idealised versions of middle- and upper-class women – Mrs B*** and her kind – were enshrined as guardians, not only of beauty and sensibility, but of preserving the culture from its own depravity.

Guest's argument is important because in many respects what I have been describing is a profoundly ideological attempt to manipulate and disguise the divisive nature of commercial culture. Once the discussion of taste has been privatised, brought to the tea-table, in Addison's phrase, it can become, properly speaking, a topic upon which the middle classes could expect to be granted a voice. Through the representation of feminine taste and refinement – always both private and domesticated – many middle-class writers sought to suggest how it would be possible for luxury goods to be reconciled with decency and politeness. The association of women with taste, and of taste with privacy, enabled a separation of tasteful consumption (choices that were informed, moderate, reasonable) from mere fashionable dissipation. Most eighteenth-century writers who endeavoured to define taste argued that a preference for an object (particularly luxury goods) could only be rendered virtuous, hence admissible, if it was associated with a refined femininity which could license such pleasure. Frances Reynolds, in particular, was emphatic in her commitment to this notion, the more so as she regarded virtuous women as a restraint against the advancing tide of luxury and extravagance. However, the commitment was made equally by many male theorists such as William Hogarth, James Usher and Allan Ramsay, each of whom offered the opinion that it was often women, and not men, who were the more sophisticated or more reliable arbiters of taste.[55]

Once such comparisons have been made, then Reynolds's *Enquiry* begins to look less the product of an overly pious or unfortunate woman, and can be seen to participate in what was a more general range of concerns. Reynolds's fear that luxury would taint the appetites of women and the taste of British culture more generally may mirror her brother's contempt for 'vulgarity and . . . new-acquired consequence', but it does so in a way which rejects the masculine pride which motivated Joshua Reynolds's contempt for mere opulence. Indeed, it is masculine cravings for show and extravagance which most seem to disturb Frances. This commitment to the virtues of retired, yet culturally significant, femininity needs to be understood, not as a mere sisterly sniping at an oppressive elder brother, but as part of a more general development in eighteenth-century culture.

In many respects, the constructions of femininity which were given prominence in eighteenth-century accounts of taste or beauty existed in a close relationship with the formation of middle-class identity. For it was by connecting an image of virtuous femininity to the acquisition of private goods and domestic services that the middle-class intellectuals sought to defend their cultural aspirations. As such, although the eighteenth century had begun with the civic and aristocratic aspirations of Lord Shaftesbury, the account of taste most readily accepted by the final quarter of the century was not that which advocated disinterested public virtue, but one which recommended a contemplation of the virtues of the middle-class. Moreover, rather than repudiating women as agents of corruption, theorists of taste argued, instead, that women could be admitted, under certain circumstances, as the more discerning of the two genders. The account of beauty which emerged from within such discursive alignments is one which enabled a reloca-tion of taste and morality within an account of the physical

appearance and social presence of women as the signs of middle-
class goodness and forbearance. As such it is a strategy which can
be found not only within discourses on taste, but in the practices
of portrait-painters such as Hogarth and Ramsay and in the mid-
century novel of sentiment, such as those by Sarah Scott and
Charlotte Lennox. Once the extent of these connections is understood, then the full significance and extent of the 'Empire of Beauty'
can be appreciated.

Notes

PREFACE

1 Edmund Burke, *A Philosophical Enquiry into the Origin of Our Ideas of the Sublime and Beautiful*, ed. and intro. J. T. Boulton (Oxford: Basil Blackwell, 1990), p. 11.
2 Ronald Paulson, *Hogarth Vol. III: Art and Politics, 1750–1764* (Cambridge: The Lutterworth Press, 1993), p. xvi. Frances Ferguson has also lamented the neglect of the Beautiful. See her *Solitude and the Sublime: Romanticism and the Aesthetics of Individuation* (London: Routledge, 1992), pp. 44–45.

INTRODUCTION: THE EMPIRE OF BEAUTY AND THE CULTURAL POLITICS OF TASTE

1 Joseph Spence [Sir Harry Beaumont, pseud.], *Crito; or, A Dialogue on Beauty* (London: R. Dodsley, 1752), pp. 58–60.
2 Charlotte Lennox, *The Female Quixote; or, The Adventures of Arabella*, ed. Margaret Dalziel and intro. Margaret Anne Doody (Oxford: Oxford University Press, 1989), pp. 149–50.
3 The work of Bourdieu and Foucault has been important in forming and giving coherence to this project. This said I am struck by, and suspicious of, the tendency to homogenise which all too often characterises their work. See Pierre Bourdieu, *Distinction: A Social Critique of the Judgement of Taste*, trans. Richard Nice (London: Routledge, 1992) and Michel Foucault, *The Order of Things: An Archaeology of the Human Sciences* (London: Tavistock, 1970).
4 I can claim, as further justification for my critical practice, the existence of Howard Caygill's excellent study, *The Art of Judgement* (Oxford: Basil Blackwell, 1989). Caygill's book, unlike mine, does treat the issue of taste from the position of a historian of philosophy.
5 J.G.A. Pocock, *Virtue, Commerce and History: Essays on Political Thought and History Chiefly in the Eighteenth Century* (Cambridge: Cambridge University Press, 1985), pp. 66–67. For an account which supports that of

Pocock's work, though with a different emphasis, see Albert O. Hirshman, *The Passions and the Interests: Political Arguments for Capitalism before its Triumph* (Princeton: Princeton University Press, 1977), pp. 9–66.

6 Paul Langford, *A Polite and Commercial People: England 1727–83* (Oxford: Oxford University Press, 1992), p. 2.

7 Lawrence Klein, 'The Third Earl of Shaftesbury and the Progress of Politeness', *Eighteenth-Century Studies*, vol. 18, no 2 (Winter, 1984–85), p. 187.

8 For an account of the social history, to which I allude, see Paul Langford, *A Polite and Commercial People*, pp. 61–121; and Nicholas Rogers, *Whigs and Cities: Popular Politics in the Age of Walpole and Pitt* (Oxford: Clarendon Press, 1989), see esp. pp. 13–129, 259–303.

9 Neil McKendrick, 'Commercialisation and the Economy' in Neil McKendrick, John Brewer and J.H. Plumb, *The Birth of a Consumer Society: The Commercialization of Eighteenth-Century England* (London: Europa, 1982), pp. 9–33.

10 Susan Staves, in an important study, has charted the ways in which concepts of property and authority changed during the course of the early modern period. See her *Player's Scepters: Fictions of Authority in the Restoration* (Lincoln: University of Nebraska Press, 1979), especially pp. 43–110. For an alternative account of this process in the eighteenth century, and its 'semiological' significance, see James H. Bunn, 'The Aesthetics of British Mercantilism', *New Literary History*, vol. 11 (1980), pp. 303–21.

11 The phrase is taken from Marx's description of the fetishised commodity. See Karl Marx, *Capital*, 3 vols., trans. Ben Fowkes, with an intro. by Ernest Mandel (Pelican Marx Library, Harmondsworth: Penguin, 1988), vol. I, p. 163. For an informed account of how commodity fetishism functions within capitalist ideology see Terry Lovell, *Pictures of Reality: Aesthetics, Politics and Pleasure* (London: BFI, 1983), pp. 56–63.

12 The most cogent account of the politics of patrician taste and the attempt to defend and redefine it in the eighteenth century, is provided by David H. Solkin. See his *Richard Wilson – The Landscape of Reaction* (London: Tate Gallery Productions, 1982), pp. 56–76.

13 I am aware that there is a problem in any attempt to represent a single or simple middle-class identity within eighteenth-century society. In many respects the middle classes did not gain political coherence, at least in the parliamentary sense, until animated by the major political events of the latter half of the century. However, work by Leonore Davidoff and Catherine Hall suggests that, 'although the eighteenth-century middling groups had many affinities with the aristocracy and gentry, the basis of their property and their value systems and, not least the non-conformity of many in their ranks, set them apart', Davidoff

and Hall, *Family Fortunes: Men, Women and the English Middle Class, 1780–1850* (London: Hutchinson, 1987), p. 18. See also Catherine Hall, *White, Male and Middle-Class: Explorations in Feminism and History* (Cambridge: Polity Press, 1992), pp. 94–107, 151–71.

14 J.H. Plumb, 'The Acceptance of Modernity' in McKendrick, Brewer and Plumb, *The Birth of Consumer Society*, pp. 316–39. For a more extended treatment of this theme, see John Brewer and Roy Porter eds., *Consumption and the World of Goods* (New York: Routledge, 1993); James Raven, *Judging New Wealth: Popular Publishing and Responses to Commerce in England, 1750–1800* (Oxford: Clarendon Press, 1992); John Sekora, *Luxury: The Concept in Western Thought, from Eden to Smollett* (Baltimore: Johns Hopkins University Press, 1977); Peter Borsay, *The English Urban Renaissance: Culture and Society in the Provincial Town, 1660–1770* (Oxford: Clarendon Press, 1989).

15 McKendrick, 'Commercialism and the Economy', pp. 24–29.

16 Edward Moore et al., *The World*, no. 12 (March 22nd, 1753) in *The World, By Adam Fitz-Adam. A New Edition*, 3 vols. (Edinburgh: A. Donaldson, 1770) vol. I, p. 55.

17 I use the term 'tactic' in the sense articulated by Michel de Certeau. See his *The Practice of Everyday Life*, trans. Steven Rendell (Berkeley: University of California Press, 1984), esp. pp. 29–42.

18 Lady Mary Wortley Montagu, *The Nonsense of Common Sense*, no. II (27th December, 1737), in *Essays and Poems and Simplicity, A Comedy*, ed. R. Halsbrand and I. Grundy (Oxford: Clarendon Press, 1977), p. 109.

19 Wortley Montagu, *Essays and Poems*, p. 111.

20 Richard Steele, *Tatler*, no. 10 (May 3rd, 1709) in Joseph Addison and Richard Steele, *The Tatler*, ed. and intro. by Donald F. Bond (Oxford: Clarendon Press, 1987), p. 87.

21 *Ibid.*, vol. I, p. 88.

22 *Ibid.*, vol. I, p. 90.

23 For an account of this process of separation see Bourdieu, *Distinction*, pp. 29–32 and Eagleton, *The Ideology of the Aesthetic* (Oxford: Basil Blackwell, 1990), pp. 13–30. Eagleton's account may be profitably contrasted with his assessment of Postmodernity in his essay 'Capitalism, Modernism and Postmodernism' in *Against the Grain: Selected Essays* (London: Verso, 1988), pp. 131–48.

24 Jerome Stolnitz, in particular, bemoans beauty's fall from cultural significance. See his ' "Beauty": Some Stages in the History of an Idea', *Journal of History of Ideas*, vol. 22, no. 2 (April/June, 1962), pp. 185–204.

25 The *Oxford English Dictionary* offers two broad definitions of the term 'aesthetic'. First, Taste considered as a science or philosophy. Although this usage originates with Baumgarten in the period 1750–58, it is not found in common English usage until the 1830s. Secondly, as a science treating of sensuous perception. This is the more etymologically accurate definition, and was being used and defended as such by Kant

in the 1780s, entering English around 1800. It is this second definition
which provides the *OED*'s sole recorded use of the word in the
eighteenth century (and this from 1798), when a W. Taylor, writing in
the *Monthly Review* (vol. 25, p. 585), refers to the 'aesthetic', only to
disparage it as part of the 'dialect peculiar to professor Kant'. See also
Caygill, *The Art of Judgement*, p. 38.

26 Among the studies which have focused on a strictly 'aesthetic' approach
to the beautiful, W.J. Hipple's *The Beautiful, the Sublime and the Picturesque
in Eighteenth-Century British Aesthetic Theory* (Carbondale: University of
Southern Illinois Press, 1957) remains the most comprehensive and the
most persuasive in its general concerns. See also W.J. Bate, *From Classic
to Romantic: Premises in Taste in Eighteenth-Century England* (New York:
HarperTorch Books, 1961), and Samuel H. Monk, *The Sublime: A Study of
Critical Theories in XVIIIth-Century England* (Ann Arbor: University of
Michigan, 1960).

27 John Gilbert Cooper, *Letters Concerning Taste* (London: R. & J. Dodsley,
1755), p. 61.

28 *Ibid.*, p. 82.

29 [Henry Baker], *The Universal Spectator. By Henry Stonecastle*, 4 vols.
(London: A. Ward, J. Clarke et al. 1747), vol. III, pp. 46–47.

30 David Hume, 'Of the Standard of Taste' in *Essays, Moral, Political and
Literary*, ed. and intro. by Eugene F. Miller (Indianapolis: LibertyClassics, 1985), pp. 226–49.

31 *Ibid.*, p. 227.

32 Samuel Johnson, *The Rambler*, no. 92 (2nd February, 1751), in *The
Rambler*, ed. W.J. Bate & Albrecht B. Strauss in *The Yale Edition of the
Works of Samuel Johnson*, 14 vols. (New Haven: Yale University Press,
1969), vol. IV, p. 121.

33 Cooper, *Letters Concerning Taste*, p. 62.

34 *Ibid.*, pp. 62, 10–11, 26–28. I provide a fuller reading of Cooper's
position in Chapter One, below.

35 Edmund Burke, *A Philosophical Enquiry into the Origin of Our Ideas of the
Sublime and Beautiful*, ed. J.T. Boulton (Oxford: Basil Blackwell, 1990), p. 1.

36 Richard Payne Knight, *An Analytical Inquiry into the Principals of Taste*
(London: T. Payne and J. White, 1805), p. 9.

37 Frances Ferguson, 'Legislating the Sublime', in Ralph Cohen ed.,
Studies in Eighteenth-Century British Art and Aesthetics (Los Angeles: University of California Press, 1985), p. 142.

38 Neil Hertz, 'The Notion of Blockage in the Literature of the Sublime'
in Geoffrey Hartman ed., *Psycho-analysis and the Question of the Text*
(Baltimore: Johns Hopkins University Press, 1978), pp. 62–85.

39 Raymond Williams, *Keywords* (London: Fontana Press, 1983), pp. 11–12.

40 Raymond Williams, *Marxism and Literature* (Oxford: Oxford University
Press, 1977), p. 21. For a more extensive elaboration of this theme, see
Keywords, pp. 11–26. Of more direct relevance to eighteenth-century

studies are his *Culture and Society* (Harmondsworth: Penguin, 1971), especially pp. 13–19, and *The Country and the City* (London: Hogarth Press, 1985), especially, pp. 60–141.

41 Williams, *Keywords*, p. 11.

42 Burke, *Enquiry*, p. 11.

43 *Ibid.*, p. 12.

44 George Coleman et al., *Connoisseur*, no. 120 (13 May 1756) in *The Connoisseur. By Mr. Town, Critic and Censor-General*, 4 vols., 4th edn (London: R. Baldwin, 1761), vol. IV, p. 121.

45 For a fuller account of these debates see, Robert Donald Spector, *English Literary Periodicals and the Climate of Opinion during the Seven Years' War* (The Hague: Mouton, 1966), pp. 241–311.

46 For a discussion of the relation of taste to conceptions of both discourse and genre, see Stephen Copley, 'The Fine Arts in Eighteenth-Century Polite Culture' in John Barrell ed., *Painting and the Politics of Culture: New Essays on British Art 1700–1850* (Oxford: Oxford University Press, 1992), pp. 13–27. See also his 'Introduction' to *Literature and the Social Order* (London: Croom Helm, 1984), pp. 2–3.

47 Peter de Bolla, *The Discourse of the Sublime: Readings in History, Aesthetics and the Subject* (Oxford: Basil Blackwell, 1989), p. 7.

48 *Ibid.*, p. 8.

49 *Ibid.*, pp. 10–11.

50 Shaftesbury, Third Earl of [Anthony Ashley Cooper], *Characteristics of Men, Manners, Opinions, Times etc.*, 2 vols., ed. with intro. by John M. Robertson (Gloucester, Mass.: Peter Smith, 1963), vol. I, p. 279.

51 John Barrell, *The Political Theory of Painting from Reynolds to Hazlitt: 'The Body of the Public* (New Haven: Yale University Press, 1986), pp. 1–68.

52 Shaftesbury, *Characteristics*, vol. 1, p. 280. The most detailed examination of this theme in Shaftesbury's work has been provided by John Andrew Bernstein. See his 'Shaftesbury's Identification of the Good with the Beautiful', *Eighteenth-Century Studies*, vol. 10, no. 3 (Spring, 1977), pp. 304–25.

53 *Ibid.*, vol. 1, pp. 293–300.

54 *Ibid.*, vol. 1, p. 82.

55 Shaftesbury, *Characteristics*, vol. I, p. 217.

56 See in particular J.G.A. Pocock's *The Machiavellian Moment: Florentine Political Thought and the Atlantic Republican Tradition* (Princeton: Princeton University Press, 1975).

57 Pocock, *Machiavellian Moment*, pp. 361–505. His discussion of Burke is also to be found in *Politics, Language and Time: Essays in Political Thought and History* (London: Methuen, 1972), pp. 202–32. See also Isaac Kramnick, *Bolingbroke and his Circle: The Politics of Nostalgia in the Age of Walpole* (Cambridge, Mass.: Harvard University Press, 1968).

58 J.G.A. Pocock, 'Between Machiavelli and Hume: Gibbon as Civic Humanist and Philosophical Historian' in *Edward Gibbon and the Decline*

and Fall of the Roman Empire, ed. G.W. Bowersock and John Clive (Cambridge, Mass.: Harvard University Press, 1977), pp. 103–104.

59 Karl Marx and Frederick Engels, *The German Ideology*, ed. C.J. Arthur (London: Lawrence and Wishart, 1970), p. 64.

60 John Barrell, *The Birth of Pandora and the Division of Knowledge* (London: Macmillan, 1992), p. 63.

61 Shaftesbury, Third Earl of [Anthony Ashley Cooper], *Second Characters; or, the Language of Forms by the Right Honorable Anthony, Earl of Shaftesbury*, ed. Benjamin Rand (New York: Greenwood Press, 1969), pp. 22–23.

62 For an account of Shaftesbury's politics relative to his views on art, see Barrell, *Political Theory of Painting*, pp. 3–13. A more explicit marxist engagement with Shaftesbury has been made by Terry Eagleton, see his *Ideology of the Aesthetic*, pp. 34–38.

63 Pocock, *Machiavellian Moment*, pp. 40–41.

64 Shaftesbury, *Second Characters*, pp. 60–61.

65 Mark Akenside, *The Pleasures of the Imagination* (London: R. Dodsley, 1744), Bk. II, ll. 62–73.

66 *Ibid.*, Bk. 101, ll. 67–69.

67 See, for example, the representation of Beauty as an abstract (though physically perceived) manifestation of truth and order, and as an inspiration to good deeds in Book I of Akenside's *The Pleasures of the Imagination*, see especially, ll. 372–75, 418–21, 474–80.

68 *Ibid.*, See the 'Argument' to Book II.

69 *Ibid.*, Bk. II, l. 6.

70 Pocock, 'Between Machiavelli and Hume', p. 105.

71 For a discussion of how Shaftesbury's work may be read as an attempt to accommodate commerical culture to the exercise of virtue, see Caygill, *The Art of Judgement*, pp. 44–51.

72 Eagleton, *The Ideology of the Aesthetic*, p. 37.

73 Shaftesbury, *Characteristics*, vol. I, pp. 116–18, 178, 213–14.

74 Shaftesbury, *Second Characters*, pp. 31–33.

75 *Ibid.*, p. 33.

76 *Ibid.*, pp. 35, 39.

77 Joseph Spence, *Polymetis, or an Enquiry Concerning the Agreement Between the Works of the Roman Poets and the Remains of the Ancient Artists* (London: R. Dodsley, 1747), pp. 28, 43.

78 Shaftesbury, *Characteristics*, vol I, pp. 162–64.

79 Spence's account of the rise, excellence and eventual fall of the Roman poets conducted over two of the dialogues which compose *Polymetis* represents the fullest version of this thesis in the text, see pp. 17–27, 28–35. Importantly, Spence believed that, under Augustus, poetry reached a respectable middle age, an era which was both 'manly and polite', *Polymetis*, p. 35.

80 *Ibid.*, p. 66.

81 *Ibid.*, p. 73.

82 *Ibid.*, p. 68.
83 *Ibid.*, p. 66.
84 *Ibid.*, p. 67.
85 Shaftesbury, *Characteristics*, vol. I, p. 93.
86 Spence, *Polymetis*, pp. 67–68.
87 For a discussion of the politics of women's taste, see Ann Bermingham, 'The Aesthetics of Ignorance: The Accomplished Woman in the Culture of Connoisseurship', *The Oxford Art Journal*, vol. 16, no. 2 (1993), pp. 3–20; and Chloe Chard, 'Effeminacy, Pleasure and the Classical Body' in Gill Perry and Michael Rossington eds., *Femininity and Masculinity in Eighteenth-Century Art and Culture* (Manchester: Manchester University Press, 1994), pp. 142–61.
88 Spence, *Polymetis*, pp. 1–2.
89 For a discussion of this process, see Peter Stallybrass and Allon White, *The Politics and Poetics of Transgression* (London: Routledge, 1986) and G.J. Barker-Benfield, *The Culture of Sensibility: Sex and Society in Eighteenth-Century Britain* (Chicago: University of Chicago Press, 1992).
90 See Amanda Vickery, 'Golden Age to Separate Spheres? A Review of the Categories and Chronology of English Women's History', *The Historical Journal*, vol. 36, no. 2 (1993), pp. 383–414; and Dena Goodman, 'Public Sphere and Private Life: Toward a Synthesis of Current Historiographical Approaches to the Old Regime', *History and Theory: Studies in the Philosophy of History*, vol. 31 (1992), pp. 1–20.
91 Caygill, *The Art of Judgement*, pp. 48–53.
92 Barrell, *Birth of Pandora*, p. 87.
93 *Ibid.*, p. 82.
94 For an account of eighteenth-century leisure in relation to both commerce and politeness, see J.H. Plumb, 'The Commercialisation of Leisure in the Eighteenth Century' in McKendrick, Brewer and Plumb, *The Birth of Consumer Society*, pp. 265–85; Terry Castle, *Masquerade and Civilisation: The Carnivalesque in Eighteenth-Century English Culture and Fiction* (London: Methuen, 1986), pp. 1–109; David Solkin, *Painting for Money: The Visual Arts and the Public Sphere in Eighteenth-Century England* (New Haven: Yale University Press, 1993), pp. 106–56.
95 Pocock, *Machiavellian Moment*, pp. 462–67.
96 Klein, 'The Third Earl of Shaftesbury', p. 190.
97 *Ibid.*, pp. 187–88.
98 Nicholas Phillipson, 'Politics, Politeness and the Anglicanisation of Eighteenth-Century Scottish Culture' in R.A. Mason ed., *Scotland and England, 1286–1815* (Edinburgh: University of Edinburgh Press, 1987), p. 235.
99 *Ibid.*, p. 237.
100 *Ibid.*, p. 233.
101 For an account of Highmore's practices as a portrait-painter, see

David Mannings, 'A Well-Mannered Portrait by Highmore' in *Connoisseur*, vol. 189, no. 760 (June, 1975), pp. 116–19.

102 Joseph Highmore, 'Of Politeness and Complaisance, as Contradistinguished' in *Essays, Moral, Religious and Miscellaneous*, 2 vols. (London: B. White, 1766), vol. II, p. 48.

103 Klein, 'The Third Earl of Shaftesbury', pp. 190–92, 197–99.

104 *Ibid.*, pp. 46–47.

105 Joseph Addison, *Spectator*, no. 177 (September 22nd, 1711) in Joseph Addison and Richard Steele, *The Spectator*, ed. and intro Donald F. Bond, 5 vols. (Oxford: Clarendon Press, 1965), vol. 11, p. 198.

106 Joseph Addison, *Spectator*, no. 10 (March 12th, 1711), in Addison and Steele *Spectator*, vol. I, pp. 44–45.

107 Jürgen Habermas, *The Structural Transformation of the Public Sphere: An Inquiry into a Category of Bourgeois Society*, trans. Thomas Burger, assist. Frederick Lawrence (Cambridge: Polity Press, 1989).

108 Habermas, *Structural Transformation*, p. 52. For a useful consideration of the themes and limits of Habermas's work, see Craig Calhoun ed., *Habermas and the Public Sphere* (Cambridge, Mass.: Harvard University Press, 1992); and Anthony J. La Vopa, 'Conceiving a Public: Ideas and Society in Eighteenth-Century Europe', *Journal of Modern History*, vol. 64, (1992), pp. 79–116.

109 Pocock, *Machiavellian Moment*, esp. pp. 467–77, 493–505.

110 Lawrence Klein, 'Gender, Conversation and the Public Sphere in early Eighteenth-Century England' in *Textuality and Sexuality: Reading Theories and Practices*, ed. Judith Still and Michael Worton (Manchester: Manchester University Press, 1993), p. 100.

111 For a critique of Habermas's gender politics, see Nancy Fraser, *Unruly Practices* (Minneapolis: Minnesota University Press, 1989); and Andreas Huyssen, 'Mapping the Postmodern' in Linda J. Nicholson ed., *Feminism/Postmodernism* (London: Routledge, 1990), pp. 234–77.

112 Robert Markley, 'Sentimentality as Performance: Shaftesbury, Sterne and the Theatrics of Virtue' in Felicity Nussbaum and Laura Brown eds., *The New Eighteenth Century: Theory, Politics, English Literature* (London: Methuen, 1987), p. 213. A more general discussion of the discursive structures in which debates about religion, politics and the arts were conducted in the seventeenth century has been provided by Michael McKeon. See his 'The Politics of Discourse and the Rise of the Aesthetic in Seventeenth-Century England' in Kevin Sharpe and John D. Zwicker eds., *The Politics of Discourse: The Literature and History of Seventeenth-Century England* (Berkeley: University of California Press, 1987), pp. 36–51.

113 Markley, 'Sentimentality as Performance', p. 218.

114 For an example of the newly social debate on virtue and beauty, see *A Discourse Concerning the Propriety of Manners, Taste and Beauty, Being an Introduction to a Work hereafter published intituled Moral Beauty and Deformity,*

exemplified and contrasted in two living characters (London: no publisher credited, 1751).

115 An appraisal of this change in terms of the criticism of the Fine Arts has been made by Stephen Copley. See his 'The Fine Arts in Eighteenth-Century Polite Culture', pp. 13–37.

1 'A WANTON KIND OF CHASE': GENDER, LUXURY AND THE
DEFINITION OF TASTE

1 For a discussion of the philosophic and ideological range of eighteenth-century aesthetics see Peter de Bolla, *The Discourse of the Sublime: Readings in History, Aesthetics and the Subject* (Oxford: Basil Blackwell, 1989), pp. 27–102; Howard Caygill, *The Art of Judgement* (Oxford: Basil Blackwell, 1989), pp. 38–103.

2 John Brewer, ' "The Most Polite Age and the Most Vicious": Attitudes towards Culture as Commodity, 1660–1800', in Ann Bermingham and John Brewer eds., *The Consumption of Culture 1660–1800* (London: Routledge, 1995), pp. 341–61. See also Albert O. Hirshman, *The Passions and the Interests: Political Arguments for Capitalism before its Triumph* (Princeton: Princeton University Press, 1977).

3 Paul Langford, *A Polite and Commercial People: England 1727–1783* (Oxford: Oxford University Press, 1991), esp. pp. 59–121.

4 J.G.A. Pocock, *Virtue, Commerce and History – Essays on Political Thought and History, Chiefly in the Eighteenth Century* (Cambridge: Cambridge University Press, 1985), pp. 70–71.

5 For a further discussion of this issue see Neil McKendrick, 'The Commericalisation of Fashion' in Neil McKendrick, John Brewer and J.H. Plumb, *The Birth of a Consumer Society: The Commercialization of Eighteenth-Century England* (London: Europa, 1982), pp. 34–56. McKendrick makes the point that while critiques of fashion and commerce have a long history they reached a new pitch of vociferousness in the eighteenth century, testimony, he suggests, to the very substantial social and economic shifts undergone in the period.

6 Jonathan Richardson, *Two Discourses. I. An Essay on the whole Art of Criticism as it relates to Painting, shewing how to Judge I. Of the Goodness of a Picture; II. Of the Hand of the Master; III. Whether 'tis an Original, or a Copy. II. An Argument in Behalf of the Science of a Connoisseur; wherein is shewn the Dignity, Certainty, Pleasure and Advantage of it* (London: W. Churchill, 1719), II, p. 8.

7 Richardson, *Two Discourses*, II, p. 7; I, p. 16. For an overview of Richardson's critical agenda, see Carol Gibson-Wood, 'Jonathan Richardson and the Rationalisation of Connoisseurship', *Art History*, vol. 7, no. 1 (March, 1984), pp. 38–56. See also John Barrell, *The Political Theory of Painting from Reynolds to Hazlitt: "The Body of the Public"* (New Haven: Yale University Press, 1986), pp. 23–27, 45–54.

8 Richardson, *Two Discourses*, II, pp. 130–4.
9 *Ibid.*, II, pp. 18–26.
10 *Ibid.*, I, p. 26.
11 *Ibid.*, I, pp. 113, 111–2.
12 *Ibid.*, II, 231.
13 *Ibid.*, I, p. 144.
14 William Hogarth, *The Analysis of Beauty. Written with a View of Fixing the Fluctuating Ideas of Taste* (London: J. Reeve, 1753), p. 3.
15 Edmund Burke, *A Philosophical Enquiry into the Origin of Our Ideas of the Sublime and Beautiful*, ed. and intro. J.T. Boulton (Oxford: Basil Blackwell, 1990), pp. 13–14.
16 Caygill, *The Art of Judgement*, pp. 83–85.
17 Burke, *Enquiry*, p. 20.
18 David Hume, 'Of the Standard of Taste' in *Essays, Moral, Political and Literary*, ed. Eugene F. Miller (Indianapolis: LibertyClassics, 1985), pp. 226–49.
19 Hume, 'Of the Standard of Taste', pp. 235–40.
20 For a general discussion of these issues see Iain Pears, *The Discovery of Painting: The Growth of Interest in the Arts in England, 1680–1768* (London and New Haven: Yale University Press, 1988), pp. 27–50.
21 For a general discussion of this moment in English culture see, James Raven, *Judging New Wealth: Popular Publishing and Responses to Commerce in England, 1750–1800* (Oxford: Clarendon Press, 1992), pp. 157–82, 201–48.
22 Edward Moore et al., *The World* no. 15 (April 12th, 1753) in *The World. By Adam Fitz-Adam, A New Edition*, 3 vols. (Edinburgh: A. Donaldson, 1770), vol. I, p. 74.
23 Moore et al., *The World*, no. 15 (April 12th, 1753) in *The World* vol. i, p. 75; see also, *The World*, no. 12 (March 22nd, 1753); *The World*, no. 26 (June 28th, 1753), in *The World*, vol. I, pp. 57–58, 134–38.
24 For further examples of this criticism in the mid-century periodical see, *Connoisseur*, no. 2 (February 7th, 1754); *Connoisseur*, no. 33 (September 13th, 1754); *Connoisseur*, no. 113 (March 25th, 1756); *Connoisseur*, no. 135 (August 26th, 1756); *Connoisseur*, no. 139 (September 23rd, 1756), in *The Connoisseur. By Mr. Town, Critic and Censor-General*, 4th edn 4 vols. (London: R. Baldwin, 1761), vol. I, pp. 11–12, 255–61, vol. IV, pp. 65–71, 223–36, 266.
25 Brewer, "The Most Polite Age and the Most Vicious", pp.342–50; Raven, *Judging New Wealth*, pp. 157–182; Robert Donald Spector, *English Literary Periodicals and the Climate of Opinion during the Seven Years' War* (The Hague: Mouton, 1966), pp. 241–311.
26 Brewer 'The Most Polite Age of the Most Vicious', p 346.
27 *Ibid.*, pp. 345–50, 354–58.
28 Terry Castle, *Masquerade and Civilisation: The Carnivalesque in Eighteenth-Century English Culture and Fiction* (London: Methuen, 1986) pp. 1–51.
29 In one of his most famous essays Raymond Williams argued that nearly

all critical theories are theories of consumption. See 'Base and Super-structure in Marxist Cultural Theory', in Rick Rylance ed., *Debating Texts: A Reader in 20th Century Literary Theory and Method* (Milton Keynes: Open University Press, 1987), p. 214. Williams provides a more specific delineation of the emergence of 'culture' in his *Culture and Society* (Harmondsworth: Penguin, 1971), pp. 13–19, 23–47. For a more elaborate investigation of the relation of consumption to the formation of 'high culture' see Pierre Bourdieu, *Distinction: A Social Critique of the Judgement of Taste*, trans. Richard Nice (London: Routledge, 1992), pp. 97–256.

30 Caygill, *The Art of Judgement*, pp. 40–41.

31 For a discussion of this process see Jürgen Habermas, *The Structural Transformation of the Public Sphere: An Inquiry into a Category of Bourgeois Society*, trans. Thomas Burger with the assistance of Frederick Lawrence (Cambridge: Polity Press, 1989), pp. 1–26, 51–56. Habermas's conception of the 'bourgeois public sphere' has received specific elaboration in the areas of literature and the arts; see Terry Eagleton, *The Function of Criticism: From 'The Spectator' to Post-Structuralism* (London: Verso, 1984), pp. 8–14; Eagleton, *The Ideology of the Aesthetic* (Oxford: Basil Blackwell, 1990), pp. 31–32; and, Peter Uwe Hohendahl, *The Institution of Criticism* (Ithaca: Cornell University Press, 1982).

32 Joseph Addison, *Specator*, 411–21 (June 21st–July 3rd, 1712) in Joseph Addison and Richard Steele, *The Spectator*, 5 vols., ed. Donald F. Bond (Oxford: Clarendon Press, 1965), vol. III, pp.536–582.

33 Addison, *Spectator*, no. 409 (June 19th, 1712), in *Spectator*, vol. III, p. 531.

34 Addison, *Spectator*, no. 412 (June 23rd, 1712), in *Spectator*, vol. III, p. 542.

35 Addison, *Spectator*, no. 412 (June 23rd, 1712), in *Spectator*, vol. III, p. 544.

36 Addison, *Spectator*, no. 411 (June 21st, 1712), in *Spectator*, vol. III, p. 538–39.

37 Shaftesbury, Third Earl of [Anthony Ashley Cooper]. *Characteristics of Men, Manners, Opinions, Times etc.*, 2 vols., ed. with intro. by John M. Robertson (Gloucester, Mass.: Peter Smith, 1963), vol. II, pp. 126–27.

38 Addison, *Spectator*, no. 411 (June 21st, 1712) and no. 412 (June 23rd, 1712), in *Spectator*, vol. III, p. 538, 543.

39 Francis Hutcheson, *An Inquiry into the Original of our Ideas of Beauty and Virtue; in Two Treatises. I Concerning Beauty, Order, Harmony, Design. II. Concerning Moral Good and Evil*, 3rd edn (London: J. and J. Knapton et al, 1729).

40 *Ibid.*, p. 11.

41 *Ibid.*, pp. 12–13.

42 *Ibid.*, pp. 6–8.

43 *Ibid.*, p. xiii.

44 *Ibid.*, p. 7.

45 *Ibid.*, pp. 26, 14.

46 *Ibid.*, p. 6.

47 *Ibid.*, pp. 6–9, 88–92. For an account of this problem in Hutcheson's

work, see Peter Kivy, *The Seventh Sense* (New York: Burt Franklin, 1976), pp. 48–55.

48 Hutcheson, *Inquiry*, pp. 94–95.

49 *Ibid.*, p. 100.

50 *Ibid.*, pp. 94–95.

51 For a more detailed consideration of Hutcheson's positions see Daniela Gobetti, *Private and Public: Individual Households and the Body Politic in Locke and Hutcheson* (London: Routledge, 1992), esp. pp. 111–37.

52 Caygill, *The Art of Judgement*, pp. 53, 62.

53 For a discussion of this aspect of Hutcheson's work, see David Solkin, *Painting for Money: The Visual Arts ond the Public Sphere in Eighteenth-Century England* (New Haven: Yale University Press, 1993), pp. 82–87.

54 For a discussion of Hogarth's indebtedness to Addison see Ronald Paulson, *Hogarth vol. I: The Modern Moral Subject, 1697–1732* (Cambridge: Lutterworth Press, 1991), p. 76, *Hogarth vol. II: High Art and Low, 1732–1750* (Cambridge: Lutterworth Press, 1993), pp. 292, 335, 378, *Hogarth vol. III: Art and Politics, 1750–1764* (Cambridge: Lutterworth, 1993), pp. 68–69.

55 Paulson, *Hogarth vol. III: Art and Politics, 1750–1764*, pp. 63–67, 73–76.

56 David Bindman, *Hogarth* (London: Thames and Hudson, 1981), pp. 151–53.

57 Hogarth, *Analysis*, pp. 40–42, 46–47, 49–50.

58 [?Samuel Johnson], *Gentleman's Magazine*, vol. 24 (January, 1754) pp. 11–15. For an account of the reception of the *Analysis*, see Paulson, *Hogarth vol. III, Art and Politics, 1750–1764*, pp. 132–51.

59 Hogarth, *Analysis*, p. 2.

60 *Ibid.*, pp. iii–v.

61 *Ibid.*, pp. 66–67.

62 *Ibid.*, pp. 64–66.

63 *Ibid.*, p. 81.

64 *Ibid.*, p. 36.

65 *Ibid.*, pp. 125–26.

66 *Ibid.*, pp. 79–80, 122–34.

67 *Ibid.*, p. 25.

68 *Ibid.*, pp. 28.

69 *Ibid.*, pp. 36–37.

70 *Ibid.*, pp. 28, 25.

71 Michael Kitson, 'Hogarth's Apology for Painters' in *Walpole Society Notes*, vol. XII (1966–68), pp. 65, 71.

72 Paulson, *Hogarth vol. III; Art and Politics, 1750–1764*, pp. 81–85.

73 A useful account of this transformation in poetry and poetry criticism has been provided by Richard Wendorf. See his *William Collins and Eighteenth-Century English Poetry* (Minneapolis: University of Minnesota Press, 1981), pp. 27–55. A more general, but less satisfactory account, can be found in Joan Pittock, *The Ascendency of Taste: The Achievement of*

Joseph and Thomas Warton (London: Routledge, Kegan Paul, 1973), pp. 1–74.

74 For a discussion of this aspect of the *Seasons*, see Ralph Cohen, *The Unfolding of 'The Seasons'* (Baltimore: Johns Hopkins University Press, 1970), pp. 73–75.

75 James Thomson, *The Seasons*, ed. and intro. James Sambrook (Oxford: Clarendon Press, 1981), 'Spring', ll. 935, 936–37.

76 John Norton, 'Akenside's *The Pleasures of the Imagination: An Exercise in Poetics'* in *Eighteenth-Century Studies*, vol. 3, no. 3 (Spring, 1970), p. 370.

77 Akenside, *Pleasures of the Imagination* (London: R. Dodsley, 1744), Bk. I, ll. 124–25, 127–29; see also Norton, 'Akenside's *Pleasures*', pp. 371–72, 382–83.

78 Paulson, *Hogarth vol. III: Art and Politics, 1750–1764*, pp. 95–96.

79 Hogarth, *Analysis*, pp. 27–28.

80 *Ibid.*, pp. 137–38, 147–50.

81 For an alternative reading of the function of the 'Country Dance', and particularly its role in *Plate 2* of the *Analysis*, see Paulson, *Hogarth vol. III: Art and Politics, 1750–1764*, pp. 112–31.

82 Hogarth, *Analysis*, pp. 28–29, 59–66.

83 The claim that Hogarth engages with an aesthetic which attempts to rationalise the taste of the middle classes has most recently been made by David Solkin, see his *Painting for Money*, pp. 78–105.

84 Ronald Paulson, *The Beautiful, the Novel and the Strange: Aesthetics and Heterodoxy* (Baltimore: Johns Hopkins University Press, 1996), pp. 81–86. This is a position Paulson has maintained with great consistency; see also *Hogarth vol. III: Art and Politics, 1750–1764*, pp. xvi–xvii.

85 Samuel Johnson, *Adventurer* (November, 27th, 1753) in *The Idler and the Adventurer*, W.J. Bate, John M. Bullit and L.F. Powell, Yale Edition of the Works of Samuel Johnson (New Haven: Yale Univerisity Press, 1963), pp. 451–56. Oliver Goldsmith, *The Bee*, no. vii (November 17th, 1759) in *The Collected Works of Oliver Goldsmith*, ed. Arthur Friedman, 4 vols. (Oxford: Clarendon Press, 1966), vol. I, pp. 486–88.

86 Burke has been the subject of a number of different and frequently opposing critical readings. Indeed his work seems available to any number of possible interpretations. Of particular interest in terms of the present study has been the work of Frances Ferguson, *Solitude and the Sublime: Romanticism and the Aesthetics of Individuation* (London: Routledge, 1992), pp. 1–96 and Tom Furniss, *Edmund Burke's Aesthetic Ideology: Language, Gender and Political Economy in Revolution* (Cambridge: Cambridge University Press, 1993), pp. 15–112, both of whom allay questions of gender with procedures derived from post-structuralist criticism. A stimulating account of the *Enquiry's* textual operations has been also provided by Peter de Bolla. See his *The Discourse of the Sublime*, esp. pp. 61–72.

87 Furniss, *Edmund Burke's Aesthetic Ideology*, p. 24. However, Furniss also notes that in comparison to Hume, Burke's *Enquiry* continues to associate luxury with indolence and effeminacy see pp. 56–59.

88 Burke, *Enquiry*, p. 112.

89 *Ibid.*, pp. 42, 51, 109, 118–19.

90 *Ibid.*, p. 115.

91 *Ibid.*, pp. 107–109, 112–17.

92 *Ibid.*, pp. 114–15. For a further discussion of this passage see Frances Ferguson, *Solitude and the Sublime*, pp. 51–53.

93 *Ibid.*, pp. 92–109, 112.

94 *Ibid.*, pp. 41–42.

95 *Ibid.*, pp. 42–45, see also pp. 92, 113.

96 The connection between feeling and sociability was an important commitment for Burke, as, in his subsequent *Reflections on the Revolution in France*, he was to demonstrate a willingness to elevate the love of a woman into a vision of social cohesion. See Edmund Burke, *Reflections on the Revolution in France*, ed. and intro. Conor Cruise O'Brien (Harmondsworth: Penguin, 1986), pp. 164, 169–72. See also Caygill, *The Art of Judgement*, pp. 84–85; and, Ferguson, *Solitude and the Sublime*, pp. 8, 21, 31. For a more extensive discussion of Burke's theories relative to his political ideology see Furniss, *Edmund Burke's Aesthetic Ideology*, pp. 113–265.

97 Burke, *Enquiry*, pp. 11–27. See also Furniss, *Edmund Burke's Aesthetic Ideology*, pp. 78–83.

98 *Ibid.*, p. 91.

99 *Ibid.*, pp. 13, 23, 51–52.

100 *Ibid.*, pp. 149–50.

101 *Ibid.*, p. 150.

102 *Ibid.*, pp. 106, 135.

103 Thomas Cole, *Discourse of Luxury, Infidelity and Enthusiasm* (London: R. and J. Dodsley, 1761), p. 50.

104 John Sekora, *Luxury: The Concept in Western Thought, from Eden to Smollett* (Baltimore: Johns Hopkins University Press, 1977), esp. pp. 7–11, 62–131.

105 For a discussion of the diversity of texts written against luxury in the mid-century see Sekora, *Luxury*, pp. 63–109.

106 John Brown, *An Estimate of the Manners and Principals of the Times* (London: L. Davis and C. Reymers, 1757), p. 29.

107 *Ibid.*, pp. 36–38.

108 Samuel Fawconer, *An Essay on Modern Luxury: or, an Attempt to Delineate its Nature, Causes and Effect* (London: James Fletcher, 1765), pp. 11–13.

109 Brown, *Estimate*, p. 62.

110 *Ibid.*, pp. 45, 58, 73.

111 Samuel Fawconer, *Modern Luxury*, pp. 4–5.

112 Brown, *Estimate*, pp. 112–19.

113 Fawconer, *Modern Luxury*, pp. 38, 44–45, 55–56. For a more general account of this ideological position in eighteenth-century culture, see J.G.A. Pocock, *The Machiavellian Moment: Florentine Political Thought and the Atlantic Republican Tradition* (Princeton: Princeton University Press, 1975), pp. 423–61, 462–505.

114 Burke, *Enquiry*, pp. 40–43.

115 Caygill, *The Art of Judgement*, pp. 80–83.

116 Lord Kames [Henry Home], *Elements of Criticism*, 3 vols. (London and Edinburgh: A. Millar, and A. Kincaid & J. Bell, 1762), vol. I, p. 263.

117 Caygill, *The Art of Judgement*, p. 62.

118 Kames, *Elements*, vol. I, pp. 255–67.

119 *Ibid.*, vol. I, p. iii.

120 *Ibid.*, vol. I, pp. 8–17; vol. III, pp. 351–74.

121 *Ibid.*, vol. I, pp. 255–56.

122 *Ibid.*, vol. I, p. 6.

123 *Ibid.*, vol. III, pp. 370–71.

124 Caygill, *The Art of Judgement*, pp. 60–62, 84. See also Eagleton, *Ideology of the Aesthetic*, pp. 52–61.

125 Kames, *Elements*, vol. III, pp. 363–65.

126 Caygill, *The Art of Judgement*, p. 69.

127 Adam Smith, 'Of the Nature of that Imitation which takes Place in what are called the Imitative Arts' in *Essays on Philosophical Subjects with Dugald Stewart's Account of Adam Smith*, eds. W.P.D. Wightman, J.C. Bryce and I.S. Ross (Oxford: Clarendon Press, 1980), p. 183.

128 A notable exception to this trend was Smith's countryman, David Hume. See his 'Of the Refinement of the Arts' in *Essays, Moral, Political and Literary*, pp. 268–80.

129 David H. Solkin, *Richard Wilson – The Landscape of Reaction* (London: Tate Gallery Productions, 1982), pp. 58–64, 68–70.

130 In a number of recent studies there has been a growing awareness of the variety of readings to which Shaftesbury's work was available. See David Solkin, 'ReWrighting Shaftesbury: The Air Pump and the Limits of Commercial Humanism' in John Barrell ed. *Painting and the Politics of Culture* (Oxford: Oxford University Press, 1992), pp. 73–100; and Robert Markley, 'Sentimentality as Performance: Shaftesbury, Sterne and the Theatrics of Virtue' in Felicity Nussbaum and Laura Brown eds., *The New Eighteenth Century: Theory, Politics and English Literature (London and New York: Methuen, 1987), pp. 210–30*.

131 John Gilbert Cooper, *Letters Concerning Taste* (London: R. and J. Dodsley, 1755), p. iii.

132 *Ibid.*, p. 1.

133 *Ibid.*, p. 16. Cooper's commitment to the ideal of a rural retreat can also be seen in his *Epistles to the Great from Aristippus in Retirement* (London: R. and J. Dodsley, 1758).

134 Cooper, *Letters*, pp. 50, 52.

135 For a discussion of this theme in *The Seasons*, see John Barrell, *English Literature in History, 1730–80: An Equal, Wide Survey* (London: Hutchinson, 1983), pp. 59–63. Compare Terry Eagleton's point that the best way to support a public culture is to privatise it – *The Function of Criticism: 'The Spectator' to Post-Structuralism* (London: Verso, 1986), see especially, pp. 69–84.

136 Cooper, *Letters*, pp. 119–21.

137 *Ibid.*, pp. 16–17, 86.

138 *Ibid.*, p. 87. For an account of the 'ideological' impact of writing-to-the-moment, see Terry Eagleton, *The Rape of Clarissa: Sexuality and Class Struggle in Samuel Richardson* (Oxford: Basil Blackwell, 1982), pp. 23–26.

139 *Ibid.*, pp. 6, 68–69.

140 *Ibid.*, p. 51.

141 *Ibid.*, pp. 59, 71–79, 80–84.

142 *Ibid.*, p. 62.

143 Disapprobation of a taste for chinoiserie was in the 1750s and 1760s a crucial mark of traditional tastes. See Spector, *English Literary Periodicals and the Climate of Opinion*, pp. 241–368.

144 Kivy, *The Seventh Sense*, p. 222.

145 Cooper, *Letters*, p. 3.

146 *Ibid.*, p. 16.

147 Hutcheson, *Inquiry*, pp. 87–91.

148 Cooper, *Letters*, p. 10.

149 *Ibid.*, pp. 11–12.

150 *Ibid.*, p. 12.

151 The image of heart strings or chords was central to much of what has recently been defined as the culture of sensibility during the eighteenth century. For a discussion of this image and its significance, see Anne Jesse Van Sant, *Eighteenth-Century Sensibility and the Novel: The Senses in Context* (Cambridge: Cambridge University Press, 1993), pp. 7–9.

152 Cooper, *Letters*, pp. 30–31.

153 Walter Jackson Bate, *From Classic to Romantic: Premises in Taste in Eighteenth Century England, (New York: HarperTorch Books, 1961), p. 54.*

154 Kivy, *The Seventh Sense*, p. 223.

155 Cooper, *Letters*, pp. 71–72.

156 *Ibid.*, p. 74.

157 *Ibid.*, p. 86.

158 *Ibid.*, p. 67.

159 *Ibid.*, pp. 115–18.

160 *Ibid.*, p. 90.

161 *Ibid.*, pp. 28, 60, 89–99.

162 *Ibid.*, pp. 27–28.

163 *Ibid.*, pp. 28, 29–31.

164 *Ibid.*, p. 26.
165 For a discussion of the relation of sensibility to commercial culture see
     G.J. Barker-Benfield, *The Culture of Sensibility: Sex and Society in Eighteenth-
     Century Britain* (Chicago: University of Chicago Press, 1992) and John
     Mullan, *Sentiment and Sociability: The Language of Feeling in the Eighteenth
     Century* (Oxford: Clarendon Press, 1988).
166 For an account of Shaftesbury's concerns, see John Barrell, *The Birth of
     Pandora and the Division of Knowledge* (London: Macmillan, 1992),
     pp. 63–64.
167 Cooper, *Letters*, pp. 68–69.
168 George Berkeley, 'An Essay towards preventing the Ruin of Great
     Britain' in *The Works of George Berkeley, Bishop of Cloyne*, eds. A.A. Luce
     and T.E. Jessop, 9 vols. (London: Thomas Nelson, 1953), vol. VI, p. 74.
169 Berkeley, 'Ruin of Great Britain', p. 76.
170 Adam Smith, *The Theory of Moral Sentiments*, ed. D.D. Raphael and A.L.
     Macfie (Indianapolis: LibertyClassics, 1982), esp. pp. 9–16, 38–43.
171 John Mullan, *Sentiment and Sociability*, pp. 43–56.
172 For a further discussion of the 'Reformation of Male Manners', see
     Barker-Benfield, *Culture of Sensibility*, pp. 37–103.

2 'THE ART OF BEING PRETTY': POLITE TASTE AND THE JUDGEMENT OF WOMEN

1 John Hawkesworth et al., *Adventurer*, no. 82 (August 18th, 1753), *The
   Adventurer*, 3rd edn, 4 vols. (London: C. Hitch and L. Hawes, J. Payne,
   1756), vol. III, p. 105.
2 *Ibid.*, p. 109.
3 *Ibid.*, p. 110.
4 *Ibid.*, p. 111.
5 *Ibid.*, p. 109.
6 *Ibid.*, pp. 110, 105.
7 The sentiment was a commonplace, but was given a particularly vivid
   and extended treatment by James Fordyce. See his, *Sermons to Young
   Women*, 3rd edn, 2 vols. (London: A. Millar and T. Cadell, 1766), vol. I,
   pp. iv–vi, 17–18.
8 Edmund Burke, *A Philosophical Enquiry into the Origin of Our Ideas of the
   Sublime and Beautiful*, ed. and intro. J.T. Boulton (Oxford: Basil Blackwell,
   1990), pp. 40–44, 115–19; William Hogarth, *The Analysis of Beauty.
   Written with a View of Fixing the Fluctuating Ideas of Taste* (London: J. Reeve,
   1753), pp. 35–36, 65–67. See also Chapter One above.
9 Hawkesworth et al., *The Adventurer*, vol. III, p. 110.
10 Michel Foucault, *The Archaeology of Knowledge* (London: Tavistock, 1972),
    pp. 102–104.
11 Jürgen Habermas, *The Structural Transformation of the Public Sphere: An
    Inquiry into a Category of Bourgeois Society*, trans. Thomas Burger with the

assistance of Frederick Lawrence (Cambridge: Polity Press, 1989), pp. 43–56.

12 David Hume, 'Of Essay Writing', in *Essays, Moral, Political and Literary*, ed. E.F. Miller (Indianapolis: LibertyClassics, 1985), p. 535. The essay appeared only in *Essays, Moral, Political and Literary*, 2 vols. (Edinburgh: A. Kincaid, 1742) before being withdrawn.

13 Hume, 'Of Essay Writing', pp. 533–34. Hume recognised that such a mixing of the sexes rested upon the new social and commodified spaces of commercial society. See 'Of the Refinement of the Arts', in *Essays, Moral, Political and Literary*, pp. 268–80.

14 *Ibid.*, p. 535.

15 *Ibid.*, p. 536.

16 For an account of Hume's anxiety about the relation of society to philosophy see John Mullan, *Sentiment and Sociability: The Language of Feeling in the Eighteenth Century* (Oxford: Clarendon Press, 1988), intro. and ch. 1.

17 Hume, 'Of Essay Writing', p. 537.

18 For a discussion of Hume's role in the formation of politeness in relation to conversation see Stephen Copley, 'Commerce, Conversation and Politeness in the Early Eighteenth-Century Periodical', *British Journal of Eighteenth-Century Studies*, vol. 18, no. 1 (Spring, 1995), pp. 63–77.

19 Lawrence Klein, 'The Third Earl of Shaftesbury and the Progress of Politeness', *Eighteenth-Century Studies*, vol. 18, no. 2 (Winter, 1984–85), pp. 186–214. See also Peter Stallybrass and Allon White, *The Politics and Poetics of Transgression* (London: Routledge, 1986), pp. 80–124.

20 Alexander Gerard, *An Essay on Taste with Dissertations on the Same Subject by de Voltaire, D'Albert and de Montesquieu* (London and Edinburgh: A. Millar and Kincaid & Bell, 1759), pp. 200–202.

21 Allan Ramsay, the younger, 'A Dialogue on Taste', 2nd edn, in *The Investigator*, 4 vols. (London: For the Author, 1762), vol. II, pp. 29–31. Rather impishly, Ramsay suggested that Spence's book was most noted for the 'figure it has given him with the misses'. More to Spence's credit is Robert Wark's suggestion that Spence may have been a source for Reynolds in the preparation of his *Discourses*, see 'Principal Books Reynolds read or may have read in preparation for writing the *Discourses*', in Joshua Reynolds, *Discourses on Art*, 2nd edn (New Haven: Yale Univeristy Press, 1975), p. 338. For Spence's influence on Hogarth, see Ronald Paulson, *Hogarth vol III: Art and Politics, 1750–1764* (Cambridge: Lutterworth Press, 1993), pp. 464–65.

22 Daniel Webb, *An Inquiry into the Beauties of Painting, and into the Merits of the Most Celebrated Painters Ancient and Modern* (London: R. and J. Dodsley, 1760), p. iii.

23 In this context it is intriguing that Spence should have published *Crito* under the pseudonym 'Sir Harry Beaumont'. Spence appears to have employed the pseudonym when writing texts less obviously scholarly

than his accounts of the Grand Tour or, indeed, his conversations with Pope. However, it seems unlikely that the name was ever intended as an effective disguise, operating rather as a more cautious self-representation. The only other title published under this name – *Moralities; or, Essays, Letters, and Fables and Translations* – exhibits a similar stress on the pleasures of sensibility alongside moral instruction. See Joseph Spence, [Sir Harry Beaumont, pseud.], *Moralities; Or, Essays, Letters, and Fables and Translations* (London: R. Dodsley, 1753). For a fuller treatment of Spence's career, see Austin Wright, *Joseph Spence: A Critical Biography* (Chicago: University of Chicago Press, 1950), esp. pp. 126, 129–35, 140–44.

24 Joseph Spence [Sir Harry Beaumont, pseud.], *Crito; or, A Dialouge on Beauty* (London: R. Dodsley, 1752), pp. 1, 5.

25 Spence, *Crito*, pp. 3–4.

26 *Ibid.*, p. 12.

27 *Ibid.*, pp. 4–5.

28 *Ibid.*, pp. 44–45, 32–33.

29 *Ibid.*, pp. 6–7.

30 Joshua Reynolds, *The Idler*, no. 82 (November 10th, 1759) in *The Works of Sir Joshua Reynolds, Knight; Late President of the Royal Academy*, 3 vols. (London: T. Cadell, jnr. and W. Davies, 1801), vol. II, pp. 235–43.

31 For an example of the application of civic-humanist principles to the criticism of painting, see Joshua Reynolds, 'Discourse III' (14th December, 1770) and 'Discourse IV' (10th December, 1771), in *Discourses on Art*, ed. and intro. Robert R. Wark, 2nd edn (New Haven: Yale University Press, 1975) esp. pp. 39–53, 55–73.

32 Reynolds, *Works*, p. 240.

33 For a discussion of Reynolds's attitude to the customary see John Barrell's 'Sir Joshua Reynolds and the Englishness of English Art' in H.K. Bhabha ed., *Nation and Narration* (London: Routledge, 1990), pp. 154–76.

34 Spence, *Crito*, p. 7.

35 *Ibid.*, p. 12.

36 *Ibid.*, pp. 14–15.

37 *Ibid.*, p. 19.

38 *Ibid.*, p. 23.

39 Burke, *Enquiry*, pp. 91–92.

40 Spence, *Crito*, p. 24.

41 *Ibid.*, pp. 25–26.

42 *Ibid.*, pp. 38, 30–31.

43 *Ibid.*, pp. 29–30.

44 *Ibid.*, p. 37.

45 *Ibid.*, pp. 44–45.

46 *Ibid.*, pp. 46–50.

47 *Ibid.*, p. 53.

48 *Ibid.*, pp. 54–55.

49 Ramsay, *Dialogue on Taste*, pp. 17–18, see also pp. 10–14, 21–24.

50 Spence, *Crito*, p. 58.

51 *Ibid.*, pp. 59–60.

52 Alexander Pope, 'Epistle to a Lady' (1735), *The Poems of Alexander Pope*, edited by John Butt (London: Routledge, 1992 p. 569). For a discussion of this aspect of Pope's work see Ellen Pollak's *The Poetics of Sexual Myth: Gender and Ideology in the Verse of Swift and Pope* (Chicago: University of Chicago Press, 1985), pp. 22–76, 108–27.

53 Spence, *Crito*, pp. 60–61.

54 Joseph Spence, *Polymetis; or an Enquiry concerning the Agreement Between the Works of the Roman Poets and the Remains of the Ancient Artists* (London: R. and J. Dodsley, 1747), pp. 66–68.

55 Henry Home, Lord Kames, *Elements of Criticism*, 3 vols. (London & Edinburgh: A. Millar, and A. Kincaid & J. Bell, 1762), vol. I, p. 93.

56 Kames, *Elements*, vol. I, p. 95. While Kames's contribution to the history of taste is vital it is important to note that his account of the pleasures of looking upon distressed virtue is comparable to many sentimental texts of the period. See Ann Jesse Van Sant, *Eighteenth-Century Sensibility and the Novel: The Senses in Context* (Cambridge: Cambridge University Press, 1993), pp. 45–59.

57 David H. Solkin, *Painting for Money: The Visual Arts and the Public Sphere in Eighteenth-Century England* (New Haven: Yale University Press, 1992), p. 188.

58 For a discussion of Webb's criticism of painting in relation to other accounts of the polite arts during the mid-century see Stephen Copley, 'The Fine Arts in Eighteenth-Century Polite Culture' in John Barrell ed., *Painting and the Politics of Culture: New Essays on British Art 1700–1850* (Oxford: Oxford University Press, 1992), pp. 13–27.

59 Webb, *Beauties of Painting*, p. ix.

60 *Ibid.*, pp. 8–9.

61 *Ibid.*, p. 18. Webb's sense that painters were not necessarily able to judge of their own productions connects him with the discourse of gentlemanly connoisseurship dominant in eighteenth-century accounts of painting. See Iain Pears, *The Discovery of Painting: The Growth of Interest in the Arts in England, 1680–1768* (London and New Haven, Yale University Press, 1988), pp. 192–93.

62 Webb, *Beauties of Painting*, p. 8n.

63 *Ibid.*, p. 37.

64 *Ibid.*, p. 36, 29.

65 *Ibid.*, p. 29n.

66 *Ibid.*, p. 29n.

67 *Ibid.*, pp. 12, 134.

68 *Ibid.*, p. 29.

69 *Ibid.*, pp. 30–31.
70 *Ibid.*, p. 15.
71 Burke, *Enquiry*, p. 108.
72 Webb, *Beauties of Painting*, p. 31.
73 *Ibid.*, pp. 66–68.
74 *Ibid.*, pp. 123–25.
75 *Ibid.*, pp. 124, 125.
76 Reynolds, 'Discourse IV', in *Discourses on Art*, p. 72.
77 Webb, *Beauties of Painting*, pp. 194–96, 185–87.
78 *Ibid.*, pp. 134–35.
79 The Third Earl of Shaftesbury [Anthony Ashley Cooper], *Characteristics of Men, Manners, Opinions, Times etc.*, 2 vols., ed. and intro. John M. Robertson (Gloucester, Mass.: Peter Smith, 1963), vol. I, pp. 89–99.
80 Webb, *Beauties of Painting*, pp. 181–82.
81 *Ibid.*, pp. 186–87, 144–46.
82 *Ibid.*, pp. 188–89.
83 *Ibid.*, p. 189.
84 *Ibid.*, p. 191.
85 Lynda Nead has provided an illuminating discussion of this theme in art criticism, see her 'Seductive Canvasses: Visual Mythologies of the Artist and Artistic Creativity', *Oxford Art Journal*, vol. 18, no. 2 (1995), pp. 59–61.
86 George Turnbull, *A Treatise on Ancient Painting, containing Observations on the Rise, Progress, and Decline of the Art amongst the Greeks and Romans* (London: for the Author, 1740), p. 45. For a discussion of Turnbull's work see John Barrell, *The Political Theory of Painting from Reynolds to Hazlitt: The 'Body of the Public'* (New Haven: Yale Univeristy Press, 1986), pp. 18–20, 24–26, 37–45.
87 Burke, *Enquiry*, pp. 40–42.
88 James Usher, *Clio; or a Discourse on Taste Addressed to a Young Lady* (London: T. Davis, 1767), p. 1.
89 Joseph Addison, *Spectator*, no. 10 (March 12th, 1711), in Joseph Addison and Richard Steele, *The Spectator*, ed. Donald F. Bond, 5 vols. (Oxford: Clarendon Press, 1965), vol. I, p. 44.
90 Usher, *Clio*, p. 91.
91 *Ibid.*, pp. 17–18.
92 *Ibid.*, pp. 18–19, 20.
93 *Ibid.*, p. 4.
94 *Ibid.*, p. 91.
95 *Ibid.*, p. 2.
96 *Ibid.*, p. 37.
97 Kathryn Shevelow, *Women and Print Culture: The Construction of Femininity in the Early Periodical* (London: Routledge, 1989), pp. 33–34, 43–44, 45.
98 Shevelow, *Women and Print Culture*, pp. 32, 47. For a further account of the ways in which the practices of conversation were gendered see

Lawrence Klein, 'Gender, Conversation and the Public Sphere in early Eighteenth-Century England' in Judith Still and Michael Worton eds., *Textuality and Sexuality: Reading Theories and Practice* (Manchester: Manchester University Press, 1993), pp. 100–12.

99 Usher, *Clio*, pp. 2–3, 5, 13–14.

100 *Ibid.*, p. 22.

101 *Ibid.*, pp. 27–28.

102 *Ibid.*, pp. 53–54.

103 *Ibid.*, pp. 60–61.

104 *Ibid.*, p. 68.

105 *Ibid.*, p. 28.

106 See, for example, *Reflections Arising from the Immorality of the Present Age* (London: M. Cooper, 1756), p. 19.

107 Usher, *Clio*, pp. 15–16. The most obvious significance of 'inward light' here is as an allusion to the Protestant, perhaps specifically Quaker, notions of the converted or redeemed soul.

108 *Ibid.*, p. 23.

109 *Ibid.*, p. 31.

110 Peter de Bolla, *The Discourse of the Sublime: Readings in History Aesthetics, and the Subject* (Oxford: Basil Blackwell, 1989), pp. 8–12, 27–102.

111 Paul de Man, *The Resistance to Theory* (Minneapolis: Minnesota University Press, 1986), p. 5.

112 Usher, *Clio*, p. 38–39.

113 *Ibid.*, pp. 79, 80.

114 *Ibid.*, p. 44.

115 [Cosmetti], *The Polite Arts, Dedicated to the Ladies* (London: Roach, 1767), p. 8.

116 *Ibid.*, p. 9.

117 *Ibid.*, pp. 26, 23–24.

118 *Ibid.*, p. 22. The patronising tone of Cosmetti's advice is not dissimilar to the general tenor of account of female 'accomplishments'. For a discussion of this theme see Ann Bermingham, 'The Aesthetics of Ignorance: The Accomplished Woman in the Culture of Connoisseurship', *Oxford Art Journal*, vol. 16, no. 2 (1993), pp. 3–20.

119 For a discussion of the theme see Nancy Armstrong, *Desire and Domestic Fiction: A Political History of the Novel* (Oxford: Oxford University Press, 1987), pp. 28–58, 108–34; Jill Campbell, *Natural Masques: Gender and Identity in Fielding's Plays and Novels* (Stanford, Stanford University Press, 1995), pp. 201–41; and John P. Zomchich, *Family and Law in Eighteenth-Century Fiction: The Public Conscience in the Private Sphere* (Cambridge: Cambridge University Press, 1993).

120 Dr J. Cosens, *The Economy of Beauty in a Series of Fables addressed to the Ladies*, 2 vols. (London: J. Wilkie, 1772).

121 Thomas Marriot, *Female Conduct: Being an Essay on the Art of Pleasing, to be practiced before and after Marriage* (London: W. Owen, 1759). For a

contrasting view of female beauty see Robert Dodsley, *Beauty; or, the Art of Charming* (London: Lawton Gilliver, 1735).

122 Usher, *Clio*, pp. 61, 68.

123 For a fuller discussion of this important theme see Peter Uwe Hohendahl, *The Institution of Criticism* (Ithaca: Cornell University Press, 1982).

124 George Coleman et al., *Connoisseur*, no. 75 (July 3rd, 1755) in *The Connoisseur. By Mr. Town, Critic and Censor-General*, 4th edn, 4 vols. (London: R. Baldwin, 1761), vol. III, p. 30.

125 Addison, *Spectator*, no. 177 (September 22nd, 1711) in Joseph Addison and Richard Steele, *The Spectator*, 5 vols., ed. Donald F. Bond (Oxford: Clarendon Press, 1965) vol. II, p. 195.

3 'SUCH STRANGE UNWONTED SOFTNESS': JOSHUA REYNOLDS
AND THE PAINTING OF BEAUTY

1 The Painting is now commonly ascribed the title, *Elizabeth Gunning, Duchess of Hamilton and Argyll*, and is in the possession of the Lady Leverhulme Art Gallery, Merseyside.

2 Desmond Shawe-Taylor, *The Georgians: Eighteenth-Century Portraiture and Society* (London: Barrie and Jenkins, 1990), p. 147. Martin Postle also begins his discussion of Reynolds with an examination of this portrait. See his *Sir Joshua Reynolds: The Subject Pictures* (Cambridge: Cambridge University Press, 1995), pp. 3–5.

3 David Mannings, 'Elizabeth Gunning, Duchess of Hamilton and Argyll' in *Reynolds*, ed. Nicholas Penny with contributions by Diana Donald et al. (London: Royal Academy of Arts, 1986), pp. 197, 199.

4 Postle provides a lengthy study of how Reynolds manipulated his portrait commission in order to satisfy his own commercial, as well as artistic, ambitions. See *Sir Joshua Reynolds*, pp. 1–57.

5 Shawe-Taylor, *Georgians*, pp. 151, 147.

6 For an account of this problem see Marcia Pointon, *Hanging the Head: Portraiture and Social Formation in Eighteenth-Century England* (New Haven: Yale University Press, 1993), pp. 1–9, 13–52.

7 A useful account of Reynolds's function as a 'third person' spokesman for the cultured elite, rather than as a commentator on his own work is provided in David Mannings, *Studies in British Portrait Painting in the Eighteenth Century with Special Reference to the Early Work of Sir Joshua Reynolds*, unpubl. PhD thesis, University of London, 1977.

8 John Barrell, *The Political Theory of Painting from Reynolds to Hazlitt: 'The Body of the Public'* (New Haven: Yale University Press, 1986), pp. 63–72.

9 There is only a handful of references to the portrayal of women in the whole of the *Discourses*. One of these praises the *Venus di Medici*, but it comes amidst a general commendation of the art of statuary.

10 An account of how portraiture could be reconciled with public virtue is

234 *Notes to pages 122–24*

provided in David Mannings, 'Shaftesbury, Reynolds and the Rediscovery of Portrait Painting in Eighteenth-Century England' in *Zeitshrift
für Kunstgeschitche*, vol. 48 (1984), pp. 319–28.

11 For a discussion of the relationship between femininity, portrayal and
desire in Reynolds's work see Marcia Pointon, 'Graces, Bacchantes and
"Plain Folks": Order and Excess in Reynolds's Female Portraits', *British
Journal of Eighteenth-Century Studies*, vol. 17, no. 1 (Spring, 1994), pp. 1–26.
See also Gill Perry, 'Women in Disguise: Likeness, the Grand Style and
the Conventions of Feminine Portraiture in the Work of Sir Joshua
Reynolds' in Gill Perry and Michael Rossington eds., *Femininity and
Masculinity in Eighteenth-Century Art and Culture* (Manchester: Manchester
University Press, 1994), pp. 18–40.

12 For a range of art historical responses to the painting see Algernon
Graves and William Vine Cronin, *The History of the Works of Joshua
Reynolds*, 4 vols. (London: Henry Graves, 1899–1901), vol. II, pp. 421–22;
Charles Robert Leslie and Tom Taylor, *The Life and Times of Sir Joshua
Reynolds: with notices of some of his contemporaries*, 2 vols. (London: John
Murray, 1865), vol. I, pp. 102, 181; R. Tatlock, *A Record of the Collections in
the Lady Lever Art Gallery*, 2 vols. (London: 1928) vol. I, pp. 60–62; and Ellis
K. Waterhouse, *Reynolds* (London: Trench Trubner, 1941), pp. 11–12.

13 Quoted in William T. Whitley, *Artists and their Friends in England, 1700–79*,
2 vols. (London: Medici Society, 1928), vol I, pp. 167–68. Horace
Walpole also identified the sitter correctly, noting in his copy of the
exhibition catalogue that the portrait represented, 'Duchess of Hamilton. Elizabeth Gunning'. See, 'Notes by Horace Walpole, Fourth
Earl of Orford, on the Exhibitions of the Society of Artists and Free
Society of Artists, 1760–91', transcribed and edited by Hugh Gatty in
Walpole Society Notes, vol. XXVII (1938–39), p. 76. The title is typically
innocuous. Reynolds exhibited a number of paintings under this title.
Its effects are twofold: firstly it hides the sitter behind a publicly
acceptable, even anonymous, façade. Secondly it places the painting in
the category in which it is to be sold: a *whole length*.

14 John Brown, *An Estimate of the Manners and Principals of the Times* (London:
L. Davis and C. Reymers, 1757), pp. 44–45.

15 George Coleman et al., the *Connoisseur*, no. 21 (June 27th, 1754) and no.
72 (26 June 1755), in *The Connoisseur. By Mr Town, Critic and Censor-General*,
4th edn, 4 vols. (London: R. Baldwin, 1761), vol. I, pp. 172–78 and vol.
III, pp. 21–28.

16 Coleman et al., *Connoisseur*, no. 36 (October 3rd, 1754), no. 38 (October,
17th 1754) and no. 44 (November 28th, 1754), in *The Connoisseur. By Mr.
Town*, vol. II, pp. 4–8, 19, 69–70.

17 The suggestion that women were walking around naked as the consequence of following fashion was quite common in the 1750s. See for
example, [Adam Eden], *Vindication of the Reformation, on foot, among the
Ladies, to Abolish Modesty and Chastity, and Restore the Native Simplicity of going*

Naked. And an Attempt to reconcile all Opposers to it, and make them join in a speedy Completion of this Glorious Design (London: R Griffiths, 1755); and, the *World*, no. 21 (May 24th, 1753) in *The World. By Adam Fitz-Adam. A New Edition*, 3 vols (Edinburgh: A Donaldson, 1770) vol. I, pp. 110–11.

18 These connections have been made most cogently by Harriet Guest. See her 'A Double Lustre,: Femininity and Sociable Commerce, 1730–60' in *Eighteenth-Century Studies*, vol. 23, no. 4 (Summer, 1990), pp. 479–501.

19 For the purposes of this argument, I am concerned exclusively with this particular moment of the painting's exhibition. Between 1764 and 1919 the painting hung at Hamilton Palace; the form of this display seems to me to be wholly different from the public visibility of either the exhibition or Reynolds's studio.

20 Iain Pears, *The Discovery of Painting: The Growth of Interest in the Arts in England, 1680–1768* (London and New Haven: Yale University Press, 1988), pp. 133–56.

21 The beginnings of such an inquiry can be found in David Mannings, 'At the Portrait Painters: How the Painters of the eighteenth century conducted their studios and their sittings' in *History Today*, vol. 27 (1977), pp. 279–87; and Pointon, *Hanging the Head*, pp. 36–52.

22 André Rouquet, *The Present State of the Arts in England* (London: no publisher credited, 1755), pp. 6–8, 11–16, 21–23.

23 *Ibid.*, p. 33.

24 *Ibid.*, p. 36.

25 *Ibid.*, pp. 38–39.

26 *Ibid.*, p. 46 (my emphasis); *The Duchess of Hamilton and Argyll* remained in Reynolds's possession for four years after the exhibition, and would probably have hung in the suite of rooms which composed his studio and reception area.

27 *Ibid.*, p. 49.

28 *Ibid.*, pp. 46–47.

29 *Catalogue of the Pictures, Sculptures, Models, Drawings, Prints etc., Exhibited in the Great Room of Society for the Encouragement of Arts, Manufactures & Commerce, 21st April, 1760* (London: For the Society, 1760). See also Ellis K. Waterhouse, *Reynolds* (London: Phaidon, 1973), pp. 177–78.

30 Charles Robert Leslie and Tom Taylor, *Life and Times of Sir Joshua Reynolds*, vol I, p. 181, n. 2.

31 Ronald Paulson has commented at some length on the Royal Academy submission of 1771, in terms of a comparison between the images of women on offer, see his *Breaking and Remaking: Aesthetic Practice in England, 1700–1820* (New Brunswick: Rutgers University Press, 1989), pp. 277–96.

32 I am thinking here of the kinds of choice and discrimination David Mannings has isolated in Reynolds's *Garrick between Tragedy and Comedy*. See his 'Reynolds, Garrick and the Choice of Hercules' in *Eighteenth-Century Studies*, vol. 17, no. 3 (Spring, 1984), pp. 260–83.

33 The phrase is Lynda Nead's. See her *The Female Nude: Art, Obscenity and Sexuality* (London: Routledge, 1992).

34 A full biography of Elizabeth Gunning is provided by W. Horace Bleackley, *The Beautiful Duchess. Being an Account of the Life and Times of Elizabeth Gunning, Duchess of Hamilton and Argyll*, 2nd edn (London: John Lane, 1927).

35 Elizabeth Montagu, quoted in E.J. Climenson, *Elizabeth Montagu – Queen of the Blue Stockings. Her Correspondence from 1720–61. By her Great-Great Niece*. 2 vols. (London: John Murray, 1906), vol. I, p. 270.

36 Their father's correspondence reveals that he and his brother, if no one else, knew exactly what business had been embarked upon by bringing his daughters to London. Indeed, his letters make it explicit that he wanted nothing less than a good 'price' for his daughters' 'virtue'. A selection from Gunning's letters has been quoted in Ida Gantz, *The Pastel Portrait: The Gunnings of Castlecoote and the Howards of Hampstead* (London: The Cresset Press, 1962), pp. 30–31, 38–41.

37 Samuel Richardson, 'Letter to Miss Westcomb', August 6th, 1750, MS in the Forster Collection, Victoria and Albert Museum, filed as FM. XIV, 3, ff 53–54. The text is quoted in part in T.C. Duncan Eaves and Ben D. Kimpel, *Samuel Richardson: A Biography* (Oxford: Clarendon Press, 1971), p. 199.

38 Horace Walpole, 'To Sir Horace Mann', June 18th 1751, Letter 327, *The Letters of Horace Walpole*, 9 vols., ed. P. Cunningham (Edinburgh: John Grant, 1906), vol. II, p. 259. The closing reference to an earthquake alludes to the tremors which struck London on 8 February and 8 March 1750. The cause of the quakes was attributed to a mixture of masquerades, the royal fireworks and *Tom Jones*; in short, the luxury of the times.

39 Walpole, 'To Sir Horace Mann', February 27th 1752, Letter 337, *Letters*, vol. II, p. 279.

40 [A.W.], 'On a Late Incident. By A Lady', in *Gentleman's Magazine*, vol. 21 (February, 1751) (London: E. Cave), p. 83.

41 Elizabeth Montagu, quoted in Climenson, *Elizabeth Montagu*, vol. I, p. 287. See also Mary Delany, 'To Mrs Dewes [sister]', 8 June 1750, letter, *The Autobiography and Correspondence of Mary Delany with Interesting Reminicences of King George III and Queen Charlotte*, ed. Rt. Hon. Lady Llanover, 3 vols. (London: Richard Bentley, 1861), vol. II, pp. 551–53.

42 'An Epistle to a Gentleman of Ireland. Written soon after the Arrival of the Miss G_____gs in London, *Gentleman's Magazine*, vol. 20 (June, 1750), p. 277.

43 Walpole, 'To George Montagu, Esq,' June 2nd, 1759, Letter 612, *Letters*, vol. III, p. 229.

44 Walpole, 'To George Montagu, Esq,' June 23rd, 1759, Letter 616, *Letters*, vol. III, p. 233.

45 The total amount raised in this way was said to be two and a half

guineas; see Ruth M. Bleackley, 'The Beautiful Miss Gunnings' in *The Connoisseur*, vol. XII (May–August, 1905), pp. 163–64.

46 Joshua Reynolds, 'To Miss Weston', 30 April 1751, Letter VII, *Letters of Sir Joshua Reynolds* collected and edited by F.W. Hilles (Cambridge: Cambridge University Press, 1929), pp. 10–11.

47 For a discussion of the kinds of dress used in eighteenth-century portraiture see Aileen Riberio, 'Some Evidence of the Influence of the Dress of the Seventeenth Century in Eighteenth-Century Female Portraiture' in *Burlington Magazine*, vol. 119 (December, 1977), pp. 834–40.

48 Gavin Hamilton, *Elizabeth Gunning Duchess of Hamilton*, 1752–53, The Hamilton Collection.

49 Francis Cotes, *Elizabeth Gunning, Duchess of Hamilton and Argyll*, Trustees of the 10th Duke of Argyll, Inverary Castle; Shawe-Taylor, *The Georgians*, pp. 152–53.

50 Sittings commenced in January, 1758 and continued sporadically through to the June of the following year. Elizabeth's husband, John, sixth Duke of Hamilton died on January 18th 1758 in between the first (cancelled) and second appointments which occurred on the 16th and 20th of the same month. Her widowhood was, however, to be short lived, as she married Col. John Campbell, later fifth Duke of Argyll, on the 3 February 1759. There were perhaps four appointments between her first husband's death and her second marriage. A concluding sitting seems to have occurred on June 2nd, though the picture was to remain with Reynolds until April, 1764.

51 It is an anxiety Elizabeth Gunning may well have shared. Indeed she was desirous of rectifying her status through the favours of George III. The endeavour was not though to receive universal acclaim, as Lady Mary Coke suggested: 'She [Lady Betty] told me the Duchess of Hamilton was asking to be made a peeress in her own right, and remainder to her son. As Lord Lorn [2nd husband, later the Duke of Argyll] had just received that favour, I thought with her that the Duchess of Hamilton, considering her Birth, cou'd have the least pretensions to such a favour', January 26th, 1767, *The Letters and Journals of Lady Mary Coke*, 4 vols. (Edinburgh: David Douglas, 1889), vol. I, p. 124.

52 Overt symbols of aristocratic rank are not unusual in Reynolds's *œuvre*. However, in this case, it would have been sufficiently striking to have attracted notice. Other examples would include *Rebecca, Countess Folkestone* (1761), *Maria, Countess Waldegrave Later Duchess of Gloucester* (1759) and *Mary Parton, Duchess of Ancaster* (1764).

53 A point emphasised by the fact that Reynolds's 1764 painting of Kitty Fisher has her both draped in an ermine, and accompanied by two doves. To an extent, such symbols merely associate the sitter with Venus; however, the significance of ermine, both as a symbol of chastity

and nobility would appear to be rendered ironic by placing it upon a woman like Kitty Fisher.

54 Alastair Smart, *Allan Ramsay: Painter, Essayist and Man Of Enlightenment* (New Haven: Yale University Press, 1992), pp. 189–90.

55 Mannings, 'The Duchess of Hamilton and Argyll', p. 198.

56 David Mannings, 'Reynolds and the Restoration Portrait', *Connoisseur*, no. 183 (July, 1973), pp. 186–93.

57 William Hazlitt, quoted in Oliver Millar, *The Tudor, Stuart and Early Georgian Pictures in the Collection of Her Majesty the Queen* (London: Phaidon, 1963), p. 124.

58 J. Douglas Stewart, 'Pin-Ups or Virtues? The Concept of the "Beauties" in Late Stuart Portraiture' in *English Portraits of the Seventeenth and Eighteenth Centuries* (Los Angeles: California University Press, 1974), pp. 3–27.

59 *The Charms of Beauty; or, the Grand Contest between the Fair Hibernians, and the English Toasts, A Poem. Occasioned by the Marriage of his Grace the Duke of Hamilton with Miss Elizabeth Gunning; and the expected marriage of her elder Sister with a certain noble Earl* (London: J. Gifford, 1752), p. 1.

60 See, for example, *Peeping Tom to the Countess of Coventry. An Epithalamium* (London: S. Price and R. Wilson, 1752).

61 Walpole, 'To Sir Horace Mann', August 31st 1751, Letter 330, *Letters*, vol. II, p. 265.

62 David Solkin, 'Great Pictures or Great Men: Reynolds, Male Portraiture and the Power of Art' in *Oxford Art Journal*, vol. 9, no. 2 (1986), pp. 42–49.

63 Joseph Spence [Sir Harry Beaumont, pseud.], *Polymetis: or, An Enquiry Concerning the Agreement between the Works of the Roman Poets, and the Remains of the Ancient Artists* (London: Dodsley, 1747), p. 143.

64 See John Barrell, *The Birth of Pandora and the Division of Knowledge* (London: Macmillan, 1992), pp. 63–88 and J.R. Hale, 'Art and Audience: The Medici Venus', in *Italian Studies*, vol. 31 (1976), pp. 37–58.

65 *The Judgement of Paris; or, the Triumph of Beauty. A Pastoral Ballad Opera in one act* (London: J Roberts, 1731) and Ralph Schönberg, *The Judgement of Paris. An English Burletta* (London: T. Beckett and P.A. de Hondt, 1768).

66 James Beattie, *The Judgement of Paris*, in *The Poetical Works of Beattie, Blair and Falconer* (Edinburgh: James Nichol, 1854), pp. 52–71.

67 Lady Sarah Bunbury, 'To Susan O'Brien', quoted in *The Life and Letters of Lady Sarah Lennox, 1745–1826*, eds. The Countess of Ilchester and Lord Stavordale, 2 vols. (London: John Murray, 1902), vol. I, p. 155.

68 Elizabeth Montagu, *Letters of Elizabeth Montagu, with some notices of her contemporaries*, 3 vols. (London: T. Cadell, 1813), vol. III, p. 166.

69 Spence, *Polymetis*, p. 140.

70 Walpole was much given to inspecting beautiful women; on one particular occasion he took it upon himself to appraise the relative merits of Maria Gunning, Lady Kildare and Lady Pitt-Rivers. See his

Memoirs of the Reign of George the Third, 4 vols. (London: Lawrence and Bullen, 1984), vol. III, p. 131, n. 1.

71 See, for example, Edward Snow, 'Theorising the Male Gaze: Some Problems' in *Representations*, vol. 25 (Winter, 1989), pp. 30–41.

72 Stephen Daniels, 'Loutherbourg's *"Chemical Theatre"* Coalbrookedale by Night' in John Barrell ed., *Painting and the Politics of Culture: New Essays in British Art, 1700–1850* (Oxford: Oxford University Press, 1992), pp. 195–230.

73 See Edgar Wind, *Hume and the Heroic Portrait: Studies in Eighteenth-Century Imagery*, ed. Jaynie Anderson (Oxford: Clarendon Press, 1986), plates 52–54.

74 For an account of Reynolds's portrait of Anne Dashwood, see Alexander S. Gourlay and John E. Grant, 'The Melancholy Shepherdess in Prospect of Love and Death', in *Bulletin of Research in the Humanities*, vol. LXXXV (1982), pp. 169–89.

75 Walpole, 'To Sir Horace Mann', October 5th, 1760, Letter 686, *Letters*, vol. III, p. 345.

76 Walpole, 'To Sir Horace Mann', November 1st 1760, Letter 693, *Letters*, vol. III, p. 358.

77 Lord Chesterfield, 'To Soloman Dayrolles', 17 March 1752, Letter 1819, *Letters of Philip Dormer Stanhope, Fourth Earl of Chesterfield*, ed. and intro. by Bonamy Dobrée, 6 vols. (London: Eyre & Spottiswode, 1933), pp. 1852–53.

78 See for example, William Mason's 'On the Death of a Lady', written on the occasion of Maria Gunning's death, in *The British Poets including Translations*, 100 vols. (Chiswick: C. Whittingham, 1822), vol. 77, pp. 86–89. For a more general discussion of the relation of beauty to the figure of Death, see Elisabeth Bronfen, *Over Her Dead Body: Death, Femininity and the Aesthetic* (Manchester: Manchester University Press, 1993), esp. pp. 59–75, 110–40.

79 Paulson, *Breaking and Remaking*, pp. 230–45.

80 John Evans, *Juvenile Pieces: Designed for the Youth of Both Sexes*, 3rd edn (London: John Phillips, 1797), p. 71.

81 Mannings, 'Duchess of Hamilton and Argyll', p. 198.

82 Waterhouse, *Reynolds*, p. 22.

83 Walpole, 'To Sir Horace Mann', November 1st, 1760, Letter 693, *Letters*, vol. III, p. 358.

84 Susan Staves, 'British Seduced Maidens', in *Eighteenth-Century Studies*, vol. 14, no. 2 (Winter, 1980–81), pp. 109–34.

85 David Solkin, *Painting for Money: The Visual Arts and the Public Sphere in Eighteenth-Century England* (New Haven: Yale University Press, 1993), pp. 178–79.

86 The phrase is Barrell's see *Birth of Pandora*, p. 67; for an account of the impact made by the foundation of the Royal Academy see Solkin *Painting for Money*, pp. 247–76.

87 Barrell, *Birth of Pandora*, pp. 80–81.
88 Malcolm Warner, 'The Sources and Meaning of Reynolds' Lady Sarah Bunbury', *The Art Institute of Chicago Museum Studies*, vol. 15 (1989), pp. 7–19.
89 Solkin, *Painting for Money*, pp. 180–90.
90 *Ibid.*, p.181.

4 'HER WHOLE POWER OF CHARMING': FEMININITY, UGLINESS AND THE REFORMATION OF THE MALE GAZE

1 Terry Eagleton, *The Rape of Clarissa: Writing, Sexuality and Class Struggle in Samuel Richardson* (Oxford: Basil Blackwell, 1982), p. 13.
2 James Fordyce, *The Character and Conduct of the Female Sex, and the Advantages to be derived by Young Men from the Society of Virtuous Women* (London: T. Cadell, 1776), pp. 4–8. Fordyce's discourse was first delivered on January 1st, 1776 at the Monkwell Street Chapel, London.
3 *Ibid.*, pp. 17–19, 20.
4 *Ibid.*, pp. 20, 23, 49–54, 88–101.
5 Erica Harth, 'The Virtue of Love: Lord Hardwicke's Marriage Act', *Cultural Critique* (Spring, 1988), p. 123. For contrasting accounts of eighteenth-century marriage, see Lawrence Stone, *The Family, Sex and Marriage, 1500–1800*, abr. and rev. edn (Harmondsworth: Penguin, 1979); and Leonore Davidoff and Catherine Hall, *Family Fortunes: Men, Women and the English Middle Class, 1780–1850* (London: Hutchinson, 1987).
6 Elizabeth A. Bohls, *Women Travel Writers, Landscape and the Language of Aesthetics, 1716–1818* (Cambridge: Cambridge University Press, 1995), pp. 3–7.
7 Janet Todd, *The Sign of Angellica: Women, Writing and Fiction, 1660–1800* (London: Virago, 1989), pp. 146, 160.
8 The critical material on *The Female Quixote* has grown exponentially in recent years. Amongst the best work is: Catherine A. Craft, 'Reworking Male Models: Aphra Behn's *Fair Vow-Breaker*, Eliza Haywood's *Fantomina*, and Charlotte Lennox's *Female Quixote*', *Modern Literary Review*, vol. 86 (1991), pp. 821–38; Laurie Langbauer, 'Romance Revised: Charlotte Lennox's 'Female Quixote', *Novel*, vol. 18 (Fall, 1984), pp. 29–49; Deborah Ross, 'Mirror, Mirror; The Didactic Dilemma of "The Female Quixote"', *Studies in English Literature*, vol. 27 (Summer, 1987), pp. 455–73; Leland E. Warren, 'Of the Conversation of Women: "The Female Quixote" and the Dream of Perfection', *Studies in Eighteenth-Century Culture*, vol. 11 (1982), pp. 367–80.
9 The exchange I have in mind is that which occupies chapters ii and iii of Book IV; '*In which a very pleasing Conversation is left unfinished*' and '*Definition of Love and Beauty – The necessary Qualities of an Hero and Heroine*'

respectively. Charlotte Lennox, *The Female Quixote; or, the Adventures of Arabella*, ed. Margaret Dalziel and intro. Margaret Anne Doody (Oxford: Oxford University Press, 1989), pp. 144–53.

10 Lennox, *Female Quixote*, pp. 149–50.
11 *Ibid.*, pp. 146–47.
12 *Ibid.*, p. 148.
13 *Ibid.*, pp. 26–30.
14 *Ibid.*, p. 148. See also notes, p. 400.
15 Fanny Burney, *Evelina; or, the History of a Young Woman's Entrance into the World*, ed. and intro. by Edward A. Bloom, with the assistance of Lillian D. Bloom (Oxford: Oxford University Press, 1989), pp. 25–29.
16 Lennox, *Female Quixote*, p. 44.
17 For an account of the problematic status of women's discourse in Lennox's fiction see Warren, 'Of the Conversation of Women', pp. 368–69, 377–78.
18 For an account of the significance of this, and other assertions, see Langbauer, 'Romance Revised', pp. 44–47.
19 Craft, 'Reworking Male Models', p. 833.
20 Burney, *Evelina*, p. 83.
21 Lennox, *Female Quixote*, p. 380.
22 *Ibid.*, p. 80.
23 *Ibid.*, pp. 88–89.
24 *Ibid.*, p. 138.
25 *Ibid.*, pp. 90, 152.
26 Langbauer, 'Romance Revised', pp. 31–32, 40–42; see also Lennox, *Female Quixote*, pp. 60–61.
27 Critical responses to the end of the novel have tended to focus on its more restrictive aspects, see for example, Langbauer, 'Romance Revisited', pp. 47–49, and Ross, 'Mirror, Mirror', pp. 467–69.
28 Tassie Gwilliam, *Samuel Richardson's Fictions of Gender* (Stanford: Stanford University Press, 1993), pp. 15–49.
29 Henry Fielding, *Amelia*, ed. David Blewett (Harmondsworth: Penguin, 1987), pp. 57–58. The initial reception of Fielding's novel was mixed, however. Not every reader was convinced that the heroine's deformed nose was the sign of virtue Fielding had intended. For an indicative selection of responses to Fielding's work see *Henry Fielding: The Critical Heritage*, ed. Ronald Paulson and Thomas Lockwood (London: Routledge and Kegan Paul, 1969).
30 See for example, Jill Campbell, *Natural Masques: Gender and Identity in Fielding's Plays and Novels* (Stanford: Stanford University Press, 1995), pp. 203–42; see also George E. Haggerty, 'Amelia's nose; or Sensibility and its Symptoms', *The Eighteenth Century: Theory and Interpretation*, vol. 36 (1995), pp. 139–56.
31 Charlotte Lennox, *Sophia*, 2 vols. (London: James Fletcher, 1762), vol. I, pp. 1–2. For an account of the text, and some speculation on its

reception, see Judith Dorn, 'Reading Women Reading History: The Philosophy of the Periodical Form in Charlotte Lennox's *The Lady's Museum*', *Historical Reflections / Réflexions Historiques*, vol. 18, no. 3 (1992), pp. 23–24.

32 Lennox, *Sophia*, vol. I, pp. 19–20.

33 *Ibid.*, vol. I, pp. 2–4.

34 *Ibid.*, vol. II, pp. 12–13.

35 *Ibid.*, vol. I, pp. 65–67, 92–93.

36 *Ibid.*, vol. I, pp. 25–26, 28.

37 Patricia Meyer Spacks, 'Sisters' in Mary Anne Schofield and Cecilia Macheski, eds., *Fetter'd or Free? British Women Novelists, 1670–1815* (Athens Oh: University of Ohio Press, 1986), pp. 137–38.

38 Lennox, *Sophia*, vol. II, p. 164.

39 *Ibid.*, vol. I, p. 35.

40 Harth, 'The Virtue of Love', p. 124.

41 Lennox, *Female Quixote*, p. 349.

42 For a contrast between Arabella's and Sophia's characters, see Lennox, *Sophia*, vol. I, pp. 131–32; and Lennox, *The Female Quixote*, pp. 348–50.

43 Lennox, *Sophia*, vol. I, p. 180.

44 *Ibid.*, vol. I, pp. 155–63. See Spacks, 'Sisters', p. 142.

45 *Ibid.*, vol. I, pp. 179–82.

46 *Ibid.*, vol. I, pp. 102–104.

47 *Ibid.*, vol. I, pp. 152–54.

48 *Ibid.*, vol. I, pp. 208–209, 211–15.

49 *Ibid.*, vol. I, pp. 60–63.

50 Spacks, 'Sisters', pp. 141–43.

51 Lennox, *Sophia*, vol. II, pp. 30–31, 213–14, 220–21.

52 *Ibid.*, vol. II, pp. 236–37.

53 *Ibid.*, vol. II, p. 205.

54 There are a number of moments in the novel when Sophia is represented in a distinctly private or domesticated character consistent with the value system of the middle classes. See Lennox, *Sophia*, vol. II, pp. 187–91, 206–208, 235–37.

55 Accounts of the beautiful woman, or 'Beauty', which viewed her as a dissipated and luxuriant wastrel with no identity beyond that of fashion, were common in the eighteenth century. See, for example, *Beauty and Proportion. A Poem* (London: T. Astley, 1735); Anon., *Female Taste: A Satire in Two Epistles inscribed to a Modern Polite Lady* (London: S. Crowder & H. Woodgate, 1755).

56 Spacks, 'Sisters', p. 138.

57 Such an opposition occurs frequently in Lennox's work, see Lennox, *Sophia*, vol. I, pp. 38, 135, 138, 224, and vol. II, pp. 28–30, 191.

58 Sarah Scott, *Agreeable Ugliness; or, the Triumph of the Graces; Exemplified in the Real Life and Fortunes of a Young Lady of Distinction* (London: R. and J. Dodsley, 1754).

59 Pierre-Antoine de la Place, *La Laideur Aimable et les Dangers de la Beauté: histoire veritable* (Londres [actually Paris]: Rollin, 1752).

60 Scott, *Agreeable Ugliness*, pp. 1, 3–6.

61 Elizabeth Bergen Brophy, *Women's Lives and the Eighteenth-Century Novel* (Tampa: South Florida University Press, 1991), pp. 16–17.

62 Caroline Gonda, 'Sarah Scott and the "Sweet Excess of Paternal Love"', *Studies in English Literature*, vol. 32, no. 3 (Summer, 1992), pp. 511–35.

63 Scott, *Agreeable Ugliness*, pp. 7–9.

64 *Ibid.*, pp. 15, 18–19.

65 *Ibid.*, pp. 12–13.

66 The relationship between parental mood and the appearance of the unborn child is discussed by Jill Campbell in *Natural Masques*, pp. 109–30. What is unusual about Scott's narrative is that it is the father's mind, not the mother's body, which determines the appearance of the child.

67 Scott, *Agreeable Ugliness*, pp. 19–21.

68 Deidre Lynch, 'Overloaded Portraits: The Excesses of Character and Countenance' in Veronica Kelly and Dorothea von Mücke, eds., *Body and Text in the Eighteenth Century* (Stanford: Stanford University Press, 1994), pp. 112–43.

69 Oliver Goldsmith, *The Vicar of Wakefield*, ed. Arthur Friedman (Oxford: Oxford University Press, 1992), pp. 11–12.

70 William Hogarth, *The Analysis of Beauty. Written with a View of Fixing the Fluctuating Ideas of Taste* (London: J. Reeve, 1753), pp. 123–31.

71 *Ibid.*, p. 36. See also pp. 80, 126, 130.

72 For an account of the importance of physiognomy in eighteenth-century culture see Roy Porter, 'Making Faces: Physiognomy and Fashion in Eighteenth-Century England', *Etudes Anglaises*, 38, no. 4 (October–December, 1985), pp. 386–96; and Graeme Tytler, 'Letters of Recommendation and False Vizors: Physiognomy in Novels of Henry Fielding', *Eighteenth-Century Fiction*, vol. 2, no. 2 (1990), pp. 93–111.

73 Scott, *Agreeable Ugliness*, pp. 13–14.

74 *Ibid.*, p. 25.

75 *Ibid.*, pp. 110, 112.

76 *Ibid.*, pp. 146–48.

77 Further instances of the folly and intrepidity of Madame de Villiers and her daughter fill the text see, for example, pp. 124–31, 145–51, 192–93. In each case what is significant is the degree to which these haughty beauties disregard middle-class sensibility and fail to recognise the worth of the men around them.

78 Sarah Scott, *The History of Sir George Ellison*, 2 vols. (London: A. Millar, 1766), vol. II, pp. 223–30.

79 *Ibid.*, vol. II, pp. 287–88.

80 This issue has, in recent years, received extensive critical work. See for

example Susan Staves, 'British Seduced Maidens', *Eighteenth-Century Studies*, vol. 14, no. 2 (Winter, 1980–81), pp. 109–34; Erica Harth, 'The Virtue of Love', pp. 123–54; and John P. Zomchick, *Family and Law in Eighteenth-Century Fiction: The Public Conscience in the Private Sphere* (Cambridge: Cambridge University Press, 1993).

81 Scott, *Agreeable Ugliness*, p. 120.
82 Marcia Pointon, *Hanging the Head: Portraiture and Social Formation in Eighteenth-Century England* (New Haven: Yale University Press, 1993), pp. 141–58.
83 William Hazlitt, 'On Sitting for one's Portrait' in *The Plain Speaker* (London: J.M. Dent, 1928), p. 108 (my emphasis).
84 Scott, *Agreeable Ugliness*, pp. 116, 118.
85 *Ibid.*, pp. 120–21.
86 *Ibid.*, p. 119.
87 *Ibid.*, pp. 163–65, 207–10.
88 Gonda, 'Sweet Excess', pp. 514–15.
89 Scott, *Agreeable Ugliness*, pp. 54–60, 67–74, 116–21.
90 Sarah Scott, *A Description of Millenium Hall and the Country Adjacent together with the Characters of the Inhabitants and such HistoricalAnecdotes and 'Reflections as may excite in the Reader proper Sentiments of Humanity*. Intro. Jane Spencer (London: Virago, 1986), p. 18.
91 While the term 'monster' changed its meaning during the eighteenth century, it retained, if only implicitly, the notion of the monstrous as that which is exhibited or displayed: as in 'de*monstrate*' and 're*monstrate*'. This complicates the initial suggestion that ugliness is the natural antithesis of resplendent, eye-catching beauty, for even at its most abject, in the form of the monstrous face, the ugly held a conceptual connection with the act of exhibition. Perhaps the most convenient illustration of this point can be found in the 'Preface' to *Joseph Andrews*. Here, Fielding uses the word monster and its cognates on a number of occasions and, in each case, identifies it with a notion of display. Hence burlesque is defined as 'the Exhibition of what is monstrous'. More significantly, the art of *caricatura* has an 'aim' which is 'to exhibit Monsters, not Men'. See Henry Fielding, *Joseph Andrews*, ed. Douglas Brookes-Davies (Oxford: Oxford University Press, 1980), pp. 4–5. The visit of Ellison and Lamont to the Monsters' 'inclosure' in *Millenium Hall* appears to retain a sense of this older usage.
92 Scott, *Millenium Hall*, pp. 194–95.
93 *Ibid.*, p. 199.
94 *Ibid.*, pp. 4–8, 12–13, 68–69, 205–207.
95 For a discussion of the 'improving' agenda of Scott's novel see Dorice Williams Elliott, 'Sarah Scott's "Millenium Hall" and Female Philanthropy', *Studies in English Literature*, vol. 35 (1995), pp. 535–53; see also James Cruse, 'A House Divided: Sarah Scott's *Millenium Hall*', *Studies in English Literature*, vol. 35 (1995), pp. 555–73.
96 Cruse, 'A House Divided', pp. 555–56.

5 'THE ACCOMPLISHMENT OF YOUR LONG AND ARDENT
WISHES': BEAUTY, TASTE AND THE FEMINISATION OF CULTURE

1 John Brewer, ' "The Most Polite Age and the Most Vicious": Attitudes towards Culture as Commodity, 1660–1800', *The Consumption of Culture, 1600–1800*, eds. Ann Bermingham and John Brewer (London: Routledge, 1995), pp. 341–61; David Solkin, *Painting for Money: The Visual Arts and the Public Sphere in Eighteenth-Century England* (New Haven: Yale University Press, 1993). See also Paul Mattick ed., *Eighteenth-Century Aesthetics and the Reconstruction of Art* (Cambridge: Cambridge University Press, 1993).

2 Joshua Reynolds, 'Discourse I' (2 January 1769), *Discourses on Art*, ed. Robert R. Wark, 2nd ed (New Haven: Yale University Press, 1975), p. 13.

3 For a full discussion of what Robert Uphaus has termed the 'ideology' of the Discourses, see John Barrell, *The Political Theory of Painting from Reynolds to Hazlitt: 'The Body of the Public'* (New Haven: Yale University Press, 1986), pp. 69–162. See also David Solkin 'Great Pictures or Great Men? Reynolds, Male Portraiture and the Power of Art', *Oxford Art Journal*, vol. 9, no. 2 (1986), pp. 42–49; Robert Uphaus, 'The Ideology of Reynolds', *Discourses on Art*, *Eighteenth-Century Studies*, vol. 12, no. 1 (Fall, 1978), pp. 59–73.

4 Reynolds, 'Discourse VII' (December 10th, 1776), *Discourses*, p. 121.

5 *Ibid.*, p. 140.

6 *Ibid.*, p. 125.

7 Reynolds, 'Discourse VIII' (December 10th, 1778), *Discourses*, pp. 149–50. For Solkin's commentary on this passage see 'Great Pictures or Great Men?', p. 49.

8 *Ibid.*, pp. 152–53.

9 Reynolds, 'Discourse III' (December 14th, 1770), *Discourses*, pp. 44–45, 47–48.

10 Reynolds, 'Discourse VI' (December 10th, 1774), *Discourses*, p. 107.

11 Harriet Guest, 'The Wanton Muse: Politics and Gender in Gothic Theory after 1760' in Stephen Copley and John Whale eds., *Beyond Romanticism: New Approaches to Texts and Contexts* (London: Routledge, 1992), pp. 133–34. See also Harriet Guest, 'Curiously Marked: Tattooing, Masculinity and Nationality in Eighteenth-Century British Perceptions of the South Pacific' in John Barrell ed., *Painting and the Politics of Culture: New Essays on British Art, 1700–1850* (Oxford: Oxford University Press, 1992), pp. 107–11.

12 Reynolds, 'Discourse VIII', *Discourses*, p. 152. Although Reynolds's position remained relatively consistent during the first nine Discourses (those written between 1769–80), in the later lectures Reynolds refined and redirected his argument allowing himself greater flexibility in his treatment of commerce and commercial art. For a discussion of the

evolution of Reynolds's critical opinions see Barrell, *The Political Theory of Painting*, pp. 70–72.

13 Reynolds, 'Discourse IV', *Discourses*, pp. 62–73. For a discussion of the relationship between refinement and decay in civic-humanist ideology see J.G.A. Pocock, 'Between Machiavelli and Hume: Edward Gibbon as Civic Humanist and Philosophical Historian' in G.W. Bowerstock and John Clive eds., *Edward Gibbon and the Fall of the Roman Empire* (Cambridge, Mass.: Harvard University Press, 1977), pp. 103–19.

14 André Rouquet, *The Present State of the Arts in England* (London: no publisher credited, 1755), pp. 6–7, 11, 14.

15 Rouquet, *Present State*, pp. 40–41.

16 Rouquet, *Present State*, pp. 6, 17–18, 41–42, 45.

17 Edmund Burke, *A Philosophical Enquiry into the Origin of Our Ideas of the Sublime and Beautiful*, ed. and intro. J.T. Boulton (Oxford: Basil Blackwell, 1990), pp. 40–42; *Connoisseur*, no. 1 (January 31st, 1754), in *The Connoisseur. By Mr. Town*, vol. I, pp. 1–2. See also Frances Ferguson, *Solitude and the Sublime: Romanticism and the Aesthetics of Individuation* (London: Routledge, 1992), pp. 8, 31, 45.

18 John Gilbert Cooper, *Letters Concerning Taste* (London: R. and J. Dodsley, 1755), p. 28.

19 Cooper, *Letters Concerning Taste*, pp. 26–29, 68–69, 82–84.

20 Frances Sheridan, *Memoirs of Miss Sidney Bidulph*, ed. Patricia Koster and Jean Coates Clearey (Oxford: Oxford University Press, 1995), pp. 361–68, 378–79.

21 Charles Robert Leslie and Tom Taylor, *The Life and Times of Sir Joshua Reynolds: with notices of some of his contemporaries*, 2 vols. (London: John Murray, 1865), vol. I, pp. 121–22.

22 Reynolds uses the expression, in a footnote, to gloss over the fact that in his eighth Discourse he neglected to mention Burke, or indeed any one else, when he appealed for a 'COMPLETE essay or inquiry into the connection between the rules of Art, and the eternal and immutable dispositions of our passions', *Discourses on Art*, p. 162.

23 James Northcote, 'Autobiography', quoted in Leslie and Taylor, *Life and Times of Sir Joshua Reynolds*, vol. I, pp. 183–84.

24 James Northcote, *The Life of Sir Joshua Reynolds*, (London: Henry Colborn, 1819), p. 103; Leslie and Taylor, *Life and Times of Sir Joshua Reynolds*, vol. I, p. 184.

25 Samuel Johnson, 'To Miss Frances Reynolds', Letter, July 21st, 1781, in *The Letters of Samuel Johnson*, 4 vols., ed. Bruce Radford (Oxford: Clarendon Press, 1992) vol. III, pp. 355–56.

26 Frances Reynolds, *An Enquiry Concerning the Principles of Taste and the Origin of Our Ideas of Beauty &c.* (London: Baker & Galabin, 1785), pp. 16, 18, 6–7, 37.

27 Peter de Bolla, *The Discourse of the Sublime: Readings in History, Aesthetics and the Subject* (Oxford: Basil Blackwell, 1989), p. 48.

28 *Ibid.*, p. 18.

29 *Ibid.*, pp. iii–iv.

30 *Ibid.*, pp. 32–34.

31 *Ibid.*, pp. 20–21. The quotation is taken from Young's 'Love of Fame, the Universal Passion. In Seven Characteristical Satires', *Edward Young: The Complete Works, Poetry and Prose*, ed. James Nichols, 2 vols. (Hildesheim: Georg Olms, 1968), vol. I, p. 393.

32 Reynolds, *Enquiry*, pp. 22–23.

33 *Ibid.*, pp. 23–24.

34 *Ibid.*, pp. 13–14, 24–25.

35 *Ibid.*, pp. 29–30.

36 *Ibid.*, p. 32.

37 de Bolla, *Discourse of the Sublime*, p. 49.

38 Reynolds, *Enquiry*, p. 30.

39 *Ibid.*, pp. 27–28.

40 *Ibid.*, pp. 30–31.

41 *Ibid.*, pp. 29–34.

42 *Ibid.*, p. 35.

43 *Ibid.*, pp. 39–40.

44 *Ibid.*, pp. 38, 42.

45 *Ibid.*, pp. 43–44.

46 *Ibid.*, p. 41.

47 *Ibid.*, p. 46.

48 Northcote, *Life of Sir Joshua Reynolds*, pp. 102–103.

49 For a discussion of the generally 'masculine' gendering of the debate about aesthetics in the late eighteenth century see Anne K. Mellor, *Romanticism and Gender* (London: Routledge, 1993), pp. 1–11, 13–29.

50 Samuel Johnson, 'To Miss Reynolds', Letter, April 8th, 1782, in *Letters*, vol. IV, pp. 30–31.

51 Ann Bermingham, 'The Aesthetics of Ignorance: The Accomplished Woman in the Culture of Connoisseurship', *The Oxford Art Journal*, vol. 16, no. 2 (1993), pp. 4–5.

52 Marcia Pointon, *Hanging the Head: Portraiture and Social Formation in Eighteenth-Century England* (New Haven: Yale University Press, 1993), pp. 159–74. For a further discussion of the development of alienation in eighteenth-century culture see James M. Carrier, 'Alienating Objects: The Emergence of Alienation in Retail' in *Man: The Journal of the Royal Anthropological Institute*, vol. 29, no. 2 (June, 1994), pp. 359–80.

53 Harriet Guest, 'A Double Lustre: Femininity and Sociable Commerce, 1730–60', *Eighteenth-Century Studies*, vol. 23, no. 4 (Summer, 1990), p. 483.

54 For a further perspective on the significance of the domestic sphere in eighteenth-century society see Dena Goodman, 'Public Sphere and Private Life: Toward a Synthesis of Current Historiographical Approaches to the Old Regime' in *History and Theory: Studies in the Philosophy of History*, vol. 31 (1992), pp. 1–20; and Amanda Vickery, 'Golden Age to

Separate Spheres? A Review of the Categories and Chronology of English Women's History' in *The Historical Journal*, vol. 36, no. 2 (1993), pp. 383–418.

55 See William Hogarth, *The Analysis of Beauty. Written with a View of Fixing the Fluctuating Ideas of Taste* (London: J. Reeve, 1753), pp. 80–81; Allan Ramsay, 'A Dialogue on Taste', 2nd edn, *The Investigator*, 4 vols (London: For the Author, 1762), vol. II, pp. 25–27; and James Usher, *Clio; or a Discourse on Taste. Addressed to A Young Lady* (London: T. Davis, 1767), pp. 43–45, 91. In each case the unaffected judgement of women is used to offset the dissipated or luxuriant tastes of the author's adversaries.

Bibliography

PRIMARY SOURCES

Addison, Joseph and Steele, Richard. *The Tatler*, ed. and intro. Donald F. Bond, 3 vols., Oxford: Clarendon Press, 1987.

The Spectator, ed. and intro. Donald F. Bond, 5 vols., Oxford: Clarendon Press, 1965.

Akenside, Mark. *The Pleasures of the Imagination*, London: R. Dodsley, 1744.

[Baker, Henry]. *The Universal Spectator. By Henry Stonecastle*, 4 vols., London: A. Ward, J. Clarke et al., 1747.

Beattie, James. *The Poetical Works of Beattie, Blair and Falconer*, Edinburgh: James Nichol, 1854.

Berkeley, George. *The Works of George Berkeley, Bishop of Cloyne*, ed. A.A. Luce and T.E. Jessop, 9 vols., London: Thomas Nelson, 1953.

Boswell, James. *Life of Johnson*, intro. Pat Rogers, ed. R.W. Chapman, Oxford: Oxford University Press, 1991.

Brown, John. *An Estimate of the Manners and Principles of the Times*, London: L. Davis and C. Reymers, 1757.

A Sermon Preached on Thursday the 16th May, 1765, at the anniversary meeting of the guardians of the asylum of deserted female orphans, London: J. Reymers, 1765.

Burke, Edmund. *A Philosophical Enquiry into the Origin of Our Ideas of the Sublime and Beautiful*, ed. and intro. J.T. Boulton, Oxford: Basil Blackwell, 1990.

Reflections on the Revolution in France, ed. and intro. Conor Cruise O'Brien, Harmondsworth: Penguin, 1986.

Burney, Fanny. *Evelina; or, The History of a Young Woman's Entrance into the World*, ed. and intro. Edward A. Bloom, with the assistance of Lillian D. Bloom, Oxford: Oxford University Press, 1989.

Catalogue of the Pictures, Sculptures, Models, Drawings, Prints etc., Exhibited in the Great Room of the Society for the Encouragement of Arts, Manufactures, & Commerce, 21st April, 1760, London: For the Society, 1760.

The Charms of Beauty; or, the Grand Contest of the Fair Hibernians, and the English Toasts, A Poem. Occasioned by the Marriage of his Grace the Duke of Hamilton with Miss Elizabeth Gunning; and the expected marriage of her elder Sister with a certain noble Earl, London: J. Gifford, 1752.

Chesterfield, Earl of [Philip Dormer Stanhope]. *The Letters of Philip Dormer Stanhope, Fourth Earl of Chesterfield*, ed. and intro. by Bonamy Dobrée, 6 vols., London: Eyre and Spottiswode, 1933.

Coke, Lady Mary. *The Letters and Journals of Lady Mary Coke*, 4 vols., Edinburgh: David Douglas, 1889.

Cole, Thomas. *Discourse on Luxury, Infidelity and Enthusiasm*, London: R. and J. Dodsley, 1761.

Coleman, George et al., *The Connoisseur. By Mr. Town, Critic and Censor-General*, 4th edn, 4 vols., London: R. Baldwin, 1761.

Cooper, John Gilbert. *Epistles to the Great from Aristippus in Retirement*, London: R. and J. Dodsley, 1758.

Letters Concerning Taste, London: R. and J. Dodsley, 1755.

The Power of Harmony, London: R. Dodsley, 1745.

Cosens, Dr J. *The Economy of Beauty in a Series of Fables addressed to the Ladies*, 2 vols., London: J. Wilkie, 1772.

[Cosmetti]. *The Polite Arts. Dedicated to the Ladies*, London: Roach, 1767.

[Delany, Mary]. *The Autobiography and Correspondence of Mary Delany with Interesting Reminiscences of King George III and Queen Charlotte*, ed. Rt. Hon. Lady Llanover, 3 vols., London: Richard Bentley, 1861

Discourse Concerning the Propriety of Manners, Taste and Beauty, Being an Introduction to a Work hereafter published intituled Moral Beauty and Deformity, exemplified and contrasted in two living Characters, London: no publisher credited, 1751.

Dodsley, Robert. *Beauty; or, the Art of Charming*, London: Lawton Gilliver, 1735.

[Eden, Adam]. *Vindication of the Reformation, on foot, among the Ladies, to Abolish Modesty and Chastity, and Restore the Native Simplicity of going Naked. And an Attempt to reconcile all Opposers to it, and make them join in a speedy Completion of this Glorious Design*, London: R. Griffiths, 1755.

Evans, John. *Juvenile Pieces: Designed for the Youth of Both Sexes*, 3rd edn, London: John Phillips, 1797.

Fawconer, Samuel. *An Essay on Modern Luxury: or, an Attempt to Delineate its Nature, Causes and Effects*, London: James Fletcher, 1765.

Female Taste: A Satire in Two Epistles inscribed to a Modern Polite Lady, London: S. Crowder and H. Woodgate, 1755.

Fielding, Henry. *Amelia*, ed. and intro. David Blewett, Harmondsworth: Penguin, 1987.

Joseph Andrews, ed. and intro. Douglas Brookes-Davies, Oxford: Oxford University Press, 1980.

Fordyce, James. *The Character and Conduct of the Female Sex, and the Advantages to be derived by Young Men from the Society of Virtuous Women*, London: T. Cadell, 1776.

Sermons to Young Women, 2 vols., 3rd edn, London: A. Millar and T. Cadell, 1766.

Gerard, Alexander, *An Essay on Taste with Dissertations on the Same Subject by de*

Voltaire, D'Albert and de Montesquieu, London and Edinburgh: A. Millar, and A. Kincaid and J. Bell, 1759.

Goldsmith, Oliver. *The Collected Works of Oliver Goldsmith*, ed. Arthur Friedman, 4 vols., Oxford: Clarendon Press, 1966.

The Vicar of Wakefield, ed. Arthur Friedman, Oxford: Oxford University Press, 1992.

Hawkesworth, John et al. *The Adventurer*, 3rd edn, 4 vols., London: C. Hitch and L. Hawes, J. Payne, 1756.

Hay, William. *Deformity. An Essay*, London: R. & J. Dodsley, 1754.

Hazlitt, William. *The Plain Speaker*, Everyman's Library, no. 814, London: J.M. Dent, 1928.

Highmore, Joseph. *Essays Moral, Religious and Miscellaneous*, 2 vols., London: B. White, 1766.

Hogarth, William. *The Analysis of Beauty. Written with a View of Fixing the Fluctuating Ideas of Taste*, London: J. Reeve, 1753.

Hume, David. *Essays, Moral, Political and Literary*, ed. and intro. by Eugene F. Miller, Indianapolis: LibertyClassics, 1985.

Hutcheson, Francis. *An Inquiry into the Original of Our Ideas of Beauty and Virtue; in Two Treatises. I Concerning Beauty, Order, Harmony, Design. II Concerning Moral Good and Evil*, 3rd ed., London: J. and J. Knapton, et al., 1729.

Johnson, Samuel. *The Letters of Samuel Johnson*, 4 vols., ed. Bruce Radford, Oxford: Clarendon Press, 1992.

The Yale Edition of the Works of Samuel Johnson, 14 vols., New Haven: Yale University Press, 1958–85.

Judgement of Paris; or, the Triumph of Beauty. A Pastoral Ballad Opera in one act, London: J. Roberts, 1731.

Kames, Lord [Henry Home]. *Elements of Criticism*, 3 vols., London and Edinburgh: A. Millar, and A. Kincaid and J. Bell, 1762.

Knight, Richard Payne. *An Analytical Inquiry into the Principals of Taste*, London: T. Payne and J. White, 1805.

Lennox, Charlotte. *The Female Quixote; or, The Adventures of Arabella*, ed. Margaret Dalziel and intro. by Margaret Anne Doody, Oxford: Oxford University Press, 1989.

Sophia, 2 vols., London: James Fletcher, 1762.

Lennox, Sarah. *The Life and Letters of Lady Sarah Lennox, 1745–1826*, 2 vols., ed. Countess of Ilchester and Lord Stavordale, London: John Murray, 1902.

Locke, John. *An Essay Concerning Human Understanding*, ed. Peter H. Nidditch, Oxford: Clarendon Press, 1975.

Marriot, Thomas. *Female Conduct: Being an Essay on the Art of Pleasing, to be Practiced by the Fair Sex before and after Marriage*, London: W. Owen, 1759.

Mob in the Pit; or Lines Addressed to the D___ch___ss of A_____ll, 2nd edn, London: S. Bladon, 1773.

Moore, Edward et al. *The World. By Adam Fitz-Adam. A New Edition*, 3 vols., Edinburgh: A Donaldson, 1770.

Montagu, Elizabeth. *Letters of Elizabeth Montagu, with some notices of her contemporaries*, 3 vols., London: T. Cadell, 1813.

Northcote, James. *The Life of Sir Joshua Reynolds*, 2nd edn, revised and augmented, 2 vols., London: Henry Colburn, 1819.

Peeping Tom to the Countess of Coventry. An Epithalamium. London: S. Price and R. Wilson, 1752.

de la Place, Pierre-Antoine. *La Laideur Aimable et les Dangers de la Beauté: histoire veritable* (Londres [actually Paris]), Rollin, 1752.

Pope, Alexander. *The Poems of Alexander Pope*, one volume, Twickenham Edition, ed. John Butt, London: Methuen, 1963.

Ramsay, Allan the younger. 'A Dialogue on Taste', 2nd edn, in *The Investigator*, 4 vols., London: For the Author, 1762.

Reflections Arising from the Immorality of the Present Age, London: M. Cooper, 1756.

Reynolds, Frances. *An Enquiry Concerning the Principles of Taste, and of the Origin of Our Ideas of Beauty &c.*, London: Baker & Galabin, 1785.

Reynolds, Joshua. *Discourses on Art*, ed. and intro. Robert R. Wark, 2nd edn, New Haven: Yale University Press, 1975.

'The Ledger of Sir Joshua Reynolds', ed. by Malcolm Cormack, in *The Walpole Society*, vol. XLII (1968–70), pp. 105–69.

The Letters of Sir Joshua Reynolds, ed. F.W. Hilles, Cambridge: Cambridge University Press, 1929.

Sir Joshua Reynolds' Notes and Observations on Pictures etc., ed. W. Cotton, London: 1859.

Portraits. Character Sketches of Oliver Goldsmith, Samuel Johnson, and David Garrick, together with other MSS of Reynolds lately discovered amongst the Private Papers of James Boswell, ed. F.W. Hilles, New York and London: Heineman, 1952.

The Works of Sir Joshua Reynolds, Knight; Late President of the Royal Academy, 3 vols., London: T. Cadell, jnr. and W. Davies, 1801.

Richardson, Jonathan. *An Essay on the Theory of Painting*, 2nd edn, London: A. Bettesworth, 1725.

Two Discourses. I. An Essay on the whole Art of Criticism as it relates to Painting, shewing how to Judge I. Of the Goodness of a Picture; II. Of the Hand of the Master; III. Whether 'tis an Original, or a Copy. II. An Argument in behalf of the Science of a Connoisseur; wherein is shewn the Dignity, Certainty, Pleasure, and Advantage of it, London: W. Churchill, 1719.

Richardson, Samuel. 'Letter to Miss Westcomb,' August 6th, 1750, MS located in Forster Collection, Victoria & Albert Museum, filed as FM.XIV, 3, ff 53–54.

Pamela: or, Virtue Rewarded, ed. Peter Sabor, intro. Margaret A. Doody, Harmondsworth: Penguin, 1985.

Rouquet, André. *The Present State of the Arts in England*, London: no publisher credited, 1755.

Schönberg, Ralph. *The Judgement of Paris. An English Burletta*, London: T. Beckett and P.A. de Hondt, 1768.

Scott, Sarah. *Agreeable Ugliness; or, the Triumph of the Graces; Exemplified in the Real Life and Fortunes of a Young Lady of Distinction*, London: R. and J. Dodsley, 1754.

A Description of Millenium Hall and the Country Adjacent together with the Characters of the Inhabitants and such Historical Anecdotes and Reflections as may excite in the Reader proper Sentiments of Humanity, intro. by Jane Spencer, London: Virago, 1986.

The History of Sir George Ellison, 2 vols., London: A. Millar, 1766.

Shaftesbury, Third Earl of [Anthony Ashley Cooper]. *Characteristics of Men, Manners, Opinions, Times etc.*, 2 vols., ed. with intro. by John M. Robertson, Gloucester, Mass.: Peter Smith, 1963.

Second Characters; or, the Language of Forms by the Right Honorable Anthony, Earl of Shaftesbury, ed. Benjamin Rand, New York: Greenwood Press, 1969.

Sheridan, Frances. *Memoirs of Miss Sidney Bidulph*, ed. Patricia Koster and Jean Coates Cleary, Oxford: Oxford University Press, 1995.

Smith, Adam. *Essays on Philosophical Subjects with Dugald Stewart's Account of Adam Smith*. ed. W.P.D. Wightman, J.C. Bryce and I.S. Ross, Oxford: Clarendon, 1980.

The Theory of Moral Sentiments, ed. D.D. Raphael and A.L. Macfie, Indianapolis: LibertyClassics, 1982.

Spence, Joseph. [Sir Harry Beaumont, pseud.] *Crito; or, A Dialouge on Beauty*, London: R. Dodsley, 1752.

Moralities; or, Essays, Letters, and Fables and Translations, London: R. Dodsley, 1753.

Polymetis; or, An Enquiry Concerning the Agreement between the Works of the Roman Poets and the Remains of the Ancient Artists, London: R. Dodsley, 1747.

Thomson, James. *The Seasons*, ed. and intro. James Sambrook, Oxford: Clarendon Press, 1981.

Turnbull, George. *A Treatise on Ancient Painting, Containing Observations on the Rise, Progress, and Decline of the Art amongst the Greeks and Romans*, London: for the Author, 1740.

Usher, James. *Clio; or a Discourse on Taste Addressed to a Young Lady*, London: T. Davis, 1767.

Walpole, Horace. *The Letters of Horace Walpole*, 9 vols., ed. P. Cunningham, Edinburgh: John Grant, 1906.

Memoirs of the Reign of George the Third, 4 vols., London: Lawrence and Bullen, 1984.

'Notes by Horace Walpole, fourth Earl of Orford, on the Exhibitions of the Society of Artists and Free Society of Artists, 1760–91', transcribed and edited by Hugh Gatty in *Walpole Society Notes*, vol. XXVII (1938–39).

Webb, Daniel. *An Inquiry into the Beauties of Painting, and into the Merits of the Most Celebrated Painters Ancient and Modern*, London: R. and J. Dodsley, 1760.

Williams, John. *Memoirs of the Royal Academicians; Being an Attempt to Improve the National Taste*, London: H. Symonds, 1796.
Wortley Montagu, Mary. *Essays and Poems and Simplicity, a Comedy*, ed. Robert Halsbrand and Isobel Grundy, Oxford: Clarendon Press, 1977.

SECONDARY SOURCES

Albrecht, W.P. *The Sublime Pleasures of Tragedy: a Study of Critical Theory from Dennis to Keats*, Lawrence: University of Kansas Press, 1975.
Allan, D.G.C. 'The Society of Arts and Government, 1754–1800: Public Encouragement of Arts, Manufactures and Commerce in Eighteenth-Century England', *Eighteenth-Century Studies*, vol. 7, no. 4 (Summer, 1974), pp. 434–52.
Armstrong, Nancy. *Desire and Domestic Fiction: A Political History of the Novel*, Oxford: Oxford University Press, 1987.
Barker-Benfield, G.J. *The Culture of Sensibility: Sex and Society in Eighteenth Century Britain*, Chicago: University of Chicago Press, 1992.
Barnauw, Jeffrey. 'Feeling in Enlightenment Aesthetics', *Studies in Eighteenth-Century Culture*, vol. 18 (1988), pp. 323–42.
Barrell, John. *The Birth of Pandora and the Division of Knowledge*, London: Macmillan, 1992.
English Literature in History, 1730–80: An Equal, Wide Survey, London: Hutchinson, 1983.
The Political Theory of Painting from Reynolds to Hazlitt: 'The Body of the Public', New Haven: Yale University Press, 1986.
'Sir Joshua Reynolds and the Englishness of English Art', in Homi K. Bhabha ed., *Nation and Narration*, London: Routledge, 1990.
Barrell, John ed. *Painting and the Politics of Culture: New Essays on British Art 1700–1850*, Oxford: Oxford University Press, 1992.
Barry, Kevin. *Language, Music and the Sign: A Study in Aesthetics, Poetics and Poetry from Collins to Coleridge*, Cambridge: Cambridge University Press, 1987.
Bate, Walter Jackson. *From Classic to Romantic: Premises in Taste in Eighteenth-Century England*, New York: HarperTorch Books, 1961.
Bermingham, Ann. 'The Aesthetics of Ignorance: The Accomplished Woman in the Culture of Connoisseurship', *The Oxford Art Journal*, vol. 16, no. 2 (1993), pp. 3–20.
Bermingham, Ann and Brewer, John eds, *The Consumption of Culture 1600–1800*, London: Routledge, 1995.
Bernstein, John Andrew. 'Shaftesbury's Identification of the Good with the Beautiful' in *Eighteenth-Century Studies*, vol. 10, no. 3 (Spring, 1977), pp. 304–25.
Bindman, David. *Hogarth*, London: Thames and Hudson, 1981.
Bleackley, Ruth M. 'The Beautiful Miss Gunnings' in *The Connoisseur*, vol. XII (May–August, 1905), pp. 163–64.
Bleackley, W. Horace. *The Beautiful Duchess. Being an Account of the Life and*

Times of Elizabeth Gunning, Duchess of Hamilton and Argyll, 2nd edn, London: John Lane, 1927.

Bohls, Elizabeth A. *Women Travel Writers, Landscape and the Language of Aesthetics, 1716–1818*, Cambridge: Cambridge University Press, 1995.

de Bolla, Peter. *The Discourse of the Sublime: Readings in History, Aesthetics and the Subject*, Oxford: Basil Blackwell, 1989.

Bonfield, Lloyd. *Marriage Settlements, 1601–1740: The Adoption of the Strict Settlement*, Cambridge: Cambridge University Press, 1983.

Borsay, Peter. *The English Urban Renaissance: Culture and Society in the Provincial Town, 1660–1770*, Oxford: Clarendon Press, 1989.

Bourdieu, Pierre. *Distinction: A Social Critique of the Judgement of Taste*, trans. Richard Nice, London: Routledge, 1992.

Brady, Frank. *James Boswell: The Later Years, 1769–95*, London: Heineman, 1984.

Brewer, John. ' "The Most Polite Age and the Most Vicious": Attitudes towards Culture as Commodity, 1660–1800', *The Consumption of Culture, 1600–1800*, eds. Ann Bermingham and John Brewer, London: Routledge, 1995, pp. 341–61.

Brewer, John & Porter, Roy eds. *Consumption and the World of Goods*, New York: Routledge, 1993.

Bronfen, Elisabeth. *Over Her Dead Body: Death, Femininity and the Aesthetic*, Manchester: Manchester University Press, 1993.

Brophy, Elizabeth Bergen. *Women's Lives and the Eighteenth-Century Novel*, Tampa: South Florida University Press, 1991.

Brown, Laura and Nussbaum, Felicity eds. *The New Eighteenth Century: Theory, Politics, English Literature*, New York: Methuen, 1987.

Bunn, James H. 'The Aesthetics of British Mercantilism', *New Literary History*, vol. 11 (1980), pp. 303–21.

Campbell, Jill. *Natural Masques: Gender and Indentity in Fielding's Plays and Novels*, Stanford: Stanford University Press, 1995.

Carrier, James H. 'Alienating Objects: The Emergence of Alienation in Retail', *Man: The Journal of the Royal Anthropological Institute*, vol. 29, no. 2 (June, 1994), pp. 359–80.

Cash, Arthur H. 'The Birth of Tristram Shandy: Sterne and Dr Burton' in Paul-Gabriel Bouce ed. *Sexuality in Eighteenth-Century Britain*, Manchester: Manchester University Press, 1987, pp. 199–224.

Castle, Terry. *Masquerade and Civilisation: The Carnivalesque in Eighteenth-Century English Culture and Fiction*, London: Methuen, 1986.

Caygill, Howard. *The Art of Judgement*, Oxford: Basil Blackwell, 1989.

de Certeau, Michel. *The Practice of Everyday Life*, trans. Steven Rendell, Berkeley: University of California Press, 1984.

Chard, Chloe. 'Effeminacy, Pleasure and the Classical Body' in Gill Perry and Michael Rossington eds., *Femininity and Masculinity in Eighteenth-Century Art and Culture*, Manchester: Manchester University Press, 1994, pp. 142–61.

Climenson, E.J. *Elizabeth Montagu – Queen of the Blue Stockings. Her Correspondence from 1720–61. By her Great-Great Niece*, 2 vols., London: John Murray, 1906.

Cohen, Ralph. *The Unfolding of 'The Seasons'*, Baltimore: Johns Hopkins University Press, 1970.

Copley, Stephen. 'Commerce, Conversation and Politeness in the Early Eighteenth-Century Periodical', *British Journal of Eighteenth-Century Studies*, vol. 18, no 1 (Spring, 1995), pp. 63–77.

'The Fine Arts in Eighteenth-Century Polite Culture' in John Barrell ed., *Painting and the Politics of Culture: New Essays on British Art 1700–1850*, Oxford: Oxford University Press, 1992, pp. 13–27.

Copley, Stephen ed. *Literature and the Social Order*, London: Croom Helm, 1984.

Copley, Stephen and Whale, John eds. *Beyond Romanticism, new approaches to texts and contexts, 1780–1832*, London: Routledge, 1992.

Craft, Catherine A. 'Reworking Male Models, Aphra Behn's *Fair Vow Breaker*, Eliza Haywood's *Fantomina* and Charlotte Lennox's *Female Quixote*', *Modern Literary Review*, vol. 86 (October, 1991), pp. 821–38.

Cruse, James. 'A House Divided: Sarah Scott's "Millenium Hall"', *Studies in English Literature*, vol. 35 (1995), pp. 555–73.

Dabydeen, David. *Hogarth, Walpole and Commercial Britain*, London: Hansib, 1987.

Daniels, Stephen. 'Loutherbourg's *Chemical Theatre* 'Coalbrookedale by Night' in John Barrell ed., *Painting and the Politics of Culture: New Essays in British Art, 1700–1850*, Oxford: Oxford University Press, 1992, pp. 195–230.

Davidoff, Leonore and Hall, Catherine. *Family Fortunes: Men, Women and the English Middle Class, 1780–1850*, London: Hutchinson, 1987.

Denvir, Brian. *The Eighteenth Century: Art, Design and Society, 1689–1789*, London: Longmans, 1983.

Derrida, Jacques. *The Truth in Painting*, trans. Geoff Bennington, Chicago: University of Chicago Press, 1987.

Dictionary of British Women Writers, ed. Janet Todd, London: Routledge, 1989.

Doody, Margaret A. 'Shakespearean Novels, Charlotte Lennox Illustrated', *Studies in the Novel*, vol. 19, no. 3 (1987), pp. 296–310.

Dorn, J. 'Reading Women Reading History: The Philosophy of the Periodical Form in Charlotte Lennox's *The Lady's Museum*', *Historical Reflections, Réflexions Historiques*, vol. 18, no. 3 (1992), pp. 7–27.

Eagleton, Terry. *Against the Grain: Selected Essays*, London: Verso, 1988.

The Function of Criticism: From 'The Spectator' to Post-Structuralism, London: Verso, 1984.

The Ideology of the Aesthetic, Oxford: Basil Blackwell, 1990.

The Rape of Clarissa: Writing, Sexuality and Class Struggle in Samuel Richardson, Oxford: Basil Blackwell, 1982.

Earle, Peter. *The Making of the English Middle Class: Business, Society and Family Life in London, 1660–1730*, London: Methuen, 1989.
Eaves, T.C. Duncan and Kimpel, Ben. D. *Samuel Richardson: A Biography*, Oxford: Clarendon Press, 1971.
Einberg, Elizabeth, introduction. *Manners and Morals: Hogarth and British Painting* (catalogue), London: Tate Gallery, 1987.
Elliot, Dorice Williams. 'Sarah Scott's *Millenium Hall* and Female Philanthropy', *Studies in English Literature*, vol. 35 (1995), pp. 535–53.
Ferguson, Frances. 'Legislating the Sublime' in Ralph Cohen ed., *Studies in Eighteenth-Century British Art and Aesthetics*, Los Angeles: University of California Press, 1985, pp. 128–47.
Solitude and the Sublime: Romanticism and the Aesthetics of Individuation, London: Routledge, 1992.
Foucault, Michel. *The Archaeology of Knowledge*, London: Tavistock, 1972.
The Order of Things: An Archaeology of the Human Sciences, London: Tavistock, 1970.
Fraser, Nancy. *Unruly Practices*, Minneapolis: Minnesota, 1989.
Furniss, Tom. *Edmund Burke's Aesthetic Ideology: Language, Gender and Political Economy in Revolution*, Cambridge: Cambridge University Press, 1993.
Gantz, Ida. *The Pastel Portrait: The Gunnings of Castlecoote and the Howards of Hampstead*, London: The Cresset Press, 1962.
Gibson-Wood, Carol. 'Jonathan Richardson and the Rationalisation of Connoisseurship', *Art History*, vol. 7, no. 1 (March, 1984), pp. 38–56.
Gillis, John R. *For Better, for Worse: British Marriages, 1600 to the Present*, Oxford: Oxford University Press, 1985.
Gobetti, Daniela. *Private and Public: Individual Households and the Body Politic in Locke and Hutcheson*, London: Routledge, 1992.
Goldsmith, M.M. 'Liberty, Luxury, and the Pursuit of Happiness' in Anthony Pagden ed., *The Language of Political Theory in Early Modern Europe*, Cambridge: Cambridge University Press, 1987, pp. 225–51.
Gonda, Caroline. 'Sarah Scott and the "Sweet Excess of Paternal Love"', *Studies in English Literature*, vol. 32, no. 3 (Summer 1992), pp. 511–35.
Goodman, Dena. 'Public Sphere and Private Life: Toward a Synthesis of Current Historiographical Approaches to the Old Regime', *History and Theory: Studies in the Philosophy of History*, vol. 31 (1992), pp. 1–20.
Gourlay, Alexander S. and Grant, John E. 'The Melancholy Shepherdess in Prospect of Love and Death', *Bulletin of Research in the Humanities*, vol. 85 (1982), pp. 169–89.
Graves, Algernon and Cronin, William Vine. *History of the Works of Joshua Reynolds*, 4 vols., London: Henry Graves, 1899–1901.
Grean, Stanley. *Shaftesbury's Philosophy of Religion and Ethics: A Study of Enthusiasm*, Athens, Ohio: Ohio University Press, 1967.
Guest, Harriet. 'Curiously Marked: Tattooing, Masculinity, and Nationality in Eighteenth-Century British Perceptions of the South Pacific' in John Barrell ed., *Painting and the Politics of Culture: New Essays on*

British Art 1700–1850, Oxford: Oxford University Press, 1992, pp. 101–34.

'A Double Lustre: Femininity and Sociable Commerce, 1730–60', *Eighteenth-Century Studies*, vol. 23, no. 4 (Summer, 1990), pp. 479–501.

'The Wanton Muse: Politics and Gender in Gothic Theory after 1760' in Stephen Copley and John Whale eds., *Beyond Romanticism: New Approaches to Texts and Contexts*, London: Routledge, 1992, pp. 118–39.

Gwilliam, Tassie. *Samuel Richardson's Fictions of Gender*, Stanford: Stanford University Press, 1993.

Habermas, Jürgen. *The Structural Transformation of the Public Sphere: An Inquiry into a Category of Bourgeois Society*, trans. Thomas Burger with the assistance of Frederick Lawrence, Cambridge: Polity Press, 1989.

Haggerty, George E. 'Amelia's nose; or Sensibility and its Symptoms', *The Eighteenth Century: Theory and Interpretation*, vol. 36 (1995), pp. 139–56.

Hale, J.R. 'Art and Audience: "The Medici Venus" c.1750–1850', *Italian Studies*, vol. 31 (1976), pp. 37–58.

Hall, Catherine. *White, Male and Middle-Class: Explorations in Feminism and History*, Cambridge: Polity Press, 1992.

Harth, Erica. 'The Virtue of Love: Lord Hardwicke's Marriage Act', *Cultural Critique* (Spring, 1988), pp. 123–54.

Haskell, Francis and Penny, Nicholas. *Taste and the Antique: The Lure of Classical Sculpture, 1500–1900*, New Haven: Yale University, 1981.

Hemingway, Andrew. 'The Sociology of Taste in the Scottish Enlightenment' in *Oxford Art Journal*, vol. 12, no. 2 (1989), pp. 3–33.

Hertz, Neil. 'The Notion of Blockage in the Literature of the Sublime' in Geoffrey Hartman ed., *Psycho-analysis and the Question of the Text*, Baltimore: Johns Hopkins University Press, 1978, pp. 62–85.

Hipple, W.J. *The Beautiful, the Sublime and the Picturesque in Eighteenth-Century British Aesthetic Theory*, Carbondale: University of Southern Illinois Press, 1957.

Hirshman, Albert O. *The Passions and the Interests: Political Arguments for Capitalism before its Triumph*, Princeton: Princeton University Press, 1977.

Hohendahl, Peter Uwe. *The Institutions of Criticism*, Ithaca: Cornell University Press, 1982.

Hope, V.M. *Virtue by Consensus*, Oxford: Clarendon Press, 1989.

Huyssen, Andreas. 'Mapping the Postmodern' in Linda J. Nicholson ed., *Feminism/Postmodernism*, London: Routledge, 1990.

Jarrett, Derek. *The Ingenious Mr. Hogarth*, London: Michael Joseph, 1976.

Johnson, E.M. *Francis Cotes*, London: Phaidon, 1976.

Jones, Robert W. 'The Empire of Beauty: The Competition for Judgement in Mid-Eighteenth-Century England', University of York, DPhil thesis, 1995.

'Such Strange Unwonted Softness to Excuse: Judgement and Indulgence in Joshua Reynolds's Portrait of Elizabeth Gunning, Duchess of Hamilton and Argyll', *Oxford Art Journal*, vol. 18, no. 1 (1995), pp. 29–43.

Jones, Vivien ed. *Women in the Eighteenth Century – Constructions of Femininity*, London: Routledge, 1990.

Kallich, Martin. *The Association of Ideas and Critical Theory in Eighteenth Century England*, The Hague: Mouton, 1970.

Kelly, Veronica and von Mücke, Dorothea E. *Body and Text in the Eighteenth Century*, Stanford: Stanford University Press, 1994.

Kitson, Michael. 'Hogarth's Apology for Painters' in *Walpole Society Notes*, vol. XII (1966–68), pp. 46–111.

Kivy, Peter. *The Seventh Sense*, New York: Burt Franklin, 1976.

Klein, Lawrence. 'Gender, Conversation and the Public Sphere in early Eighteenth-Century England' in Judith Still and Michael Worton eds., *Textuality and Sexuality: Reading Theories and Practices*, Manchester: Manchester University Press, 1993, pp. 100–116.

'The Third Earl of Shaftesbury and the Progress of Politeness', *Eighteenth-Century Studies*, vol. 18, no. 2 (Winter, 1984–85), pp. 187–214.

Kramnick, Isaac F. *Bolingbroke and his Circle; The Politics of Nostalgia in the Age of Walpole*, Cambridge, Mass: Harvard University Press, 1968.

Langbauer, Laurie. 'Romance Revised: Charlotte Lennox's *The Female Quixote*', *Novel*, vol. 18 (Fall, 1984), pp. 29–49.

Langford, Paul. *A Polite and Commercial People: England 1727–83*, Oxford: Oxford University Press, 1992.

La Vopa, Anthony J. 'Conceiving a Public: Ideas and Society in Eighteenth-Century Europe', *Journal of Modern History*, vol. 64 (1992), pp. 79–116.

Lee, R.W. *Ut Pictora Poesis: The Humanist Theory of Painting*, New York: Norton, 1967.

Leppert, Richard. *Music and Image: Domesticity, Ideology and Social Formation in Eighteenth-Century England*, Cambridge: Cambridge University Press, 1988.

Leslie, Charles Robert and Taylor, Tom. *The Life and Times of Sir Joshua Reynolds: with notices of some of his contemporaries*, 2 vols., London: John Murray, 1865.

Lipking, Lawrence. *The Ordering of the Arts in Eighteenth Century England*, Princeton: Princeton University Press, 1970.

Lovell, Terry. *Pictures of Reality: Aesthetics, Politics and Pleasure*, London: BFI, 1983.

Lynch, Deidre. 'Overloaded Portraits: The Excesses of Character and Countenance' in Veronica Kelly and Dorothea von Mucke eds., *Body and Text in the Eighteenth Century*, Stanford: Stanford University Press, 1994, pp. 112–43.

Lynch, J.J. 'Romance and Realism in Charlotte Lennox's *The Female Quixote*', *Essays in Literature*, vol. 14, no. 1 (1984), pp. 51–63.

McKendrick, Neil, Brewer, John and Plumb, J.H. *The Birth of a Consumer Society: The Commercialization of Eighteenth-Century England*, London: Europa, 1982.

McKeon, Michael. 'The Politics of Discourse and the Rise of the Aesthetic in Seventeenth-Century England', in Kevin Sharpe and John D. Zwicker eds., *The Politics of Discourse: The Literature and History of Seventeenth-Century England*, Berkeley: University of California Press, 1987, pp. 36–51.

de Man, Paul. *The Resistance to Theory*, Minneapolis: Minnesota University Press, 1986.

Mannings, David. 'An Art Historical Approach to Reynolds's *Discourses*', *British Journal of Aesthetics*, vol. 16 (Autumn, 1976).

'At the Portrait Painters: How the Painters of the eighteenth-century conducted their studios and their sittings.' *History Today*, vol. 27 (1977), pp. 279–87.

'Reynolds, Garrick, and the Choice of Hercules', *Eighteenth-Century Studies*, vol. 17, no. 3 (Spring, 1984), pp. 260–83.

'Reynolds, Hogarth and Van Dyck', *Burlington Magazine*, vol. 126, no. 890 (November, 1984), pp. 689–90.

'Reynolds and the Restoration Portrait', *The Connoisseur*, vol. 183 (July, 1973), pp. 186–93.

'Shaftesbury, Reynolds and the Rediscovery of Portrait Painting in Eighteenth-Century England', *Zeitschrift für Kunstgeschichte*, vol. 48 (1984), pp. 319–28.

'Studies in British Portrait Painting in the Eighteenth Century with Special Reference to the Early Work of Sir Joshua Reynolds', unpublished PhD thesis, University of London, 1977.

'A Well-Mannered Portrait by Highmore', *The Connoisseur*, vol. 189, no. 760 (June, 1975), pp. 116–19.

Markley, Robert. 'Sentimentality as Performance: Shaftesbury, Sterne, and the Theatrics of Virtue' in Felicity Nussbaum and Laura Brown eds., *The New Eighteenth Century: Theory, Politics, English Literature*, London and New York: Methuen, 1987, pp. 210–30.

Marshall, David. 'Writing Masters and Masculine Exercise in *The Female Quixote*', *Eighteenth-Century Fiction*, vol. 5, no. 2 (January, 1992), pp. 125–48.

Marx, Karl. *Capital*, 3 vols., trans Ben Fowkes, Pelican Marx Library, Harmondsworth: Penguin, 1988.

Marx, Karl and Engels, Frederick. *The German Ideology*, ed. and intro. C.J. Arthur, London: Lawrence and Wishart, 1970.

Mattick, Paul, ed. *Eighteenth-Century Aesthetics and the Reconstruction of Art*, Cambridge: Cambridge University Press, 1993.

Mellor, Anne K. *Romanticism and Gender*, London: Routledge, 1993.

Millar, Oliver. *The Tudor, Stuart and Early Georgian Pictures in the Collection of Her Majesty the Queen*, London: Phaidon, 1963.

Mitchell, W.J.T. ed., *Iconology: Image, Text, Ideology*, Chicago: University of Chicago Press, 1986.

Moore, James. 'The Two Systems of Francis Hutcheson: On the Origins of the Scottish Enlightenment' in M.A. Stewart ed., *Studies in the Philosophy of the Enlightenment*, Oxford: Clarendon Press, 1990, pp. 37–59.

Monk, S.H. *The Sublime: A Study of Critical Theories in XVIIIth-Century England*, Ann Arbor: University of Michigan, 1960.

Monod, Paul. 'Painters and Party Politics in England, 1714–60', *Eighteenth-Century Studies* vol. 26, no. 3 (Spring, 1993), pp. 367–99.

Mullan, John. *Sentiment and Sociability: The Language of Feeling in the Eighteenth Century*, Oxford: Clarendon Press, 1988.

Myers, Sylvia H. 'Learning, Virtue and the Term "Bluestocking"', *Studies in Eighteenth-Century Culture*, vol. 15 (1986), pp. 279–88.

Nead, Lynda. *The Female Nude: Art, Obscenity and Sexuality*, London: Routledge, 1992.

'Seductive Canvasses: Visual Mythologies of the Artist and Artistic Creativity', *Oxford Art Journal*, vol. 18, no. 2 (1995), pp. 59–61.

Nicholson, Majorie Hope. *Mountain Gloom, Mountain Glory: The Development of the Aesthetics of the Infinite*, Ithaca: Cornell University Press, 1959.

Norton, John. 'Akenside's *"The Pleasures of the Imagination"*: An Exercise in Poetics', *Eighteenth-Century Studies*, vol. 3, no. 3 (Spring, 1970), pp. 366–83.

Okin, Susan Moller. 'Patriarchy and Married Women's Property in England: Questions in Some Current Views', *Eighteenth-Century Studies*, vol. 17, no. 2 (Winter, 1983–84), pp. 121–38.

Paulson, Ronald. *The Beautiful, the Novel and the Strange: Aesthetics and Heterodoxy*, Baltimore: Johns Hopkins University Press, 1996.

Breaking and Remaking: Aesthetic Practice in England, 1700–1820, New Brunswick: Rutgers University Press, 1989.

Emblem and Expression: Meaning in English Art of the Eighteenth Century, Cambridge, Mass: Harvard University Press, 1975.

Hogarth Vol I: The Modern Moral Subject, 1697–1732, Cambridge: Lutterworth Press, 1991.

Hogarth Vol II: High Art and Low, 1732–1750, Cambridge: Lutterworth Press, 1993.

Hogarth Vol III: Art and Politics, 1750–1764, Cambridge: Lutterworth Press, 1993.

Satire and the Novel in Eighteenth Century England, New Haven: Yale University Press, 1967.

Pears, Iain. *The Discovery of Painting: The Growth of Interest in the Arts in England, 1680–1768*, London and New Haven: Yale University Press, 1988.

Perry, Gill. 'Women in Disguise: Likeness, the Grand Style and the Conventions of Feminine Portraiture in the Work of Sir Joshua Reynolds' in Gill Perry and Michael Rossington eds., *Femininity and Masculinity in Eighteenth-Century Art and Culture*, Manchester: Manchester University Press, 1994, pp. 18–40.

Phillipson, Nicholas. 'Politics, Politeness and the Anglicanisation of

Eighteenth-Century Scottish Culture; in R.A. Mason ed., *Scotland and England, 1286–1815*, Edinburgh: University of Edinburgh Press, 1987, pp. 226–46.

Pittock, Joan. *The Ascendency of Taste: The Achievement of Joseph and Thomas Warton*, London: Routledge, Kegan Paul, 1973.

Pocock, J.G.A. 'Between Machiavelli and Hume: Gibbon as Civic Humanist and Philosophical Historian' in *Edward Gibbon and the Decline and Fall of the Roman Empire*, ed. G.W. Bowersock and John Clive, Cambridge, Mass.: Harvard University Press, 1977, pp. 103–19.

The Machiavellian Moment: Florentine Political Thought and the Atlantic Republican Tradition, Princeton: Princeton University Press, 1975.

Politics, Language and Time: Essays in Political Thought and History, London Methuen, 1972.

Virtue, Commerce and History: Essays on Political Thought and History, Chiefly in the Eighteenth Century, Cambridge: Cambridge University Press, 1985.

Pointon, Marcia. 'Graces, Bacchantes and "Plain Folks": Order and Excess in Reynolds's Female Portraits', *British Journal of Eighteenth-Century Studies*, vol. 17, no. 1 (Spring, 1994), pp. 1–26.

Hanging the Head: Portraiture and Social Formation in Eighteenth-Century England, New Haven: Yale University Press, 1993.

Naked Authority: The Body in Western Art, 1830–1908, Cambridge: Cambridge University Press, 1990.

Pollak, Ellen. *The Poetics of Sexual Myth: Gender and Ideology in the Verse of Swift and Pope*, Chicago: University of Chicago Press, 1985.

Porter, Roy. 'Making Faces: Physiognomy and Fashion in Eighteenth-Century England', *Etudes Anglaises*, 38, no. 4 (October–December, 1985), pp. 386–96.

Postle, Martin. *Sir Joshua Reynolds: The Subject Pictures*, Cambridge: Cambridge University Press, 1995.

Potkay, Adam. 'Classical Eloquence and Polite Style in the Age of Hume', *Eighteenth Century Studies*, vol. 25, no. 1 (Fall, 1991), pp. 31–56.

Pottle, Frederick A. *James Boswell. The Earlier Years, 1740–1769*, London: Heineman, 1966.

Raven, James. *Judging New Wealth: Popular Publishing and Responses to Commerce in England, 1750–1800*, Oxford: Clarendon Press, 1992.

Riberio, Aileen. 'Some Evidence of the Influence of the Dress of the Seventeenth Century in Eighteenth-Century Female Portraiture', *Burlington Magazine*, vol. 119 (December, 1977), pp. 834–40.

Rogers, Nicholas. *Whigs and Cities: Popular Politics in the Age of Walpole and Pitt*, Oxford: Clarendon Press, 1989.

Ross, Deborah. 'Mirror, Mirror; The Didactic Dilemma of *The Female Quixote*' in *Studies in English Literature*, vol. 27 (Summer, 1987), pp. 455–73.

Said, Edward W. 'Opponents, Audiences, Constituencies, and Community' in *The Politics of Interpretation*, ed. W.J.T. Mitchell, Chicago: University of Chicago Press, 1983, pp. 7–32.

Sedgwick, Eve Kosofsky. *Between Men: English Literature and Male Homosocial Desire*, New York: Colombia University Press, 1985.

Sekora, John. *Luxury: The Concept in Western Thought, from Eden to Smollet*, Baltimore: Johns Hopkins University Press, 1977.

Shawe-Taylor, Desmond. *The Georgians: Eighteenth-Century Portraiture and Society*, London: Barrie and Jenkins, 1990.

Shevelow, Kathryn. *Women and Print Culture: The Construction of Femininity in the Early Periodical*, London: Routledge, 1989.

Smart, Alastair. 'Dramatic Gesture and Expression in the Age of Hogarth and Reynolds', *Apollo*, vol. 82, no. 42 (new series) (August, 1965), pp. 90–97.

Allan Ramsay: Painter, Essayist and Man of Enlightenment, New Haven: Yale University Press, 1992.

Snow, Edward. 'Theorising the Male Gaze: Some Problems', *Representations*, vol. 25 (Winter, 1989), pp. 30–41.

Solkin, David H. 'Great Pictures or Great Men? Reynolds, Male Portraiture and the Power of Art', *Oxford Art Journal*, vol. 9, no. 2 (1986), pp. 42–49.

Painting for Money: The Visual Arts and the Public Sphere in Eighteenth-Century England, New Haven: Yale University Press, 1993.

'ReWrighting Shaftesbury: The Air Pump and the Limits of Commercial Humanism' in John Barrell ed., *Painting and the Politics of Culture: New Essays on British Art 1700–1850*, Oxford: Oxford University Press, 1992, pp. 73–100.

Richard Wilson – The Landscape of Reaction, London: Tate Gallery Productions, 1982.

Spacks, Patricia Meyer. 'Sisters' in Mary Anne Schofield and Cecilia Macheski eds., *Fetter'd or Free? British Women Novelists, 1670–1815*, Athens, Oh.: University of Ohio Press, 1986, pp. 136–51.

'The Subtle Sophistry of Desire: Dr Johnson and *The Female Quixote*', *Modern Philology* (May, 1988), pp. 532–42.

Spector, Robert Donald. *English Literary Periodicals and the Climate of Opinion during the Seven Years' War*, The Hague: Mouton, 1966.

Spenser, Jane. *The Rise of the Woman Novelist from Aphra Behn to Jane Austen*, Oxford: Basil Blackwell, 1986.

Stallybrass, Peter and White, Allon. *The Politics and Poetics of Transgression*, London: Routledge, 1986.

Staves, Susan. 'British Seduced Maidens', *Eighteenth-Century Studies*, vol. 14, no. 2 (Winter, 1980–81), pp. 109–34.

'Matrimonial Discourse in Fiction and in Court: The Case of Anne Masterman' in *Fetter'd or Free? British Women Novelists, 1670–1815*, ed. Mary Anne Schofield and Cecilia Macheski, Athens, Oh: University of Ohio Press, 1968, pp. 169–85.

Player's Scepters: Fictions of Authority in the Restoration, Lincoln: University of Nebraska Press, 1979.

Stewart, J. Douglas. 'Pin-Ups or Virtues? The Concept of the 'Beauties' in Late-Stuart Portraiture' in *English Portraits of the Seventeenth and Eighteenth Centuries*, Los Angeles: California University Press, 1974, pp. 3–27.

Stolnitz, Jerome. ' "Beauty": Some Stages in the History of an Idea', *Journal of the History of Ideas*, vol. 22, no. 2 (April–June, 1962), pp. 185–204.

Stone, Lawrence. *The Family, Sex and Marriage, 1550–1800* rev. edn, Harmondsworth: Penguin, 1979.

Tatlock, R. *A Record of the Collections in the Lady Lever Art Gallery*, 2 vols., London: 1928.

Todd, Janet. *The Sign of Angellica: Women, Writing and Fiction, 1660–1800*, London: Virago, 1989.

Women's Friendship in Literature: The Eighteenth-Century Novel in England and France, New York: Colombia University Press, 1980.

Trumbach, Randolph. *The Rise of the Egalitarian Family*, New York: Academic Press, 1978.

Turner, Cheryl. *Living By the Pen: Women Writers in the Eighteenth Century*, London: Routledge, 1992.

Uphaus, Robert. 'The Ideology of Reynolds' *Discourses on Art*', *Eighteenth-Century Studies*, vol. 12, no. 1 (Fall, 1978), pp. 59–73.

'Shaftesbury on Art: The Rhapsodic Aesthetic', *Journal of Aesthetics and Art Criticism*, vol. 27, no. 3 (Spring, 1969), pp. 341–48.

Van Sant, Ann Jesse. *Eighteenth-Century Sensibility and the Novel: The Senses in Context*, Cambridge: Cambridge University Press, 1993.

Vickery, Amanda. 'Golden Age to Separate Spheres? A Review of the Categories and Chronology of English Women's History', *The Historical Journal*, vol. 36, no. 2 (1993), pp. 383–414.

Voitle, Robert. *The Third Earl of Shaftesbury, 1671–1713*, Baton Rouge: Louisiana State University Press, 1984.

Warner, Malcolm. 'The Source and Meaning of Reynolds' Lady Sarah Bunbury', *The Art Institute of Chicago Museum Studies*, vol. 15 (1989), pp. 7–19.

Warren, Leland. 'Of the Conversation of Women: *The Female Quixote* and the Dream of Perfection', *Studies in Eighteenth-Century Culture*, vol. 11 (1982), pp. 367–80.

Waterhouse, Ellis K. *Reynolds*, London: Kegan Paul and Trench Trubner, 1941.

Reynolds, London: Phaidon, 1973.

Weiskel, Thomas. *The Romantic Sublime: Studies in the Structure and Psychology of Transcendence*, Baltimore: Johns Hopkins University Press, 1976.

Wendorf, Richard. *The Elements of Life: Biography and Portrait-Painting in Stuart and Georgian England*, Oxford: Clarendon Press, 1990.

William Collins and Eighteenth-Century English Poetry, Minneapolis: University of Minnesota Press, 1981.

Whitley, William T. *Artists and their Friends in England, 1700–79*, 2 vols., London: Medici Society, 1928.

Williams, Raymond. 'Base and Superstructure in Marxist Cultural Theory', in Rick Rylance ed., *Debating Texts: A Reader in 20th Century Literary Theory and Method*, Milton Keynes: Open University Press, 1987, pp. 204–16.

The Country and the City, London: Hogarth Press, 1985.

Culture and Society, Harmondsworth: Penguin, 1971.

Keywords, London: Fontana Press, 1983.

Marxism and Literature, Oxford: Oxford University Press, 1977.

Wind, Edgar. *Hume and the Heroic Portrait: Studies in Eighteenth-Century Imagery*, ed. Jaymie Anderson, Oxford: Clarendon Press, 1986.

Wright, Austen. *Joseph Spence: A Critical Biography*, Chicago: University of Chicago Press, 1950.

Zomchick, John P. *Family and the Law in Eighteenth-Century Fiction: The Public Conscience in the Private Sphere*, Cambridge: Cambridge University Press, 1993.

Index